PREDICTABLE PLEASURES

At Table

PREDICTABLE PLEASURES

Food and the Pursuit of
Balance in Rural Yucatán

LAUREN A. WYNNE

University of Nebraska Press
LINCOLN

Portions of this book originally appeared as "Transformations in Body and Cuisine in Rural Yucatán, México" in *Food and Identity in the Caribbean*, ed. Hanna Garth, 2013, Bloomsbury Academic, an imprint of Bloomsbury Publishing Plc. Chapter 5 is derived in part from "'I Hate It': Tortilla-Making, Class, and Women's Tastes in Rural Yucatán, Mexico" published in *Food, Culture and Society*, 2015. ©Association for the Study of Food and Society (ASFS), available online: http://www.tandfonline.com/. DOI: 10.1080/15528014.2015.1043104.

LIBRARY OF CONGRESS CATALOGING-IN-PUBLICATION DATA

Names: Wynne, Lauren A., author. Title: Predictable pleasures: food and the pursuit of balance in rural Yucatán / Lauren A. Wynne. Description: Lincoln: University of Nebraska Press, [2020]. | Series: At table | Includes bibliographical references and index. | Summary: "Wynne examines the centrality of food in rural Yucatán and how residents practice care, as exercised through food, to negotiate anxieties, achieve desired bodily and social status, and maintain valued cultural forms"—Provided by publisher. Identifiers: LCCN 2019027691 ISBN 9781496201317 (hardback)

ISBN 9781496221087 (epub) ISBN 9781496221094 (mobi) ISBN 9781496221100 (pdf) Subjects: LCSH: Food habits—Yucatán Peninsula. | Food habits—Mexico—Yucatán (State) | Food preferences—Yucatán Peninsula. | Food preferences—Mexico— Yucatán (State) | Mayas—Food. | Indians of Mexico—Food. | Yucatán Peninsula— Social life and customs. | Yucatán (Mexico: State)—Social life and customs. Classification: LCC GT2853.M6 W96 2020 | DDC 394.1/209726—dc23 LC record available at https:// lccn.loc.gov/2019027691

Set in Garamond Premier by Laura Ebbeka. Designed by N. Putens.

In memory of Gaspar

CONTENTS

ILLUSTRATIONS

.

ACKNOWLEDGMENTS

The work is itself the product of great care, much of it originating out-side of my own mind and typing hands. The University of Pennsylvania's study abroad program in Oaxaca, which sadly no longer exists, provided my first extended stay in Mexico. It was in Oaxaca City and its outskirts that I first conducted ethnographic research. Paola Sesia was particularly supportive of that first endeavor, generously introducing me to the region's indigenous midwives and trusting in my nascent ethnographic skill set. At Columbia University I was lucky enough to find my way to the Institute for Research on Women and Gender, where the faculty nurtured my intellectual growth. Lila Abu-Lughod and Lesley Sharp offered encouragement and valuable feedback both in my research and in my consideration of a career in anthropology; they gave me confidence and direction when I needed it most. Robert Smith and Molly McNees welcomed me into their Mexican Health Project, providing valuable experience.

At the University of Chicago Judith Farquhar inspired a critical approach to food studies by bringing my attention to processes of embodiment and questions of agency and pleasure. Her appreciation for ethnographic detail gave me confidence to pursue even the smallest nuggets of data I found interesting. Joseph Masco provided an important grounding in science and technology studies and was a source of encouragement and insight in the earliest phases of this project. His calm and kindness kept me going during periods of discouragement. John Lucy instructed me in both the intricacies of the Yucatec Maya language and the canon of historical and ethnographic texts written about the region. He also greatly informed my understandings of everyday life in the area. I offer abundant thanks to

John and to Suzanne Gaskins for helping me find my way to Juubche' and for continuing to act as liaisons to my friends there when I am home in the United States. Both John and Suzanne offered a wealth of cultural and practical knowledge without which my field research would have been far less successful. Furthermore, they have modeled engagement and care for the community they study in a way that has deeply influenced me. Anne Ch'ien was invaluable on all practical matters during my time at Chicago. Friends in Chicago, especially Meghan Hammond, Jenifer Lawless, and Jason Ramsey, provided laughter and support during the early stages of this project and have continued to do so from afar since then.

The Center for Latin American Studies at the University of Chicago helped me fund early visits to the field and secure FLAS funding for my study of the Yucatec Maya language. The Whatcom Museum Society's Jacobs Research Fund Grant and a Fulbright-Hays Doctoral Dissertation Research Abroad Fellowship made the longest stretch of this research possible. At various points the Doolittle-Harrison Fellowship, the Marion R. & Adolph J. Lichtstern Fund Travel Grant, and the Mark Hanna Watkins Post-Field Fellowship provided essential material support for writing and conference expenses. As part of the UNC-Duke Yucatec Maya Summer Institute, Sharon Mújica, Miguel Güémez Pineda, and Fidencio Briceño Chel were wonderful ambassadors to the peninsula during my first academic visit to the region in 2004. Several scholars offered their support to me as I planned my research, including Miguel Güémez Pineda, María Dolores Cervera Montejano, and Alejandra García Quintanilla. Unfortunately, my many health problems in the field limited my ability to meet with them. Crisanto Kumul Chan and his gifted Yucatec Maya language students offered much assistance over the course of my research. Many individual readers, workshop participants, discussants, and conference attendees offered valuable feedback on parts of this work over the last decade. This includes participants in the Medicine, the Body, and Practice Workshop at the University of Chicago; the Food Networks, Gender, and Foodways Conference at Notre Dame University; the Feast and Famine Colloquium of the Food Studies Program at New York University; and many American Anthropological Association Annual Meetings.

During my time in upstate New York, I was lucky to have colleagues and friends who kept me laughing and well fed while I balanced plenty of teaching with attempts at keeping this project alive. In particular I thank Carla Barrett, Helen Blouet, Jan DeAmicis, Doug and Priscilla Eich, Kyle Green, Luke Perry, Kimberly Radtke, Christopher Riddle, and, most of all, Jessica Singer Brown. At Ursinus College I thank Jonathan Clark for his support—especially in making sure that I had time to complete this book; Cathy van de Ruit, Kate Davis, and Jasmine Harris for good company and social science comradery; students Carter Timon, Megan Burns, Sydney Dickson, and Neve Durrwachter for working diligently to help me finish the manuscript; and Christine Angermeier for her frequent assistance and patience. Both Utica College and Ursinus College provided support for this project at critical junctures, including research travel and equipment. I have had students at both institutions who have made me think better and harder about my discipline and my own work; it has been a privilege to teach you all.

I am grateful for the trust and patience of those I have worked with at the University of Nebraska Press, especially Alicia Christensen, who saw potential in this project early on. Thank you to Emily Wendell for support as well. Three anonymous reviewers pushed me, all in very different ways, to think harder and write better. Portions of chapter 5 were previously published in the essay "Transformations in Body and Cuisine in Rural Yucatán, Mexico" in the edited volume *Food and Identity in the Caribbean*. Thanks to Hanna Garth for edits that greatly improved that piece. Earlier versions of parts of this book appeared in "'I Hate It': Tortilla-Making, Class, and Women's Tastes in Rural Yucatán, Mexico" in the journal *Food, Culture and Society*. Anonymous reviewers for that journal aided in the refinement of my arguments.

In a work that explores practices of care, I must offer thanks to the people who have made it possible to write this book by caring—and doing so extraordinarily well—for my children. Their teachers at Monmouth Day Care Center, the Clinton Early Learning Center, and Flanagan's Preschool have made it far easier for me to complete this project and still come home to happy and flourishing little people. I respect those teachers' work tremendously; their skill, creativity, and patience amaze me.

My parents, Ann and Robert, have offered remarkable and generous support over the years. They made this work and the years of study and research that preceded it possible, and they have nurtured my bookish tendencies from the start and supported my academic endeavors in numerous ways. They are two of the most observant and perceptive people I know; if my work here shows any trace of these qualities, my parents are due some credit. I thank my sisters Kristin and Karin, their families, and all the members of the Wynne and Forgione families for much laughter and love. Thank you also to Lori Camelo, the late Dennis Nevin, Karin Nanning de Vries, Barbara Weitkamp, and Marjee Ellis-Dean for welcoming me into your families and fully supporting me. Many old friends have provided encouragement and distraction over the years, including Dan Bloch, Helen Han, Gina Kline, Teresa Mulaikal, Kate Polson, Susie Schwarz, and especially Gareen Hamalian.

Justin Nevin has offered love and expertise in matters of grammar for a decade and a half. He has taken the lead on childcare innumerable times in recent years to give me time to write or rest from writing. He has embraced my obsession with food; I couldn't ask for a better dining companion. And when I've lost my nerve to try new-to-us foods, I could count on him to eat toasted bee larvae and roasted pig ears—and to reflect on the experience thoughtfully. Henry and William bring joy and beautiful chaos to our lives each day. They inspire me to produce better work, make it matter, and care more.

The people of the community I call Juubche' have been remarkable in their warmth and openness. I am honored to have been part of their networks of care even for a brief while, and I often reflect on the lessons they have taught me about how to live well. There are too many of them to thank everyone individually, but don Máximo deserves special gratitude for taking a leap on letting a young anthropologist into his home and for helping me find laughter in my many missteps. I owe my greatest thanks to the woman I call here doña Esmeralda. My arrival at her home was the indirect result of her greatest loss. I will always be in debt to her for opening her heart to me when it was so freshly broken. Her willingness to share her love and her pain is a gift for which I am grateful every day.

PREDICTABLE PLEASURES

Introduction

One day in early 2009 in the community of Juubche' in Yucatán, Mexico, I returned to my temporary home from a visit to a friend. As I entered the gate and approached the house, I heard the voice of doña Antonia, the elderly mother of my hostess doña Esmeralda, in the kitchen. Before I could enter and offer her the proper greeting—anyone who enters a home in this community must offer greetings to the elders inside—doña Esmeralda ran out to me and ordered me not to greet her mother. Doña Antonia, she explained, was grinding squash seeds. I gave her a puzzled look. Squash seeds are very jealous, she continued, and they would resent my greeting doña Antonia and would spoil in anger. As important as etiquette is in this community—and indeed to not offer a proper greeting to an elder would be unthinkable in most other situations—the taste of the ground squash seeds necessitates the prioritizing of one human action over another; what felt to me a breach of the social norms was for doña Esmeralda and doña Antonia essential to the proper care of the squash seeds and, by extension, the economic well-being and gustatory pleasure of their family.

In their everyday interactions with their worlds, residents of Juubche' create and test boundaries between themselves and those worlds through such practices of care, which in its many forms ranges from the ingestion of pharmaceuticals to requests for favors from deities. Control of nonhuman entities, like those temperamental squash seeds, always remains at least a bit out of reach. Yet human action is still a critical component of the maintenance of order and the inextricable pursuits of well-being and survival here. Over the last half century in this community, a dramatic shift from subsistence agriculture to wage labor has transformed the ways in which people there define and achieve survival and well-being. Archaeological and historical research conducted in this region often notes that bodily, social, and cosmic well-being for indigenous people has long been dependent upon an ideal of balance toward which constant human effort was expended (Castellanos 2010; Farriss 1987; Kray 1997; Reilly 2002; Sigal 2000). Generally speaking, the Mesoamerican ideal of balance necessitated, above all, human participation in food labor and attendant rituals in which human agency together with an array of cosmogonic forces perpetuated the order of the universe and its many life forms. Some scholars writing on Yucatán have argued specifically that the continuity of this ideal is the product of its persistent utility: shaping strategies for action in the ever-shifting circumstances of human existence, its usefulness in multiple spheres of life only amplifies in times of more profound change (Barrera-Bassols and Toledo 2005; Farriss 1987). Rather than suggest stability or an essential core at the heart of this ideal (Fabian [1983] 2002; Hervik and Kahn 2006), I argue that balance for the people of Juubche', in the local terms I describe in the following paragraphs, represents that which makes life good, something that in and of itself is fluid and contextual. I resist the lure of essentializing such an ideal, of staking it to a particular form of identity, whether imposed from the outside or constructed from within, but I share Armstrong-Fumero's (2011) view that "healthy skepticism of positivist models of representation does not necessarily imply that the discussion of cultural continuity and non-discursive experience should be bracketed off to the degree that it has been" (66). While the pursuit of balance in Juubche' sometimes includes the embrace of change, it also often consists of the reproduction of seeming continuity, the maintenance of order or the pursuit of pleasure through that which is predictable or familiar. Frequently it is the change itself that becomes routinized, making the strange familiar, incorporating new ingredients into older culinary practices or placing a novel object on the altar of a deceased loved one.

In Juubche' practices related to balance are often talked about in this context and in the Yucatec Maya language as forms of *kalan* and *kanan*. They are concentrated in those spheres of life in which human action is most meaningful and consequential, in those spheres in which life, human and nonhuman, is sustained. As the twentieth century intensified the commodification of labor and objects, and hastened the weakening of a cosmology tied to food production and collective religious life, what changes have come to pass for the people in Juubche' as squash seeds and others forms of life lose their spirits? When the comestibles and other entities that have long been seen to give life are themselves transformed, what are the consequences for human bodies and lives?

There is perhaps no realm of life in rural Yucatán in which recent economic and social changes are more visible, tangible, *and consequential* than in what I broadly categorize as human relationships with food. It is perhaps even misleading to suggest that these relationships comprise a "realm," for food in Juubche' permeates much of everyday existence, bleeding out of the leaky boundaries of production, distribution, and consumption into the very ways in which people imagine themselves and much of what inhabits their worlds. *U meyaj kool* (the work/creation of the milpa, or cornfield) and *u meyaj janal* (the work/creation of food) have long been foci of human activity on the Yucatán Peninsula for several thousand years (Colunga-García Marín and Zizumbo-Villarreal 2004; Terán, Rasmussen, and Cauich 1998). The anthropologist Mary Elmendorf ([1976] 1978) writes that Alfonso Villa Rojas, with whom Robert Redfield produced the classic Yucatec Maya ethnography *Chan Kom*, clarified for her the translation of *meyaj*, a Yucatec Maya word often glossed as "work." *Meyaj*, according to Villa Rojas, is in fact closer to the Spanish *crear* (to create) than to the Spanish *trabajar* (to work) (117). Similarly, in Juubche' the Spanish *ganar* (to earn) is used to describe wage labor, while *meyaj* is usually reserved for agricultural labor and domestic work, especially cooking.[1] These distinctions are significant ones that reflect, first, the role that food production and preparation play in the maintenance and (re)creation of life here and, second, the depth of the challenges that wage labor presents to the agriculturally based cosmology found in many rural Yucatecan communities. Wages sustain human life (materially, at least), but, unlike milpa agriculture, wage labor can offer such material support without having to nurture other life forms. In this way it disentangles human labor from broader networks of care, reshaping it to care in other, new ways (or not to care at all).

This book analyzes the challenges that contemporary material and social conditions pose for the residents of Juubche' as they seek to survive, achieve balance, and create good lives for themselves. Care, as it is enacted and discussed in this community, refers mostly to a set of practices that in motive, process, or effect produce or aim to produce balance as a desirable state of bodily, social, and cosmic well-being. Some of these strategies are enacted with calculation, with clear intentionality: for example, weighing the benefits of a pharmaceutical drug with that of a plant-based treatment or limiting one's alcohol consumption to make a household more tranquil. Others, with time, have developed into naturalized dispositions, embodiments of time-tested strategies for well-being and survival: for example, the acquisition of palates to which certain food qualities taste "right" or the ability to sense imminent shifts in the weather. Attention to anxiety and suffering have also been fruitful sites of analysis for this work; failures of care are then made visible, suggesting that the significance of care is defined as much by its positive effects as by the negative implications of its lack. Yet the residents of Juubche' with whom I spoke also participate in newer ways of caring, some of which, like the old, seek to maintain balance, and others that operate with motives contrary to established values. Implicit in long-standing care habits is the fluidity between human bodies and all that exists outside of their permeable and oft-changing boundaries, and their interconnectedness to each other and other entities. Notions of the good life in Juubche' tend toward the relational, and self-interest is broad: an individual's physiological and emotional tranquility is dependent upon fair and balanced social relations, and patterns of reciprocity sustain a wide array of life forms and the larger social order. On one hand, care becomes exceedingly important in contemporary times; under shifting conditions, imbalance—pain, inequality, alienation—is a constant threat, requiring more human attentiveness. On the other hand, what it means to be balanced and how one goes about it are in flux, dependent upon bodies, social collectives, and ecosystems that seem themselves less stable than in the past.

The New Disorder

Many people in Juubche' articulate the constraints under which they live, the obstacles that sometimes, though not always, jeopardize their well-being. In the following conversation about the growth of Cancún in January of 2009, don Máximo and doña Esmeralda had this exchange:

Don Máximo: All those big, nice buildings in Cancún, just people like us—*masewaloob* [Yucatec Maya peasants]—built them.
Doña Esmeralda: But there is an engineer. He draws what it is to be like on paper, and they build it. Like I do with sewing.
DM: But he's a *ts'uul* [wealthy, often white person]?
DE: Yes, and he pays.

Don Máximo and doña Esmeralda understand the political and economic inequalities that are manifest in material processes and objects, like the visible and rapid growth of Cancún in just a few decades. In rural Yucatecan communities, there has long been acknowledgment that one's agency can be constrained by external forces, from the Mexican state to the lords of the forest or fluctuating tourism industry, and yet there has remained a deep confidence in the human ability to act, often in small ways, to live as well as one can: with pleasures, no matter how simple, and balance. Nancy Farriss (1987) writes that for colonial-era Yucatec Maya peoples, "Evil is disorder, represented by the chaos that preceded creation and which constantly threatens to reassert itself. The drama of creation is therefore an ongoing one, for the cosmic order must continually be reaffirmed in the face of this ever-looming chaos" (574). Since the Conquest, the lives of indigenous people in Yucatán have, to some degree, been subject to the exploitation and interventions of political and economic elites.[2] Under threat of force or out of necessity, the indigenous people of this region have long participated in colonialist and capitalist projects, many of which were seen as disruptive to the duties with which their communities and cosmos entrusted them. Of course, the region and the larger nation have transformed in a multitude of ways since the colonial era. From the persistence of debt peonage in the nineteenth century to the assimilationist policies of *indigenismo* to the turn toward neoliberalism and multiculturalism in the late twentieth century, indigenous people in Yucatán have engaged with the world outside of their own communities. From the colonial period on, many settled in larger towns and cities such as Mérida, Tizimín, and Valladolid, adapting to town and urban life, pursuing entrepreneurship or wage labor, and adopting decidedly "Yucatecan" or, less frequently, "Mexican" identities.

For those who remained in rural communities, however, food production and preparation remained an organizing structure of everyday life. Although some residents of Juubche' came to the community after childhoods in urban centers or other rural communities, for most residents this place has always been home. While I heed Gupta and Ferguson's (1992) caution about linking identity to place, place matters to people in Juubche', not in the form of essentialized notions of ethnicity but through practice, especially food work, that has for generations connected people to this place in a grounded and material way. This relationship with place is as much a product of colonization and nation-building as it is resistance to those processes, as I explore in chapter 2.

What is different about the last four decades in rural Yucatán is that wage labor has become a permanent substitute for agricultural labor rather than a supplement to it, fracturing the centrality of place and food in the formation of subjectivities here. According to Gálvez (2018), the implementation of the North American Free Trade Agreement (NAFTA) in 1994 was a particularly critical juncture, more fundamentally threatening to what she calls "milpa-based cuisine" and rural Mexico's food system than any other period after the conquest. As I explore throughout this text, the shifting contents of diets and forms of food production and preparation are evidence of this, but labor patterns are an inextricable part of this trend as well. In Yucatán full-time farmers are aging, clear from my own findings and those of others (Ebel and Castillo Cocom 2012).[3] Like some of Ebel and Castillo Cocom's (2012) informants in X-Pichil, many young men in Juubche' see the milpa as a labor pursuit that promises no social or economic mobility. Even some older residents sometimes speak of the milpa in that way. Doña Paola, a seamstress in her fifties and wife of a farmer, told me: "We didn't buy gold or anything to lift ourselves up. Everything went toward eating or drinking. But if we had learned to invest, to lift ourselves up, we would have had something to show for our work. I say to my old man, if we had learned to care for money, if we had been [wage] workers, we wouldn't have squandered everything we worked for." Doña Paola links wage labor to investment and wealth accumulation, to something different from what seems to her a waste or, in her words, a squandering. Tellingly she links this squandering with eating and drinking, but, of course, wageworkers must also eat. I suspect that doña Paola is not just referencing the possibility of surplus cash that some wage work produces but also particular ways of eating and drinking that are increasingly challenged by new economic logics and practices.

Castellanos (2010) points out that participation in new economies usually requires commitments that may replace those to which individuals and communities devoted themselves in the past. Formal education, for example, makes it difficult for boys to learn the agricultural skills upon which their fathers and grandfathers relied to make a living. And yet they often cannot utilize the skills they acquired through schooling in ways that offer significant benefit to themselves or their families. Without the interest or ability to labor in ways more deeply rooted in their home community, they become subject to the harsh conditions and unjust wages of construction, commercial agriculture, and other large-scale industries, or worse, comparable to what Green (2011) refers to in post-CAFTA (Central American–Dominican Republic Free Trade Agreement) Central America as the "nobodies," those who are seen as disposable or without value under capitalist logics. Many of the outcomes of the late twentieth-century transition from agricultural subsistence to wage labor have been contingent on political and economic factors outside of the control of rural indigenous people such as those in Juubche'. The development of a regional tourist industry and the concerted efforts to integrate rural peasants into the capitalist economy and national culture have exploited these individuals and threatened their well-being on a number of levels.

Some indigenous Yucatecans have embraced and facilitated the economic transition, joining the middle class thanks to early participation in the tourist industry and the strategic use of existing or new material resources (Castellanos 2010; Re Cruz 1996). While some of my older informants

1. Field on the outskirts of Juubche'. Courtesy of Justin Nevin.

lamented the widespread reliance on cash, the decline in agricultural practice, and the new foods of contemporary life, many others expressed a preference for life as they now know it over the conditions of the past as they remember it. While participation in capitalism usually limits time for social obligations, new funds earned through wage labor can also be used to cement ties, allowing laborers to contribute more funds to valued rites of passage such as weddings and acts of religious devotion.[4] Furthermore, as with the cultivation of nontraditional crops for export in one Maya community in Guatemala (Fischer and Benson 2006), participation in tourism and supporting industries provides many Juubche' residents with economic resources that support other members of their households to continue participating in milpa agriculture.

Despite some continuities, changes in the religious, medical, and political spheres of life in rural Yucatán have compounded the spiritual, material, and social consequences of economic transformations. The impossibilities produced through the weakening of subsistence agriculture—that is, the failure of established care practices to ensure balance and survival through milpa agriculture—were made comprehensible through the introduction of new logics for care: Protestant condemnations of long-standing rituals and exhortations for individual salvation; biomedical notions of wellness and danger; and new caregiving and care-receiving roles embedded in the rhetoric of citizenship. These changes augment the capitalist qualities of indigenous communities, qualities that Patch (1993) distinguishes from capitalist qualities of the "colonial *economy*" under which the ancestors of the contemporary indigenous Yucatecans worked (247). That is, the transformation of capitalism from one economic system that often functioned, for centuries, alongside subsistence agriculture to a hegemonic structure that shaped all facets of everyday life was a gradual process. Throughout rural Mexico the pace of this process quickened under the conditions of twentieth-century life in the region, especially during the last few decades of that century (Fitting 2011; Gálvez 2018; González 2001). The conversions of some indigenous Yucatecans to non-Catholic religions have altered cooperative practices of care for supernatural entities and challenged the human social connections they foment. New religious groups decenter the town as a geographical and social site for collective care practices, and their members' understandings of human responsibility draw narrower boundaries for the exercise of care.[5] Young people's styles of consumption often contrast with older people's ideologies of humility and equality, creating tensions by way of jealousy and gossip.[6] Biomedicine and nonlocal culinary practices challenge assumptions about taste, race, and biological transformations.[7] Certainly social tensions, especially as produced by gender and class inequalities, are not new here, but the gradual detachment of caring from what has long been the primary form of sustenance complicates the ways in which residents of Juubche' care for and through food, and how they experience themselves to be cared for by other entities.

Care acts as a force for human agency and is a productive force among many equally powerful nonhuman forces. In making tangible human action, producing desired sensations, and cultivating particular types of social and cosmic relations, care can be an unalienated form of labor, historically tied to other, more materially evident forms of human labor. For humans, individual bodies serve as the sites at which care originates and to which it returns; the remaking of the world through care also remakes the body in ways that, ideally, bring wellness and pleasure. Amid the recent social and economic changes for the people of Juubche', however, the ways in which one cares through food have multiplied and continue to diversify. Many of these new forms of care emerge not in conjunction with unalienated and valued human activities but rather in response to the alienation produced through newer and increasingly unavoidable labor practices. The forms of care in which people in Juubche' engage increasingly conflict with one another as they grow more diverse in motive, in kind, and in result. At other times alienation provokes failures of care; in new worlds that seem full of imbalance, what is the point? Today, as in the past, care, through its promotion of well-being, works to ensure balance, but the worlds and bodies to be balanced are in flux. Contemporary conditions threaten older forms of caring, but newer care practices emerge in response to new dangers, new possibilities for pleasure, and the new materialities that produce and engage all these things.

The Work of Care and the Desire for Balance

Well-being, articulated most clearly through a local concept of balance, is an active project in Juubche'. Residents manage the dangers of life through careful management of their bodies' exposures to external forces that can alter bodily states, as well as through the careful use of techniques to restore their bodies back to desired states. Care is a prominent way in which residents accomplish processes central to the reproduction of material and social life in their community. Care remakes and classifies bodies—as vulnerable to danger, as unruly, as well or unwell, as male or female or young or old, as *mayero* (Maya speaker) or *yucateco* (Yucatecan). Care as a process acknowledges human vulnerabilities, both physiological and moral, and human reliance on the external world, especially food. For residents of Juubche' the boundaries between the body and the external are fluid, however, and desires for balance embody moral expectations that link self-interest to the well-being of larger collectives, such as the community and the cosmos.

Care also acts as a more explicit practice of creation and management, one through which residents of Juubche' consciously fashion the lives they want to live. As Mol, Moser, and Pols (2010) note, care is not just something that is done to people but also something that people do to and for themselves. Care requires what Mol, Moser, and Pols call "adaptive tinkering," the development of a set of skills in response to the unpredictable, unruly, and fragile nature of the human body in the world (15). Residents of Juubche' tinker in such ways not only through the exercise of what we might call self-care but also by caring for the world around them, for kin and friends, for animals and plants, and for the spiritual entities that populate their universe. These care practices require certain sets of knowledge that must be accrued over the individual's lifetime: one must know her own body, recognize its shifts, and understand how it fits into the larger universe. One must also know how to read the needs of other entities and how and when to meet those needs.

In bodily practice and in discourse, many residents of Juubche' demonstrate the conviction that all individuals from about the onset of puberty, if not earlier, until death have the responsibility to care for themselves in various ways in response to the frightening and often immediate threats that populate their environment. They live in the world with the understanding that the entities around them, everything from the tourist industry to squash seeds to housecats, exercise agency and act in ways that they as individuals are not always able to control. In the pursuit of pleasure and sheer survival, humans must engage with the world. What they can attempt to control is, first, the degree to which these acts cause harm to themselves and to their kin, and, second, the potential harm their own actions may bring to other humans, spiritual entities, and the natural world. For people in Juubche', imbalance can be experienced directly or indirectly; for example, imbalance in the cosmos may lead one's crop to fail, contributing to hunger, an indirect consequence. Though inseparable in many ways from the fields outside it, the human body is the site at which many imbalances are directly experienced. Human illness and suffering are thought to originate in forces external to the material body. The body itself is fluid and dynamic; shifts in bodily state may make it more or less vulnerable to these external forces over the course of a day or a lifetime, but nobody is ever immune to them. A disturbing argument with kin or getting caught in the rain after a hard day's work in the *milpa* (cornfield) can produce suffering on a physiological level. Imbalances in the larger universe, such as anger on the part of the lords of the forest or hunger on the part of the *pixaan* (souls) of deceased loved ones, can do the same. Some effects of imbalance manifest over time, resulting in chronic conditions like *nervios*.

Historians, archaeologists, and cultural anthropologists have explored the underlying cosmology and social pressures that have perpetuated Yucatec Maya emphasis on human agency and the imperative for it to maintain cosmological balance (Castellanos 2010; Farriss 1984, 1987; Re Cruz 1996; Redfield and Villa Rojas [1934] 1962; Villa Rojas 1988). However, the shared logic according to which contemporary human practices that undertake these tasks unfold has never been systematically examined as comprising a single category of practice, albeit one that is, by its very nature, dynamic and adaptive. Scholars have organized this set of practices as something that ensures social reproduction, redistributes resources, or provides emotional or physiological well-being, and, in fact, I argue many of those same things in this work, but there remains a linkage that has received little to no attention. The constant appearance of the words *kalan* and *kanan* in everyday discourse in Juubche' reveals a conceptual thread that holds together the logics by which residents of this community live.

There has been a recent proliferation of research on care in an array of settings (e.g., Han 2012; Mulla 2014; Stevenson 2014; Ticktin 2011), something Smith-Morris (2018) has referred to as "medical anthropology's decade of 'care'" (426). Prior to this, studies of care had been largely limited to paid caregiving in medical and childcare settings (e.g., Nelson 1990; Wrigley 1995) and to unpaid domestic caregiving, especially for children, spouses, and elderly kin (e.g., Abel 1990; DeVault [1991] 1994). Similarly, older theoretical contributions to the study of care developed out of ethical or professional concerns (e.g., Noddings 1984; Tronto 1993). For example, Engster (2005) argues that care sustains life by satisfying three aims, as sought by any human or group of humans on behalf of another: first, providing that which is necessary for survival and basic functioning, such as food and shelter; second, cultivating in others the capabilities and skills essential for living good lives, as understood in a particular place and at a particular time; and third, helping avoid suffering or pain. For Engster, care requires certain qualities on the part of the caregiver as well, specifically a set of three virtues—attentiveness, responsiveness, and respect—without which care cannot accomplish its aims (54–55). Likewise, the influential theories on care of Gilligan (1982) and Noddings (1984) posit affection as central to caregiving. However, an insistence on these virtues limits caregiving to human organisms, and yet certainly the aims of care can be accomplished by other entities without comprising the affective and sensorial experiences of being cared *for*. Engster also restricts the objects of care to humans and perhaps other living entities, writing, for example, that the construction of homes "is usually not considered caring because in our society it is most often performed for the direct purpose of transforming the physical world and making money (which may or may not be put to caring ends)" (56). The theories of Engster, Gilligan, or Noddings may indeed be applicable to some indigenous Yucatecan social relations. However, they fail to account for the expansiveness of care as it operates in rural Yucatán: enacted on, by, or through nonhuman entities; reflecting a multitude of motives and intentions, capitalistic and noncapitalistic; and producing experiences and interests that reshape the limits of bodies and worlds.

Both within and beyond the rural Yucatecan context, care is a process embedded in other practices. It cannot be contained in motives or effects alone, and yet it is very real, a quality in the impulse that propels an action forward or the well-being produced, even unintentionally, through action. Care is not always entirely altruistic, if motives could ever even truly be disentangled enough to inspect, and its consequences will include the unintended and, sometimes, the violent (Ticktin 2011; Bocci 2017). The state and other institutions can come to harness care as a biopolitical force; when this happens, and even when it does not, forms of care may clash (Lavis 2015; Yates-Doerr 2015; Zivkovia et al. 2015). In Juubche' a form of self-care might counter long-term self-preservation, as when men drink to excess to reduce stress, while caring for others can produce benefits for oneself, indicating complexity in the very notion of self-interest.

Furthermore, care is often multiple: numerous entities may be cared for through any given practice (Besky 2013; Nading 2014). Nor are the motives or methods of care always consistent or compatible, even within what seems a single practice. What Law (2010) calls "care multiple" relies "upon routines for separating moments and objects of care and (possibly even more important) the subjectivities that go with them . . . these routines . . . are themselves a form of trial and error, involving the creation of new practices for separating and handling tensions between different subjectivities and objectives" (68). In fact, my engagement with the growing literature on nonhuman, specifically nonhuman animal, agency came largely *after* my friends in Juubche' identified for me ways in which nonhuman agents acted both with and against their own efforts at care. For example, some people in Juubche' understand nonhuman animals to have protectors who sometimes foil the efforts of humans. This includes a supernatural entity known as the *sip* that protects deer from hunters and reminds humans to exercise care in their extraction of resources from the forest. Each hunt requires a fresh assessment of how the hunters ought to care for themselves and other entities. Should they even dare to hunt at all? Should they take care not to hunt while drunk so that they are better able to spot the sip? And who and why might be engaging in their own practices of care out in the forest?[8] The need to secure meat for one's family must be balanced with the need to maintain a stable ecosystem and with the self-care, in the form of self-preservation, of prey. Similarly, Besky (2013) situates tea plantation laborers, planters, and tea bushes within what she calls a "moral economic system" and a "tripartite moral economy" (99); the bushes become like family to laborers, who engage with them in a relationship of mutual care.

Writing on veterinary caring, Law (2010) uses Charis Cussins's (1998) application of "choreography" to capture the many materialities and subjectivities that are ordered and distributed in practices of care, and how what might seem like a seamless process actually requires an "extreme degree of *effort*" (67–68). "As a repertoire that allows situated action" (Law 2010, 67), dispositions for caring comprise a form of habitus (Bourdieu 1977). Like the indigenous Yucatecan women Greene (2002) interviewed in the 1990s, most of my informants were befuddled or even amused by my attempts to invoke reflexive analysis from them, for many of the behaviors about which I asked them were largely, if not entirely, naturalized. Social and economic changes have endowed some habits with surplus meanings, connotations of ethnicity or economic status, that increasingly render them something to be pondered, but, with repetition, they too may grow more in sync with the new worlds they inhabit. Care is attuned to and, in fact, utterly dependent on the unpredictable or unaccountable, on what López et al. (2010) describe as "what threatens or might transform the limits that define it [the entities on or through which care unfolds]" (82). Care is the enactment of the recognition that one's survival depends upon external forces: the Mexican state, the patron saint, the chickens in one's yard. In each moment of care there unfolds an attempt to make things—humans, nonhumans, elements of nature, commodities—live together better. For residents of Juubche', care is the umbrella under which a vast network of reciprocal relations keeps their worlds in order, balanced, and functional.

Whether for purposes of profit or subsistence, food production must entail care in one form or another. Such is the nature of the processes of domestication by which particular plants and animals come to live with and for humans. Residents of Juubche' display affection and attention in their relations with the plant and animal world, often speaking of corn, domestic animals, and other entities as *sáantoj* (holy or blessed). At the same time, caring for the plants and animals on which food producers depend is central to the reproduction of those humans' existences, directly, through the ingestion of the foodstuffs these plants and animals are likely to become, or indirectly, through their transformation into cash or commodities of use to the producers. Yet the network of care is wider than just these organisms. For farmers in Juubche', one must be attentive to, indeed must care about, the subtle and nonsubtle signs of future weather; the appearance of organisms who, in the context of the milpa, are seen as pests; one's own bodily states; the status of government subsidies; and the price fluctuations of the global marketplace.

Engster (2005) argues that the work done by care is that of sustaining life, fundamentally different from that of generating life. In fact, he contrasts the sustaining effects of feeding with the life-generating effects of sexual reproduction (51–52). Yet, in the case of indigenous Yucatecans and other Mesoamerican groups, archaeological, historical, and ethnographic accounts often posit the two, sustenance and reproduction, as inseparable. Remember again Villa Rojas's translation of *meyaj*, the Yucatec Maya word often glossed as "work," as *crear* (to create) (Elmendorf [1976] 1978, 117). The Maya myth of creation recounts the forming of human flesh from ground corn (Gustafson 2002), and the good favor of the saints and other deities, largely sustained through food offerings, ensured human survival and reproduction (Chojnacki 2010; Redfield and Villa Rojas [1934] 1962; Taube 1988; Watanabe 1990). As don Teodoro, a shaman in Juubche', explained, "There are days we might say we won't give a little [food] to our beautiful God. We're all eating, we're giving life to ourselves, but if we forget God, he won't give anything [back to us]." Likewise, an emphasis on social cooperation and consensus may have emerged, in part, out of historical necessity, but it was reproduced through relationships of reciprocity and redistribution, most often involving food (Farriss 1984; Holmes 1978; Kramer 2005). The span from procreation to death is itself not seen as fundamentally different from other cyclical processes; hence, for example, the symbolic importance of the east with regard to fertility, for that is where the sun is reborn each morning, after death at sunset (Faust 1998). The maintenance of life is about keeping the cycles to their regular rhythms as much as it is about ensuring the survival and well-being of individual entities or groups.

Is care, as it is talked and written about in English, really akin to the Yucatec Maya *kalan* or *kanan*?[9] Not exactly, I am sure, but nor are the specific usages of the term *care* in English even equivalent across social spaces. While translation is always an act of transformation and often a form of violence (Venuti 1996), I have embraced Mol, Moser, and Pols's characterization of care as "adaptive tinkering" (2010, 15), a more general notion that communicates the sets of practices by which different entities live together. I have also followed the lead of those scholars of the Yucatec Maya language who have come before me in attempting to translate *kalan* and *kanan* into Spanish and English. In their Spanish-Maya dictionary, Bastarracha Manzano and Canto Rosado (2003) translate *kalan* and *kanan* to the Spanish *cuidar* (to care), *guardar* (to guard, to maintain, or to preserve), and *vigilar* (to look after, to guard) (112, 360, 400, 473).[10] Andrade (1955) defines *kanan* as "guard." Using a different orthography, Bricker,

Po'ot Yah, and Dzul de Po'ot (1998) define *kaláan* as "guard" and "protect" (121). Verhoeven (2007) defines it as "guard" and "watch" (206); to signify caring for or tending to, she claims, *yàabilt* or *yàakunt* are more appropriate, although they are used more often to signify "love," "like," and "appreciate" (222–29). Meanwhile, Atran (1993, 679) and Ford (2006, 106) gloss *kanan* as "care" in a context of milpa agriculture.[11] Furthermore, the English *care* is used by historians and anthropologists to describe practices for which Juubche' residents use *kanan* or *kalan*; for example, when discussing the ways in which saints are cleaned, dressed, and fed, or the ways in which farmers contend with weeds and animals (Anderson 2009; Farriss 1984; Watanabe 1990). In Juubche' the roots *kalan* and *kanan* are often formed into the phrase *Kanáant aba* (care for yourself, take care), used as a farewell greeting, or when one is issuing a more immediate and specific imperative for self-care. For example, don Milo frequently walked around his yard without his shirt early in the morning. His sister, doña Paty, could see him do so from her own home. When he frequently complained of a myriad of symptoms, she would urge him to "*Kanáant aba*" (Care for yourself) and, specifically, to do so by keeping himself warm with a shirt in the cool morning air.

In Juubche' *kalan* and *kanan* never refer to thought alone, as when one "cares about" in English. For this reason, *kanan* and *kalan* are not used to refer to what we might categorize as negative forms of caring, such as being nosy or gossiping. Rather, they are used both to categorize practices (e.g., "These are the ways in which I care for myself") and to provide the logic behind a particular practice (e.g., "I do it to care for myself"). The diverse range of practices I address in this work and categorize as care could be classified and reclassified in numerous ways, pulled apart into forms of gendered labor, moments of commensality, and processes of identity formation, to suggest just a few. A common strain here—in motive, in processual form, or in effect—urges us to think more broadly about what exactly is at stake in engagement with the world for rural indigenous Yucatecans. Specifically, we must ask why caring works or seems to work for the people of Juubche' and other entities in their social worlds in fulfilling cosmogonic duties and in achieving desired bodily, social, and cosmic states; where and how it unfolds; and whether its twenty-first-century remaking will render it more or less important. First, I want to consider why it is through and with food that so much of this caring transpires.

Why Food?

My initial research plans in Yucatán were to examine rural inhabitants' engagement with biomedicine and other ethnomedical systems, but after stays in three rural communities and then in Juubche', I noticed the frequency with which people talked about food and, less surprising given the rural locales, the substantial amount of time spent on food production and preparation. As the field of food studies was growing and increasingly legitimized within academia, it seemed logical to me to pursue what was already a personal interest, what was now a more respected object of study in my discipline and others, and, most importantly, what seemed to matter tremendously to the members of the community in which I planned to live for at least a year.

As Rozin (1999) succinctly and deftly concludes, food is significant in human life for a multitude of reasons. Food is incorporated into human bodies in a most intimate fashion, and it is a source of both pleasure and anxiety for humans throughout the world. As Sutton (2014) argues for the people of Kalymnos, Greece, "cooking is valued . . . *in and of itself, because taste matters*" (182). Cooking on Kalymnos, he explains, should not be seen as a mere analytical "window" into other aspects of human experience; rather it is itself a critical part of life on the island. Sutton's point is applicable to rural Yucatán and indeed must be further extended to the broader food system, in which production and distribution is tightly tied to preparation. Even more, the food system in rural Yucatán must be understood as something that, for at least several centuries, has in fact structured most aspects of life. This has been true of other Mesoamerican food producers as well. González (2001) writes, "Not only was maize reliant on humans, but humans became reliant upon the material conditions and social structures that maize itself played a part in creating. Maize, in short, engaged human society dialectically" (120).

The conditions of life in Yucatán may have even heightened this relationship, necessitating more care for maize and other crops on the part of humans. Michael Coe (2005) argues that the intensity of agricultural ceremonies in Yucatán is evidence of a high level of anxiety surrounding food production, notable even in comparison to the Maya highlands further south in Chiapas and Guatemala. Ethnographies of contemporary indigenous Yucatecans also make note of the anxieties that must be negotiated in the distribution and consumption of food, from the careful pairing of foodstuffs for individual eating to the attentiveness shown to social and cosmological hierarchies during moments of commensality (Callahan 2005; Hanks 1990; McCullough 1973; Redfield and Villa Rojas [1934] 1962). The myriad of food-related anxieties in rural Yucatán is the product of multiple material and social conditions, including the challenges presented by the local topography and climate; systems of knowledge for managing human and ecological well-being that weave together indigenous, colonial, and biomedical elements; and a history of social stratification, often reproduced through the marginalization of indigenous peoples and the exploitation of their labor (Castellanos 2010; Early 2006; Farriss 1984; Kray 1997; Villa Rojas 1981). Residents of Juubche' are deeply concerned with the manner in which particular qualities of foodstuffs affect their bodies, with both food scarcity and abundance, with the tensions implicit in commodity exchanges between themselves and other members of the community, with the hunger and satisfaction of supernatural entities, and with the repercussions that these and other potential sites of disruption might hold for individual and collective well-being.

Archaeological, historical, and ethnographic accounts of indigenous groups in this region frequently remark on the centrality of food in multiple spheres of Mesoamerican life (e.g., Farriss 1984; Hendon 1997; Searcy 2011; Staller 2010). Farriss (1984) argues that ability of indigenous Yucatecans to produce their own food has long been essential to their survival as a social group. Under conditions of oppression and exploitation, milpa agriculture made survival possible when larger support systems, such as extended kin networks and community-wide redistribution, were lacking. The migration of some indigenous people away from colonial persecution and civil unrest followed patterns of settlement that prioritized access to land and water, whereas most colonial-era indigenous people lived in towns organized through colonial *congregación* policies. In these towns, indigenous residents worked together to worship saints and other deities and to cultivate crops and produce other goods for subsistence and tribute to colonial authorities (Eiss 2010; Farriss 1984; Restall 1997). In the twentieth century, land reforms and the resurgence of the *ejido* system of collective land ownership fashioned new collaborative efforts at survival (Castellanos 2010), but these took shape under nationalist ideologies that partly supplanted the cosmological and religious bonds of the past. While current settlement patterns reflect political projects of the past, they are also products of indigenous survival strategies, material evidence of efforts at, and often successes in, care. For these individuals and communities, certain conditions including access to land and, for many individuals, the safety net promised by an extended network of kin and neighbors, have permitted them to survive under regular circumstances.[12] Ironically today that reliance on broader social networks, such as extended kin and town, threatens access to land. Twentieth-century population growth made rural communities ripe for the economic and social changes to come, especially the alternatives to agriculture presented by the development of regional tourism.

While various forms of government assistance increasingly aid residents of Juubche' in their day-to-day survival and may in fact encourage participation in the cash economy and consumption of industrial foods (Gálvez 2018), the household production of food remains an important source of sustenance. Voicing frequent lamentations about the decline in agricultural productivity and the contemporary requirement for cash, residents of Juubche' express some unease with their growing reliance on the global economy and the *ts'uulo'ob* (whiter, wealthier people) who are thought to control it. Histories of scarcity that pepper the family tales handed down from generation to generation may amplify these anxieties. Despite the seeming abundance of food available to residents of Juubche', as seen on store shelves and in television advertising, these tales of scarcity resonate with many families, as pasts to which they do not wish to return, as specters that arise when money is tight and the land less than fruitful, or as lingering feelings of shame. Emphases on balance and cooperation have characterized rural life for centuries, but these values are ideals that must compete with household-based divisions of labor and an ever-expanding repertoire of human desires. Patterns of reciprocity, as they long functioned between marital couples, parents and children, extended kin, larger social groups, and (super)natural entities, were processes of care, whose unity was produced through what were ideally common goals. Today expectations of reciprocity are challenged by the stagnation of life forms under late capitalism: infertile fields, bad or frozen óoloʼob (centers of consciousness, life forces), and refrigerators that store clothes and toiletries because owners can't afford the electricity to run them.

For the people of Juubche' some of these anxieties are rooted in the specific material qualities of foodstuffs, in sensorially experienced traits and the ways in which they are thought to act on bodies, while others infuse food vis-à-vis the social contexts under which it is produced and consumed, including acts of labor, interpersonal relations, and engagements with natural and spiritual entities. Often the qualities and contexts cannot be disentangled: the bodily effects of foodstuffs on humans are often linked to changes in the qualities of the foodstuffs themselves, sometimes related to the conditions of their production or preparation. As in other ethnographic settings (Hugh-Jones 1979; Munn 1986; Weiss 1996), the socially knowable qualities of foodstuffs available in Juubche' embody a host of social and cosmic relations. These relations are often obscured in the case of commodity foods. The mysterious conditions behind the production of such foods makes some older residents of Juubche' question such foods' life-sustaining potential. Such immediate critiques and the anxieties they embody are often more visible, but the longer-term effects of food on bodies are also of deep interest to residents of Juubche'. Food speaks through bodies and the sensations it produces in them, but bodies also, often more gradually, speak of food and the care it enacts and embodies. Human materiality embodies multiple values: expertise and the powerful forms of caring it makes possible; failures of care and imbalanced social relations; and social mobility and the embrace of novel care practices. People point out thin neighbors, especially the elderly, as poorly cared for by their kin. Lighter skin sometimes marks one's transformation from peasant to proletariat, making visible the lack of hard outdoor labor in one's daily routine, suggesting upward social mobility and the detachment from older care practices.

Care works to achieve balance—bodily, social, and cosmic—in ways that are at once rigid and flexible. As care emerges from the unpredictability of the world, the success of care strategies depends, in part, upon the expectation, or even prediction, of that unpredictability. Still, care's success also requires a confidence in one's ability to act in the world and the confidence that care—in its significance, in its motives, in its form, in its outcome—should fit coherently in that world in one way or another. We see this, for example, in the standardization that characterizes cuisine in Juubche', examined in greater detail later. The insistence on order is replicated down to the smallest of scales, such as the pizza, a recently introduced food that the residents of Juubche' expect to be topped in very particular ways. In doing so, they reproduce their ideologies of consensus and cooperation through the incremental development of shared tastes, collective connoisseurship that connects bodies at the most material of levels. We see similar processes in other cultural realms: through expressions and treatments of bodily suffering, through displays of desire and affection, and through engagement with natural and supernatural entities.

The Pleasures of Predictability

As a whole, indigenous Yucatecans remain an economically and politically marginalized population (Castellanos 2010; Daltabuit and Leatherman 1998), but their contributions to the development of Mexico's most profitable and popular tourist region, Cancún and its neighboring coastal areas, are multiple, from providing labor to becoming idealized and objectified showpieces for local culture (Castañeda 1996; Sandoval 2009; Torres 2011). Many of those contributions, material and cultural, have brought relatively little financial or political benefit to their own communities and quite often negative effects on health (Daltabuit and Leatherman 1998; Leatherman and Goodman 2005; Pi-Sunyer and Thomas 1997). However, some migrants benefited economically from early participation in the growing tourist economy in the 1970s and 1980s (Castellanos 2010; Re Cruz 1996). Many individuals in Juubche', and elsewhere on the peninsula (Eiss 2010; Heusinkveld 2008; Juarez 1996), appreciate improved infrastructure and access to greater educational and labor opportunities. Additionally, the temporary or circular migration of rural indigenous people within Mexico's borders, and the ongoing flow of both cash *and* community members, has slowed international migration, at least from the eastern part of the peninsula, and has provided new resources for valued cultural forms, such as religious rituals and cuisine.[13] And even among those indigenous Yucatecans for whom participation in capitalist economies has offered few benefits, there remains, according to my research and that of other anthropologists, much pleasure in everyday life. The most valued form of pleasure comes from achieving balance, from a feeling of well-being and tranquility. Rugeley finds a reoccurring lesson in Yucatec Maya folktales, "that caution and prudence are necessary for a long, happy life—and afterlife" (2001b, 25). Well-being and tranquility, often in the form of balance, are states or sensations to be maintained, not default settings on the registers of the lives of the people of Juubche'. Rather, they are projects and processes that depend on manifold types of collaboration.

Of course, "caution and prudence" exist alongside the lure of the promise or potential embedded in desire and produced through incorporation into the modern capitalist economy. In contrast to stability and equality, some young residents of Juubche', especially young men, find pleasure in risks and the promise of rewards. They may detach care from its nesting spheres of responsibility and reciprocity. But today the work of care is itself not always clearly defined, especially for younger generations for whom the rhythms and routines of farming life are but one of many competing logics of practice. For many of my friends in Juubche', what they see as recently installed desires, appetites beyond those that propagate care, can in fact threaten established notions of the good life: excess can bring certain pleasures, but this kind of pleasure is seen at best as harmless but ephemeral, and at worst as dangerous and destructive, corporeally, socially, and cosmologically. In Juubche' participation in the global economy, through circular migration to work on the coast or through the sale of crafts locally, just to give a few examples, is seen as a necessity, a basic form of care to ensure that one eats.

This participation is a form of labor essential for contemporary survival when both the land and the state regularly fail the rural poor. However, some residents also see such participation, especially when it is economically successful, as a suspect strategy, as a way of fulfilling desires that can threaten established ideologies of cooperation and equality. Some also see the barrenness of money: it is without the life-sustaining powers of most other actors, human and nonhuman, in rural life, offering no care in and of itself.

The tensions between the life of the subsistence farmer and that of the wage laborer is no mere matter of collective versus individual interests, however; rather, the very notions of the collective and the individual are themselves changing. Following this, alterations in what comprise one's material being and one's social world demand adjustments in the manner in which one acts in the world. One must make the unpredictable, the many changes in recent decades, more predictable in order to exercise control in the world. If, as I argue here, care is an underlying category of practice, human and nonhuman, in Juubche', then as the community continues to adapt to change, the meaning of care too will expand and contract, express new motives and assume new forms, and produce new bodies and worlds.

"The Yucatec Maya"

The Yucatán Peninsula is a site, both physical and discursive, of important and sometimes fierce debate about some of the core concepts of anthropology itself, including culture and identity. How to, and whether to, categorize people in this region is a contentious matter (e.g., Castañeda 2004; Castillo Cocom 2004; Hervik 2003; Reyes-Foster 2012). According to Hostettler (2004) and Restall (2009), theories of race dominated colonial and nineteenth-century discourse, and such theories persisted in early studies of indigenous Yucatecans (e.g., Goodner 1930; Redfield and Villa Rojas [1934] 1962; Shattuck and Benedict 1931). The historical and twentieth-century ethnographic literature most commonly used the terms "Yucatec Maya" or "Maya" to describe the indigenous population of the Yucatán Peninsula. Of course, the recognition of indigeneity itself is highly contested and contextual. In this region it has typically included a combination of the following traits: people who are thought to be descended mostly from native non-Europeans, who might speak an indigenous language, and who might still participate in "traditional" lifestyles. Within the broader category of "Maya," indigenous Yucatecans have been distinguished in the literature by the term "lowland Maya," used to contrast them from those "highland Maya" that populate Guatemala and the Mexican state of Chiapas.

The term "Maya" has been critiqued as an identity produced by archaeological and ethnographic discourse and as an identity reified by the Mexican state's turn toward multiculturalism and its increasing reliance on cultural tourism. The latter is exemplified by the state's deployment of this term to describe an entire region, the "Riviera Maya," a region in which the people to which that term is ascribed are often exploited and only visible as tokens of a presumed static culture (Hervik 1999, 2003; Castañeda 1996, 2004; Castillo Cocom 2012; Loewe 2009). For good reasons many of these scholars are reluctant to link identity in Yucatán to any externally perceived continuity in practice or material culture. Others have argued that it is, however, critical to recognize persistent cultural forms, but the way in which they do so has varied. For example, Fischer (1999) describes a "Maya cultural logic spanning community boundaries that simultaneously conditions individual agency and reflects changing consensual ethics that have emerged from practical activity in local and global contexts" (478). López Austin (2001), writing on Mesoamerica more broadly, identifies *el núcleo duro*, a cultural hard core, while Nash (1995) writes of "the extraordinary durability of distinctive cultures in Middle America" (9). In Yucatán local articulations of Mayanness as identity can be traced to the late twentieth-century embrace of multiculturalism by the Mexican state and by the increasingly marketable nature of indigeneity from that period through the present. Amid all of this the term is increasingly claimed by indigenous people themselves. This is happening in a multitude of ways, in ways that are sometimes clearly linked to the commodified value of Mayanness in the tourist industry but also in ways that suggest attempts to wrestle meaning making away from regional and global elites (Taylor 2014). Yet, as Armstrong-Fumero (2011) notes, "the words and things that are often invoked in narratives about Mayan identity had a presence in local life-worlds that preceded the articulation of contemporary identity politics" (66). The ways in which rural indigenous people in this region think about themselves and experience their worlds is not shaped solely by notions of Mayanness imposed by the state, by archaeologists and anthropologists, or by tourism. These have indeed been critical forces, but they circulate among other forces: close ties to kin, living and deceased; attachment to land, attachment that is affective and embodied; and habitual, though never fixed, practices such as cooking and eating that sustain ties to the human and nonhuman.

In his work on the colonial period, Restall (1997) emphasizes the importance for indigenous people of membership in patronym groups and in the *kaj*, a Yucatec Maya community and geographical entity that comprised its members and their individually and collectively owned properties. During the colonial period, again during the mid-nineteenth-century Caste War, and then in the twentieth century, Restall (2004) identifies the process of Mayan ethnogenesis, the reification of a Mayan ethnic identity, an identity that was often refused by the very people it sought to categorize. Castillo Cocom (2007) notes his own tendency and those of other Yucatec Maya speakers he encounters in a Mérida café to identify primarily, though not exclusively, with the communities from which they come. In Juubche' origin in the community is a primary way in which people identify themselves; as described earlier in this introduction, place matters for people in Juubche'. Meanwhile, Reyes-Foster (2012) notes that it is often through other forms of language—in her article, *elegancia* and *mestizaje*—that more meaningful claims to identity, or a lack thereof, take shape.

During one meal in Juubche' don Máximo and doña Esmeralda drank Coca-Cola while I chose to have only water. As don Máximo watched me drink my water, he held up his soft drink. "Look," he said, smiling, "We're the ts'uulo'ob." The category of *ts'uulo'ob* is used to described non-indigenous Yucatecans and other non-indigenous Mexicans, as well as *turistas* (literally "tourists" but also can refer more generally to white individuals) and *gringos* (tourists, usually white but not always). Don Máximo's playful inversion of class and ethnic stereotypes common among the older generation was an important reminder that expressing the connections between people, objects, and other entities is made possible by words, despite the problems they present, and by the material, in this case food. At the same time, for younger residents, for whom Coca-Cola has always been part of life, the rhetorical use of the beverage in this moment would carry less resonance. In fact, my rejection of a beverage some younger people now see as unhealthy might very well match their expectations for the consumption habits of a visiting *gringa*. This too is a reminder of the flexibility of food as a marker of difference, a marker whose meaning is deeply dependent on positionality in this community. In Juubche' I have heard people talk about themselves use terms ranging from *wayilo'on* (we from here) to *paisano* (countryman) to *mayero* (Yucatec Maya speaker) to *masewal* (poor Yucatec Maya speaker) to *yucateco* (Yucatecan, frequently used by younger people). Many residents used the term *Maya* to refer to ancient peoples in whom they see little connection to themselves. Importantly though, over my decade and a half of visits to the community, I have noticed an increase in the usage of this term to describe living people, including residents themselves. In general, people in Juubche' use such a variety of identifying terms that it would be impossible for me to use them all appropriately to describe members of the community or its subgroups unless I devoted the whole of this work to such matters. Forms of identification in the community and elsewhere in the region are, and always have been, in flux.

In her critique of culture and the concept's reliance on generalizations, Abu-Lughod (1991) called for "ethnographies of the particular" (149), a means of resisting the othering and dehistoricizing tendencies of much twentieth-century ethnography. At times this text focuses on individual stories, interrogating the convergence of forces that have shaped that individual's experiences. Quite often common threads have appeared in numerous stories, across individuals and families. When appropriate, I speak specifically of the people of Juubche', I use "residents" or, if appropriate, "informants." In extending my arguments to the larger indigenous or rural indigenous population of the region, which I do with caution, I broaden my terminology to, respectively, "indigenous Yucatecans" or "rural indigenous Yucatecans." When I am talking about other residents of the region, I use

"Yucatecans," recognizing that many factors, such as wealth, phenotypical appearance, and language use, may lead someone to be recognized or to identify as non-indigenous or nonrural. I attempt to distinguish between the categorizations of my informants and my own reliance on problematic but, I hope, ultimately useful terminology.

The Field

First and foremost, "Juubche'" is a pseudonym, one derived from a local name for a kind of tree. My use of a pseudonym is not an attempt to present the town as a generalizable or "typical" community but rather simply an effort to maintain the privacy of the people who have so generously shared their homes and experiences with me. That being said, I realize that such efforts at creating anonymity are not always effective, and that, as Scheper-Hughes (2000) writes, they can sometimes make anthropologists "too free with our pens, with the government of our tongues, and with our loose translations and interpretations of village life" (128). As such, I have tried to write this text with great care for those I write about and as though I was not relying on pseudonyms.

I first visited Juubche' during the summer of 2005 and returned again in the summer of 2006. I conducted formal research in the community between September 2007 and May 2008 and again between January and April 2009, for a total of thirteen months. I returned for shorter visits in January 2014 and the summer of 2017. During the longest stretch of my research, in 2007 and 2008, I spent several weeks in both Mérida and Playa del Carmen to receive medical care. These periods of urban residence allowed me to observe circular migration from another perspective and to compare the economic and social conditions of the two cities. Mérida is a common destination for Juubche' residents for specialized medical care or for bureaucratic matters at the state level, but Playa del Carmen is a far more common migratory destination for rural people from the eastern part of Yucatán, where Juubche' is located. While there, I had opportunities between medical appointments to observe the conditions under which migrant men labor (on construction sites, in hotels, and in restaurants), eat (in the supermarkets and small groceries that dot the city, on curbs and on the floors of work sites), and relax (on public park benches, strolling on the beach, and inside inexpensive bars). While living in Juubche', I spent most of my time in the town itself, making occasional visits to a nearby city or to neighboring communities, often but not always with residents of Juubche'.

During my time in the community I conducted 120 recorded, semistructured interviews with 116 residents in Juubche'. In interviews ranging from a half hour to three hours, informants provided life histories and responses to questions regarding work experiences, religion, food practices, and change in the community. I conducted second interviews with a small number of informants in order to ask more specific questions about food and health issues. I selected some of these informants due to their respected roles in the community; they included several midwives and a shaman. Others were selected for their direct involvement in specialized food practices, including food vendors, store owners, and bakers. The informants ranged in age from late teens to late eighties and represented a variety of religions, occupations, and economic positions. I conducted all interviews in the Yucatec Maya language; while many of my informants were also proficient Spanish speakers, all had spoken Yucatec Maya in their households as children, and few spoke Spanish while at home.

I also compiled a large collection of written field notes based on participant observation in Juubche'. These notes are the products of both everyday and special occasion observations. I observed daily food preparation, food consumption, and other domestic labor in several dozen homes and recorded every single meal I ate in Juubche'. I sometimes participated in food labor, when my offers to help were accepted and when my participation did not hinder the food work (sometimes my lack of skill would have only slowed work or lessened the quality of the food being prepared). I observed food preparation and sales by multiple vendors; biomedical and other ethnomedical healing practices; agricultural labor; and rituals in milpas, in and affiliated with the Roman Catholic Church and popular Catholicism, and in a Jehovah's Witnesses temple. I attended many community events, including ritual gatherings to honor deities and the dead, baptism and jetsmek ceremonies (the latter a rite of passage ceremony held for infants), school recitals, birthday parties, an engagement party, and holiday gatherings. On multiple occasions my stays coincided with the distribution of cash, services, and personal items through federal and local assistance programs. I was also able to attend lectures and work activities organized by the town's health clinic. Thanks to many generous invitations from my informants, I accompanied them on religious pilgrimages, to fiestas in neighboring towns, and in search of medical care. I shared taxi rides and conversations with dozens of residents on our way to and from nearby cities. In May 2008 I was present for the town's annual saint's day fiesta, a weeklong affair featuring communal food gatherings, food sales, and dances.

As a woman in a community in which large numbers of men engaged in circular migration patterns that temporarily skewed the gender ratio each week, I spent far more time with women than men in Juubche'. This was compounded by the fact that residents saw food preparation, with a few exceptions, as women's work. I interviewed many more women than men and had fewer opportunities to speak with men informally. Much of what I learned about masculine spaces such as the milpa and cantina came from formal and informal conversations with men, rather than direct observation. In contrast, I enjoyed tremendous access to feminine spaces such as kitchens. However, some gendered roles and spaces are flexible in Juubche', allowing me to, for example, observe women on cattle ranches and men in kitchens. Nonetheless I acknowledge that this work skews toward analysis of feminine spaces and voices.

Chapter Outline

This book explores the intersections of food and care in what might be understood as nesting spheres of life in Juubche': the interrelated realms of the body, the social, and the cosmological. Within these conceptual realms circulate spaces (the kitchen, the milpa, the town, the world of both living and nonliving) and social groups or entities (the marital pair, the extended family, the community, the state, and the nation). Each chapter explores the ways in which shifting foodways are themselves transformative, often through care, in how people think of and experience their bodies (chapter 2), engage with each other (especially in chapter 3), with their faith, deities, and attendant rituals (chapter 4), and with food work and food itself (chapter 5).

First, however, chapter 1 focuses on the community of Juubche', the prominence of food in the community, and the ways in which it is woven into the routines of daily life. In this chapter I make a case for my focus on the "local" as the nexus for experience in the lives of the people with whom I lived, worked, and ate. I explore everyday encounters with food in Juubche', with a focus on the embeddedness of local values into culinary culture, especially the emphasis on balance and consensus. The chapter also considers the ways in which residents experience and articulate some of the changes in food practices that have occurred over their lifetimes, positioning these anxieties and complaints as openings through which we can understand more widely accepted values attached to food.

The next chapter, chapter 2, first widens it gaze, considering the evolution of material, political, and social conditions that have contributed to the local emphasis on balance in rural Yucatán. Juubche', as a community, is of course a historical construction. While its settlement dates back to before the Conquest, life here is not, and never has been, bound by its geographic boundaries. While cognizant of the way in which this community has long engaged with and been acted on by external forces, I also recognize the centrality of the physical place for its inhabitants. It is this place—its climate and topography, its both shifting and enduring social networks—that has shaped so many of the prominent values and logics explored in this chapter. The chapter then narrows its lens to examine the embodiment of these values and logics through notions of well-being, the relationship between well-being and food, and the manners in which care seeks to maintain well-being on the level of the human body. The chapter's description of local ideas of anatomical organization and function help the reader map sicknesses and sensations to material and corporeal spaces, with a focus on the qualities of foodstuffs and their effects on bodies.

In chapter 3 I examine the increasing commodification of food and its effects on interpersonal relations, from the larger community down to the marital pair. This chapter considers how contemporary exchanges of food challenge or upload the ideals described in chapter 1, and how they manifest the anxieties provoked by social and economic changes. The chapter describes those forms of pleasure thought to threaten individuals and the community and traces their connectedness to food. Through the lens of food practices, this chapter tracks ongoing transformations in social conditions as they intersect with ideas about human nature and social relationships. First, the chapter presents local ideals for how the exchange of food is to occur, both in the gift and market economies. This portion builds on the previous chapter's analysis of the cultural values of consensus and cooperation, but it also scrutinizes local notions of human nature, especially assumptions about the threats posed by inherent self-interest. The chapter investigates the tensions that recent social and economic changes present to ideals for exchange and for human relations more generally. Close analysis of gossip about extramarital sex and the consumption of food commodities presents the case for how novel foodstuffs and changing relationships challenge local social norms, provoke anxieties, and heighten existing inequalities.

Chapter 4 examines the ways in which Catholicism, as it is practiced in Juubche', supports a particular kind of relationship with food, one that relies on care, without forsaking the pleasures of the material. New faiths challenge this and suggest alternative forms of caring that reflect fundamental shifts in human relationships with food. Chapter 4 reveals, yet again, how particular values such as consensus and balance often persist in food practices, but the chapter also argues for the challenges changing relationships with food may pose for long-standing care practices. I analyze the place of food in Catholicism and the indigenous religious practices with which it is entwined, focusing on rituals such as *janal pixaan* and the annual fiesta in honor of the community's patron saint, while also considering the place of food in the ideology and practice of other religious groups in the community.

Chapter 5 explores how new foods provide new ways of caring and new pleasures and how their gradual adoption can have transformative effects. It demonstrates the continued centrality of food in everyday life and the enduring emphasis on consensus despite new conflicts about how food is to be exchanged, prepared, and consumed. The chapter links the larger cultural values of consensus and balance to culinary and gustatory culture in the region and Juubche' in greater depth, making the argument that food culture reflects these cultural values in its emphasis on standardization. I use examples from language, food preparation, and food consumption to demonstrate the persistence of these values. I offer a detailed description of the acquisition of culinary and gustatory expertise as it has typically occurred during the lifetime of my informants in Juubche'. I then analyze the preparation and consumption of new foods, beginning with dishes prepared by younger women from mostly nonlocal ingredients and, following that, snack foods consumed by local children. I follow the effects of these new forms of gastronomic diversity while also noting the sustained expectation for standardization in food practices and products. Like the chapter before it, this chapter is interested in two parallel processes: first, how new beliefs and practices often uphold established values, and, second, how they sometimes, often gradually, diminish those values among some, leading to conflict in the community.

Finally, this work reflects on predictions of the continued decline of small-scale farming, concerns about the sustainability of tourism in the region, and the consequences these and other changes might hold for the future of food in rural Yucatán. Under a new presidential administration and with shifting growth strategies in the tourist industry, the conditions under which the people of Juubche' live and work will continue to shift, perhaps even more dramatically. The conclusion questions how care will evolve as it is increasingly disentangled from the work of the milpa.

CHAPTER 1

The Force with Which We Live

For decades cultural anthropologists have been critiquing, and rightfully so, essentialized links between geographical place and identity, pointing out that such links obscure "the ability of people to confound the established spatial orders" (Gupta and Ferguson 1992, 17). For the most part, place matters in Juubche'. But its mattering is unstable, made clear by the more fragile connection some people have to the community than others, the latter those who are happy to settle in urban areas. Most residents of Juubche' were raised in the community, and many are staying to build their own lives and families, even when opportunities to move to larger towns or cities present themselves. For these individuals, too, the way in which Juubche' matters is not fixed. Their attachment to Juubche' is a continually remade one, renewed through material and social acts that bind them to the community, even if they must regularly leave it to work. Thus my focus on Juubche' as a geographical space that matters more than others in this book follows the orientation of the people with whom I lived, ate, and conversed there. As noted elsewhere in the region (Castillo Cocom 2007), communities of origin often carry more weight in how individuals think of themselves than do broader, often externally applied notions of ethnic or national identity. While this book does not assume a universal and unproblematic link between place and identity, it follows the lead of scholars who have studied the topic in far more depth than I (Farriss 1984; Restall 1997, 2004), in arguing that local communities in rural Yucatán are, for those born or raised in them, meaningful spaces for the construction of selves. The meaningfulness of communities of origin is itself a product of historical conditions explored in greater detail in chapter 2.

For these reasons, this chapter attempts to orient the reader to Juubche' as a material and social space, first in a general sense, describing the layout of the community, its notable spatial features, and its place in the regional economy. The chapter then presents a "thick" descriptive introduction to foodways in Juubche', detailing the variety of engagements with food that are typical of the community on an everyday basis. Included in this are the reflections of residents on recent culinary and gustatory transformations, and consideration of how those transformations challenge or reinforce what are often the agreed-upon desirable traits of local cuisine.

Juubche'

The town of Juubche' is fairly large for rural communities of the region, with a population of several thousand. Nearly all of its adult population identify as native speakers of Yucatec Maya, though some younger families are opting to speak Spanish at home with their children. Yucatec Maya, also known as simply Yucatec, is an indigenous language spoken in southeastern Mexico and in parts of Belize by more than three-quarters of a million people (Instituto Nacional de Estadística y Geografía 2010). Geographically Juubche' is in the heart of the peninsula's maize-growing region, several hours from the former henequen zone to the west and from the major coastal tourist areas to the east. The town, with its current name, was inhabited as far back as the sixteenth century, but my older informants who were born in the 1920s and 1930s report it being home to only about two dozen households during their childhoods. Lower mortality rates, improved educational opportunities in the community itself, and a decline in agricultural practice, with a consequent reduction in the need to find farmland in more distant areas, have contributed to the population growth of Juubche' in the last three decades.

The layout of Juubche' follows the grid pattern common to rural Yucatán, with a large colonial-era Catholic church dominating the town plaza. The church is flanked by older homes and a tiny food stand patronized by local men and truck drivers. At the center of the plaza lies a basketball court, more often used for soccer games and school recess, a series of covered benches, and a taxi stand. Just a few years ago a several-stories-high cover was constructed over the basketball court, protecting those who use it from the sun and rain. Like the public spaces Miller describes in another community in this part of the state (1998, 313), this plaza is a common site for male social interactions, including athletic activities and social drinking, though this becomes more the case after dark. Children play soccer on the basketball court, and women attend events for government assistance programs in this space. Also bordering the plaza is the town hall where business is conducted by the *comisario* (roughly, mayor) and *comisario ejidal* (a similar figure who organizes the distribution and use of collective land). The same building also hosts a DICONSA store, where staple goods are sold at subsidized prices.[1] Next to the town hall is the state-sponsored health clinic, which, on a good day, is staffed by one doctor and two nurses.

There are a number of more isolated homes and ranches once one leaves the paved roads, and in recent years state-sponsored projects have built and improved several roads that lead to neighboring communities. In other directions unpaved paths lead deep into the forest, to distant ranches and eventually other communities. The occasional truck barrels through these paths to reach a ranch, but residents use them more frequently to travel by foot or bicycle for the purpose of reaching cornfields, tending cattle, and collecting wood and medicinal herbs. The most traveled roads are paved but narrow, leading to two major highways: one that heads toward a nearby city, a popular destination for shopping and medical care, and another that heads toward Cancún, where many young men spend the bulk of their working hours. A more recently paved road heads toward a neighboring town; as with the other paved roads, trucks use this one to make deliveries to local stores, and residents use it to travel for social visits or religious worship in other communities. All the paved roads weave through miles of cornfields and a few other rural communities before hitting the highways. Speeding taxis dodge bicycling corn farmers and the occasional errant cattle.

Although there is diversity in multiple forms—religious, economic, generational, among others—shared inhabitance of this place, in addition to the historical forces I explore in the next chapter, shapes a more collectivist orientation. During my interviews I of course heard unique stories, and yet many ended with one of the two same phrases: "That's the life *we* have around here" or "That's just like *our* lives." Most people in Juubche' refer to others being like themselves when those individuals are relatively poor and living in rural areas. Following this, they compare themselves, as a community, to other communities. According to residents of Juubche', the town's population is fairly typical with regard to socioeconomic status among the region's rural towns and villages. Residents point to tangible markers like masonry houses and pickup trucks as markers of economic progress while also noting the continued existence of some dirt roads and homes without toilets. By national standards, the town is economically marginalized, with recent census data showing that, at that time, less than half of households had tap water and just 1 percent of households owned computers (Instituto Nacional de Estadística y Geografía 2010). During my first visit in 2005, I noted only a handful of homes with landline telephones. Since that time, many more residents have acquired cellular phones, including smart phones with which they can access the internet. A small number of families own automobiles, but very few women drive them. Many men who own automobiles work as taxi drivers, serving their fellow townspeople who rely on shared taxis to go between Juubche' and Valladolid or coastal cities. Some drivers take the occasional tourist to an archaeological site near Juubche' or to one of the *cenotes* (sinkholes) in the area, which are mostly managed by a few resident families.

The proximity of Juubche' to the popular tourist destinations of Cancún and Playa del Carmen has changed life in town in profound ways. Since the development of regional tourism on the Caribbean coast in the 1970s, more and more men have taken up the practice of traveling weekly to the coastal cities for work in construction or service industries. Some men do still participate in swidden agriculture, however, walking or bicycling each day to the milpas that surround the community. A small number of men live full-time in town but commute to work at the nearby archeological site or cenote or, in the case of a few young men, in service industry jobs in Valladolid. Other men, though still a minority, supplement or opt out of agricultural labor to tend cattle on neighboring ranches. However, circular migration to and from the coast is the most attractive option for many men. One young man who was studying for an undergraduate degree explained to me that while he would prefer to work locally, there simply are not well-paying jobs in or close to Juubche'. For the majority of young men who are far less educated than this informant, working on the coast presents the only opportunity to earn a living wage. Furthermore, many boys and young men are uninterested in farming, which they equate with poverty and low social status.[2] Yet, while there, most perform menial labor; a majority of migrants from Juubche' work in construction, ironwork, or carpentry, while smaller numbers work directly in tourism, as groundskeepers or busboys for hotels or restaurants. Like indigenous workers from other communities in this region (Castellanos 2010; Sandoval 2009; Torres 2011), these men are often compensated poorly for their labor. Although many communities have their success stories, migrants who have found prosperity on the coast, for many men, long hours of difficult and often dangerous work bring few rewards: at best, enough cash to feed a family back home and to make payments on a television or stereo purchased in more optimistic times. In many ways the tourist industry and the migration it encourages have reproduced existing inequalities in the region and globally (Torres 2011), with consequences for human well-being and ecology that concern many scholars and rural residents alike (Daltabuit and Leatherman 1998; Leatherman and Goodman 2005; Pi-Sunyer and Thomas 1997). In Juubche' residents note increases in diabetes, gastrointestinal diseases, infertility, pregnancy and childbirth complications, and alcoholism.

Due to the weekly migration of most men, the town takes on a vastly different appearance on weekends; men, often drunk, socialize outside of cantinas or in the town square, while others bicycle around town visiting family. On weekdays, in contrast, the town is fairly sedate, populated by mostly women, children, and older men. Outside of the annual fiesta, which attracts hordes from neighboring towns and cities, visitors to Juubche' are usually limited to the teachers who commute in each day, mostly from larger towns and cities; itinerant vendors; and deliverymen from food companies. Occasionally tourists might be seen bicycling through town or visiting the handicraft market run by one local family, drawn to the area by the nearby archaeological site.

Juubche' is home to a preschool, an elementary school, and a secondary school. Children usually study through the end of secondary school, until age fifteen or sixteen. Small numbers of students continue with a preparatory education, until recently in the municipal seat but now in Juubche' itself, or at language schools in a nearby city, where they study English (mostly), French, and Italian to prepare themselves for work in tourism. A very small number follow secondary school with college-level training in business, nursing, and other professional fields. Pursuit of higher education, though uncommon, appears to be relatively balanced between young men and young women in Juubche'; in families with available funds, educational resources are concentrated on those children who are the brightest and most studious, seemingly regardless of gender. In fact, it may be easier for girls and young women to defer marriage to continue their studies than for boys and young men to defer wage labor to do the same. Despite the increase in educational opportunities, nearly all children still actively participate in household labor, performing tasks such as caring for younger siblings, carrying out basic food preparation, and chopping wood. In most families this labor is highly gendered from young ages, with girls doing domestic work inside the home and boys more likely to be sent out to assist with farming and wood collection. Like Castellanos (2010, 67–68), I found that age ten seemed the age at which children were entrusted with such duties. Prior to this their most frequent contribution to domestic labor seemed to be running minor errands, such as shopping for low-cost items such as cilantro and soft drinks.

Some entire nuclear families in Juubche' have made permanent moves to Cancún or other coastal cities, but few women have taken on the role of temporary migrants, in contrast to some other communities in the region (Castellanos 2010; Greene 2002). In Juubche' women's labor is based largely in the home but often includes various local entrepreneurial enterprises. In addition to the unpaid work of caring for children, *u meyaj janal* (the work/creation of food), and cleaning their homes and clothing, many women embroider *iipiles*, a regional dress worn by some women, weave hammocks, and sew clothing for sale locally or through middlemen in regional tourist markets. For some women these activities are minor supplements to the earnings of their husbands and government assistance, but for others these activities can be more profitable. The sale of garden produce such as habanero peppers and cilantro contributes to the earnings of women as well, providing a small but regular source of cash. Other women also wash clothes for extended family or neighbors, administer injections, or cut and style hair. Other labor activities may provide less consistent income but prove more lucrative or demanding; several women in the community have participated in state-sponsored midwifery training and attend low-risk pregnancies, referring high-risk cases to biomedical practitioners or one of the regional hospitals. Several women sell prepared foods and snacks to students at the local schools, and a small number, all relatively young and unmarried, commute to factory jobs in or near the closest city, where they assemble undergarments and other products for sale to American and European consumers. As the flow of cash earnings into Juubche' has increased with the development of tourism, many more families have invested in small businesses, such as general stores, *tortillerías* (tortilla factories) and *molinos* (corn mills), and meat markets. In most cases women run these businesses day to day, but investment in them usually binds together members of a nuclear or even extended family. In one family three adult children, two brothers in their late twenties and their younger sister in her early twenties, opened a store in their parents' compound, pooling together earnings from wage labor in Cancún and Juubche'. The sister, who is unmarried, manages the inventory and finances, while her mother and her brothers' wives occasionally help with customers. The family of doña Cristina found some success with a molino attached to their home. They saved enough to open a second mill on the property of doña Cristina's sister and her husband. One of doña Cristina's teenaged daughters moved there to run the molino with her aunt and uncle, the property owners.

Still, most households do not have the resources to invest in potentially profitable businesses like molinos and groceries. Nor do most migrants engage in salaried labor that promises a steady flow of cash. A majority of households are dependent on any combination of milpa agriculture, small-scale handicraft sales, sporadic wage labor, and government assistance. All families rely on cash, although to varying degrees. An elderly couple who

2. Home garden. Courtesy of Justin Nevin.

farm and raise animals may only require cash for foodstuffs such as salt and soft drinks, the occasional clothing purchase, and medical expenses, plus occasional ritual expenditures. In contrast, a young family with many children will need significantly more money for those same expenses plus diapers and school materials, as well as transportation funds and possibly tuition if a child pursues education beyond secondary school. Although this book rests upon particular premises about life in Juubche'—that certain ways of being in the world are valued above others—it also interrogates the range of experiences residents have and the conflicts created by sometimes disparate beliefs and practices.

Foodways in Juubche'

Despite the clear aging of the farming population, as noted elsewhere in the region (Ebel and Castillo Cocom 2012), most extended families in Juubche' have at least one member who still cultivates corn, but those farmers are often over the age of forty. If the farmer is not a member of

3. Feeding young turkeys. Courtesy of author.

their nuclear family, they may obtain corn through the exchange of cash or services (e.g., the construction of a home), but most residents purchase corn from stores in town. Even farming families buy at least some of their other staple foods such as beans and squash from neighbors with a surplus or, more commonly, from stores in town. With little to no market for these crops outside the town—local farmers simply cannot compete in price or quantity with imported staples—the occasional surplus becomes a source of cash for farmers who benefit from the fact that many kin and neighbors no longer work their own milpas.

Among farming and nonfarming families alike, most have at least a small home garden, known as a *soólar* (*solar* in Spanish), in which they raise animals and grow fruit, chiles, herbs (for cooking and medicine), and other greens. The exceptions tend to be households headed by younger women who disdain the labor required by gardening and raising animals.[3] They are in the minority; for most of the community, domesticated animals offer food in the form of meat and eggs, and these animals, especially pigs, are important forms of investment during periods of great economic need, such as times of illness or in preparation for a wedding. Chicken, beef, and pork are consumed at most a few times a week and are almost always freshly slaughtered, either within the household or by fellow residents for a fee or in exchange for cuts of meat. Loudspeaker announcements in the evening and then again in the early morning hours announce the details: what type of meat, where it can be purchased, and the selling price per kilogram. Increases in wealth have made both raising livestock and eating their meat more accessible. On weekend mornings, when the cash influx into the community is greatest, just after male migrants have returned, a half-dozen or more animals may be slaughtered, and the loudspeaker announcements play out price wars between sellers. Slaughtering and butchering is gendered labor: men slaughter and butcher pigs, cattle, and deer, and women slaughter and butcher chickens, turkeys, and small game.

When wage labor jobs are few and far between, more men hunt for local game such as deer, agouti, peccary, and gophers, though such animals are increasingly scarce. Eggs, from residents' own hens or purchased from neighbors, are a more common part of the everyday diet and may make their way to the table every other day in some households. Soft drinks such as Coca-Cola have been a regular part of most residents' diets since the construction of major roads in the 1980s. Some families have taken to buying bottled water, largely upon the advice of the local clinic.[4] Residents supplement produce, eggs, and meat with store-bought goods such as sugar, salt, instant coffee, and crackers, and some purchase more expensive processed foods such as sweetened yogurts, hot dogs, and sandwich bread. While many households purchase prepared tortillas from local stores, others pay to grind corn at the same stores and then pat out homemade tortillas; most families do both, making the decision based on such factors as available time, access to corn, and individual taste preferences. Midday sees lines of women and girls streaming out of the most popular molinos and tortillerías, most with buckets of soaked corn in hand or balanced on heads. When the cash is available, many families regularly buy fresh-baked French bread and *pan dulce* (sweet breads) for light breakfasts or dinners. Juubche' is home to one baker, but several bakers from neighboring towns sell their goods from their cars each evening.[5] The beeps of bakers' car horns frequently interrupt evening viewing of popular telenovelas, as drivers stop and pop their trunks or van doors open to showcase their wares.

Meals are fairly structured in Juubche' with three a day as the norm. However, whether individual members of the household eat together and at what time depends upon labor demands and educational obligations. In most homes breakfast consists of heavily sweetened instant coffee and some sort of bread product, usually bread from local bakers or packaged crackers from a grocery store. If a woman prepared tamales and empanadas the day before or purchased them from a neighbor, members of the household may eat those. When men head out to the milpa, their wives are more likely to prepare something more substantial such as eggs scrambled with onion, tomato, salt, and habanero chile, and served with fresh tortillas, or *piim*, thick tortillas often served with a mixture of lard and dried red chiles. This is an example of how labor activities structure meals, in this case manifesting a locally important distinction between *janal* (food) and *uk'ul* (drink/breakfast). Uk'ul always consists of beverages, usually hot, but can also include nondrinkable components, such as pan dulce. It is just as much defined by what it is not as what it is: uk'ul does not include tortillas or *ki' waaj*, any of a range of savory dishes served with tortillas. Together, tortillas and ki' waaj comprise janal.

The main meal of the day, served between eleven and two in the afternoon, depending upon the schedules of household members, almost always consists of janal. This includes fresh tortillas (made by a female in the family or purchased in town just before the meal), ki' waaj (the savory accompaniment), and soft drinks. The base of ki' waaj usually consists of meat (most often chicken, beef, or pork), eggs, beans (usually some variety of black beans but when in season lima beans too), squash seeds, or a vegetable such as squash, potato, or chaya. Less frequently women may prepare ki' waaj with lentils or noodles. Meat is usually grilled or boiled over the cooking fire by women or roasted in the *piib* (underground pit) by men, though the latter is usually reserved for special occasions or ritual meals. Eggs are scrambled with onions, habanero chile, and tomato; baked over the fire like a frittata with mint and onion; or fried and topped with sour orange juice, crushed habanero chile, and salt. Beans are usually boiled, salted, and served with cilantro, diced onion, and a piece of habanero chile (to be dabbed at with each piece of tortilla or added to the beans). Boiled beans, especially those left over from a previous meal, are often fried with lard and liquefied in a blender to make *tsabil bu'ul* (refried beans). Chaya, a local green, is boiled and served with lime and dried, ground squash seeds. Squash seeds are also mixed with pureed cooked tomato, habanero chile, sour orange juice, and salt to make a dish known as *sikil p'aak*, while vegetables such as squash and potatoes are usually sautéed with onions, habanero chile, and salt. Some dishes are more labor intensive but still are usually reserved for weekdays rather than weekends. Most of these dishes do not contain meat, which is more widely available on weekends and often specifically requested by returning male migrants. Younger women are often less confident in their preparation of more elaborate meatless dishes and may invite their mothers or mothers-in-law to cook and eat with them. These dishes include *onsikilbil je'*, a spiced broth made of ground squash seeds, corn dough, and lard, containing several dozen hard-boiled eggs; *x-pipian*, shaped patties of ground squash seeds and spices cooked in a broth with noodles, more spices, chaya, chayote, sweet potato, salt, lard, and sour orange juice; and *k'olbil je'*, hardboiled eggs in a spiced broth made of ground squash seeds, corn dough, and lard.[6] Students attending schools or universities outside of the town or those who commute daily to nearby cities may purchase *tortas*, sandwiches on crusty rolls, or other inexpensive fast foods while away from home.

The last meal of the day is usually eaten between seven and nine in the evening. It may consist of leftovers from the afternoon meal, a newly prepared "fast food" meal such as tacos with cold soft drinks, or pastries and breads with coffee or hot chocolate. Over the course of the day, the average adult also snacks on fruit such as apples or grapes purchased in local stores or from itinerant vendors, or fruits picked in the soólar, such as oranges, mamey, or cherimoya. Occasionally farmers bring back crops such as squash or cassava from their milpas for women to boil and serve with honey. Adults and children in wealthier families may also eat sandwiches (on mass-produced bread or bakery rolls), yogurt, or packaged chips and cookies. Children in particular snack often in Juubche' and elsewhere in rural Yucatán (Gaskins 1999; Leatherman and Goodman 2005). Snacks sold at the schools, usually by women from the community, consist of packaged chips and cookies, cups of fruit-flavored gelatin, or homemade foods such as empanadas and pork rinds.

In January of 2009 I joined doña Teófila, who sold snacks at the elementary school, to watch her prepare her goods at her home. Each school day that year, she sold three kinds of *chicharrones* (fried wheat chips served with hot sauce, not the pork rinds of the same name); either *panuchos*, *salbutes*, or *empanadas* (all fried, corn-based snacks); and orange wedges with chile powder. Every Saturday, she told me, she would purchase bags of uncooked chicharrones and seven bottles of vegetable oil in the closest city. On the day I visited, she fried the chicharrones in oil, sitting on a stool in front of her cooking fire, letting them swell up before removing them, letting them cool and draining the oil. Her husband and daughter-in-law helped her distribute them into several dozen small plastic bags. Doña Teófila sealed each bag by touching the open end to a piece of burning wood, melting the plastic together. Early in the mornings, she explained, she prepared the other foods she sells, the panuchos, salbutes, or empanadas, sometimes waking up at 4 a.m. to do so. Children's appetites for snacks and their parents' willingness to provide money for those snacks help sustain this informal industry, upon which women such as doña Teófila rely. As circular migration and other forms of wage labor have brought more cash into the community, these women have capitalized on such opportunities to earn, but their goods must compete in price and taste with the industrially produced chips and cookies available in local stores, reflecting an unprecedented range of options for consumers.

Transformation

As in other communities in the region (Fernández-Sousa 2015; O'Connor 2012), the content and cooking technologies of contemporary diets in Juubche' reveal both continuity—the centuries-old prominence of corn, beans, squash, and chiles, and a reliance on grinding, for example—and change. The oil doña Teófila uses to fry the chicharrones, as described above, is slowly replacing lard in many households, but lard and the practice of frying are both colonial adoptions, made possible by the arrival of pigs in the region. Some of these changes are looked upon favorably. Although most older residents remarked on the paucity of milpa products today compared to the past, many noted that there is far more variety in the average diet today. Doña Cristina came of age and married during a period of severe land shortages in and around Juubche' in the 1960s, and she and her husband settled deep in the forest in order to find available land for farming. Back then, when they were living alone and isolated, she remembered getting sick of eating the same foods. In contrast, she explained, "Now if you get bored and have the money, you can find something else to eat."

Chapter 5 explores in greater detail the ways in which such shifts have unfolded in recent history, but I detail here residents' responses to these shifts because they aid in my framing of what constitutes "good food" in this community. For example, for some residents, the new variety of foodstuffs available today is outweighed by the limited ability of some of those foods have to sustain life. Even today's potable water, according to some in the community, contains bleach or other chemicals that kill most plants. Don Teo, in his fifties, compared the paltry fruits of his garden with those of his late grandmother: "Back then, we had to grab water from the well, from the cenotes. . . . Today the water's changed. Back then, my grandmother had onions, listen to this, she had garlic, she had cilantro . . . lettuce . . . carrots. Everything my grandmother planted grew." Don Belchor, in his eighties, lamented the abundance of processed foods now available in Juubche': "Pure science," he declared them with disdain. Chips, cookies, and soft drinks, he explained, are not natural or healthy. In fact, they cause new illnesses, he argued. Doña Cristina, who once described machine-made tortillas as tasting like "cats' ears," expressed similar sentiments: "Well, in the past, we drank *atole* [a corn-based drink] every day. Just a little because we didn't have a lot, but we didn't drink any milk. But life now, the life of the children who are growing up now, they drink milk and they get one or another sickness. We [older people], in contrast, ate yucca, sweet potato . . . all these types of things. They gave us the force with which we live now. That's the nourishment from plants and their roots."

Such discourse privileges the local as more suited for local bodies and positions the "natural" as inherently healthier. Many Juubche' residents mentioned to me that local eggs do not go bad as quickly and hence do not so easily cause bodily harm as those produced on factory farms. Tortilla dough ground from locally grown corn feels smoother to the hand, "smoother" and "more natural," than that purchased from local stores and shipped in from other parts of Mexico or the United States. Some people complained about the taste of most pork raised in the community today; now fed commercial feed, contemporary pigs grow too large, they claimed. Their meat is too fatty and lacks the subtle flavors imparted by a diet of corn, sweet potatoes, and squash, which nearly everyone in Juubche' fed their pigs prior to the 1980s. The commodification of pig food, linked both to the decline of local agriculture (which produced the crops pigs ate in the past) and to the availability and growing appeal of commercial pig feed, produces other material effects that reshape interspecies care practices. Don Máximo and doña Esmeralda frequently complained that commercial food made the pigs' waste smell worse. This combined with the growth in the town's human population and the consequent requirement that pig owners keep their animals in pens meant that this foul-smelling waste collects in the owners' yards. Doña Esmeralda gave up raising pigs entirely for several years, citing the high cost of commercial feed and her disgust with the smell of the waste, especially while eating. Here food practices order time and space: choosing not to raise pigs led doña Esmeralda to reorganize spaces for economic activity in her yard, making room, for example, for more chickens, with their different feeding schedules and space requirements. But while chickens may provide small and consistent income, pigs are reliable forms of long-term investment, useful in times of financial need. It is not just the use of space in the soólar that shifts with such a decision then, but also the allocation and access to resources over time.

Commentary on shifting food practices does not always privilege the past or the local. Doña Elda insisted that beans always smell better cooked on a stove rather than over a fire: "Even if you weren't hungry, you will become hungry." Doña Patricia and don Elicier agreed that the homemade tablets of drinking chocolate that they bought from a neighbor were unpleasantly grainy compared to the store-bought kind. Doña Patricia and don Elicier's critique may have been as much of their neighbor's entrepreneurial endeavor, seen perhaps as a threat to economic equality in the community, as of the chocolate's material qualities, but these cases remind us that commodities such as stoves and mass-produced drinking chocolate, although far more numerous now than in the past, can possess pleasurable qualities that can be old or new, invoking pleasures of the past or pleasurable promises of the future. These pleasures sometimes fit well with deep-rooted habits of cares: the commensality and reciprocity enacted in the sharing of a pot of beans with extended kin or sipping drinking chocolate with one's spouse.

Increasingly food provokes sensations and dispositions through the embodiment of biomedical and nutritional assumptions as much as through older indigenous sets of knowledge. Elsewhere in the world the embodiment of these assumptions has shaped new tastes and sensations that link food to beauty, morality, and biomedical health (Braziel and LeBesco 2001; Caplan 1997; Hardin 2013; Solomon 2016). In Juubche' the embodiment of new forms of knowledge is sometimes self-conscious, making reference to foods' changing qualities and even transformations in the nature of bodies, as I explore in the next chapter. In recent years residents note a slight decline in the consumption of soft drinks, linked to concerns about diabetes, and more people consume processed foods targeted at certain populations, such as women and children. In the household of one upwardly mobile young family, I saw both a box of individual servings of "women's" oatmeal and a container of "children's" powdered chocolate milk fortified with vitamins and minerals. I then began noticing the powdered chocolate milk in other households with small children. While previously local food may have been prepared with children in mind with less chile or lard, for example, the dishes were not fundamentally different from those consumed by adults. The intensity with which industrial food producers have targeted Mexico post-NAFTA relies not only upon the identification of Mexicans as a group of consumers (Gálvez 2018), but also upon the identification, or rather creation, of consumer subgroups within that larger body, such as children.

Pharmaceutical marketing has also inspired new ways of understanding bodily experience and bodily needs. Many residents insisted to me that they suffered from gastritis, despite having not seen biomedical practitioners for formal diagnoses. Their symptoms, clearly sources of genuine suffering for these individuals, mirrored those on a frequently aired television commercial for a gastritis medication. Yet, they insisted to me that older generations hadn't suffered such symptoms; the conditions of contemporary life, including the weaknesses of modern bodies, made gastritis possible. Of course, as in other parts of the world, biomedicine and nutritional science contends with alternative food logics and distinct concrete social and material conditions. In rural Yucatán nutritional and biomedical information is appropriated or rejected through careful consideration of its value against other systems of knowledge, including the hot-cold syndrome. While none of these systems are necessarily discrete, their logics can support and reproduce each other or call each other into question (Counihan 1999; Farquhar 2002; Yates-Doerr 2015). Consequently bodies can be slow to integrate biomedical and nutritional assumptions into their repertoires of sensory responses. Doña Angelina complained about having to adjust her diet due to a diagnosis of diabetes twenty years ago. Since then she has used oil instead of lard for cooking, but she continues to be disgusted by the way it floats to the top of her food. The oil, a distantly produced commodity, is an apt metaphor: it doesn't finely coat or seep into doña Angelina's eggs or beans the way the lard she purchases from the local butcher does. Rather it lingers apart, only drawing attention to its difference.

Access to cash has also diversified the kitchen technologies and what Christie (2008) describes as "kitchenspaces," the boundaries of which "are evidently defined by social activity and gendered relationships rather than by physical structures" (2). In most households in Juubche', men roast certain meats and vegetables in the *píib*, an underground pit constructed in house yards, usually in a corner or other spot where it will not interfere with gardening or the care of livestock. In contrast, the kitchenspace is a feminine space, more fixed but also flexible. Women, who do most of the cooking work, use three-stone hearths located in their homes, but usually only in thatch-roofed structures, or in a sheltered part of their yard. In these spaces they boil, fry, and grill foodstuffs. A minority of households own stoves or ovens, or a combination of the two; these tend to be households headed by younger, upwardly mobile couples such as Elena, whose notable culinary practices are examined later in chapter 5.[7] In a few households headed by middle-aged couples, stoves and ovens are used to supplement cooking hearths, providing additional cooking space to more efficiently feed their large families. Doña Valentina, a mother in her forties, explained that the stove was useful for heating water and reheating beans, but she preferred to cook tortillas on a griddle atop the fire. Doña Elda explained that her stove was nice to have when she ran out of wood for the hearth, but, despite my frequent visits, I never saw her cooking with the former. However, on a few occasions, I did witness her daughter-in-law or her oldest daughter boiling beans or pasta on the stovetop, while doña Elda or her elderly mother patted out tortillas near the hearth. Other cooking technologies were more universally accepted; nearly all women use blenders occasionally for pureeing beans or tomato sauce. And some technologies are resigned to more specialized or ritual uses. Like Fernández-Sousa (2015), I found that in those households in which stone *metates* were still present, they are used to grind only occasionally, such as in preparing a spice mixture, rather than for the everyday grinding of nixtamalized corn. For this, metates have been replaced, first, by manual metallic mills and then by the electric molinos owned by a few families in town.

Duty and Pleasure

The labor required for contemporary food preparation, even with the aid of blenders and electric molinos, can be burdensome. Some women shirk as much of this labor as is socially acceptable (Wynne 2015). But providing pleasure through food is an important form of caregiving for all of the women I met in Juubche'. A woman may make something because "Tak in jantik" (I want to eat it), but her cravings are but one of many factors that she considers in planning any meal. Although women might decide to prepare a dish because they want to eat it, they will rarely do so if that dish does not please their husbands and children. Children are the most finicky eaters: they may refuse to eat certain dishes and thus oblige their mothers to prepare something else. Husbands, especially those who spend much of the week working away from home, may also voice requests for particular dishes. However, during the workweek, when many men are away on the coast, women may join their mothers or sisters to prepare less common dishes for their own consumption and that of their children. During visits to members of one extended family with six adult sisters, most of whom were married to migrants, I frequently found them visiting one another, working together to produce a meal under the close watch of their elderly mother. The many children of the sisters flowed in and out of houses, dropping off their school bags and heading out to fetch Coca-Cola and cilantro. Male migration makes such forms of shared food labor possible (Wynne 2015); when men are in Juubche', most expect their wives to be preparing food in their own homes.

Women's food consumption is constrained in other ways as well. As I argue in chapter 3, women who do not share food, who prepare foods that their husbands and children do not eat, and who frequently purchase snacks for their consumption alone, are seen as selfish, stingy, or even sexually deviant, content to satisfy their own appetites while failing to meet their responsibilities for care. A relatively new diversity of labor and education opportunities leads to household members often dining at different times, but husbands usually expect their wives to be available to prepare hot tortillas for them or, at the very least, toast the cold ones or send a child out for a machine-made batch. Women often order their days around this duty; many I know went out of their way to avoid obligations outside of the home around mealtimes. On the weekends invitations to join kin for celebratory meals in honor of birthdays, baptisms, or weddings eases the labor of cooking more complex dishes for returning migrants. The foods served on weekends also break up the well-loved but oft-repeated staples of the workweek, as women gather the ingredients and recruit labor to prepare more elaborate dishes like *chocolomo*, a stew of beef, offal, tomato, garlic, onion, and sour orange or lime juice, served with tortillas and a *salpicón*, or salad mixture, of diced radish, onion, cilantro, chile, and sour orange juice; or *puchero*, a stew of chicken, pork, eight kinds of vegetables, the local spice marinade known as *xak*, and sour orange juice, served with tortillas, pickled jalapeños, fried noodles, and a sauce made of sour orange juice, cilantro, white onion, habanero chile, and salt. On occasion, women prepare the favorite for weddings and fiestas, *relleno negro*, turkey or, more commonly, chicken with pork in a sauce of blackened chiles, toasted onion and garlic, and achiote and other spices, served with tortillas. If men are successful in hunting, their families might enjoy *piibil kej*, pit-roasted venison, often served in a broth with cilantro, habanero chile, and tortillas; or a salpicón of *u bak'el jaaleb*, pit-roasted agouti meat shredded and mixed with cilantro, diced radish and habanero chile, and salt, and marinated with sour orange juice, served with tortillas.

Women are expected to be capable of feeding their families by the time they are married, but in reality most newlywed couples spend a year or more in the home of the husband's parents. New brides defer to their mothers-in-law on most important household matters, including the preparation of meals. Within a few years, most young couples find the funds to build homes of their own, either within the compound of the husband's parents or on newly purchased property of their own. At that time, women begin to cook for their own nuclear families, but they also become active participants in the exchange of food with extended kin, including adult siblings, parents, and in-laws. Generosity and commensality are valued; not only are food exchanges between households everyday occurrences, but adults offer food to any guests who arrive during meals. Hosts usually insist on serving food or drink to particularly esteemed guests, such as kin from out of town, religious leaders, or teachers at any time of day. Frequent opportunities for commensality and the prominent role of food in daily conversations contribute to a degree of consensus on tastes and other material qualities of food. While individuals may have particular *gustos* (tastes) and contestations are not unheard of, certain qualities mark food as "good."

What Makes Food Good

Despite the hard and sometimes dangerous labor they require, food practices are still perhaps the most culturally valued of activities in Juubche'. These interactions are sources of great pleasure, when they are carefully managed and when they manifest qualities that conform with how residents understand themselves and their needs. The word *ki'* (tasty) is used, above all, with respect to the taste of food; an example is *ki' tin chi'* (tasty to my mouth). *Ki' waaj*, defined earlier, literally translates to "tasty tortillas" but actually refers to food eaten with tortillas. Of people who are pleasingly plump, it is common to hear *ki' u janal* (her eating is tasty), implying that the person finds more than perhaps the typical pleasure from eating. *Ki'imak in wóol*, a frequently uttered phrase, expresses joy and happiness. *Ki'* is also used to describe a select few other activities: bathing, sleeping, and resting in a hammock. Importantly, these activities all provide one with a sense of satisfaction—refreshment, relaxation, or fullness—that feels good to the body. They are not extraordinary sensations but rather those that are thought to characterize a good life, inclusive of pleasure, balance, and a lack of suffering.

How does food contribute to this sensation in particular ways? For people in Juubche', food cannot truly bring pleasure unless it *ku naktal* (fills). For most of my older informants, memories of food scarcity persist. Many recalled eating tortillas with just a small amount of chile when food was in short supply. Doña Esmeralda recounted that during a particularly trying time some neighbors even begged for the water in which she had soaked her corn prior to grinding it. It was more filling than plain water, she explained to me. For the elderly, this history of lack inspired an appreciation of humble food, and for many of them, a simple bowl of beans with chile, cilantro, and lime juice, served with hot tortillas, was an ideal meal. Such a meal, an everyday example of janal (the pairing of ki' waaj and tortillas), is that which fuels work in the fields or around the house. Don Pascual explains, "When you begin to make movements, to work, your body wakes up. If you're just laying down, you don't feel hunger." For the residents of Juubche', for whom hard work is often a necessity from puberty until death, food must nourish them in such a way that they are able to perform each day's labor, which for many years entailed growing and processing food. Hanks (1990) claims that for indigenous Yucatecans, the body is made up of those substances that fill the material world around them. In Juubche' the consumption of beans and corn, for example, made possible certain forms of labor, including the production of those very crops, for generations. Together, particular forms of production and consumption comprise something comparable to the *mantenimiento* concept that characterizes the interconnected activities of Zapotec farmers in Oaxaca (González 2001), linking not only food production and consumption together but also activities such as child rearing, with recognition of the role said activities play in the reproduction of life, human and nonhuman. What then does it mean to feed the body unfamiliar substances? If one cannot consume the foods that she or her kin produce, what then is one's place in the cycle of material and social reproduction? These are the sorts of questions about food with which some community members grapple, particularly because these interwoven processes of reproduction, of humans and plants, have for generation dominated not only daily rhythms and routines but ritual life as well, as discussed in chapter 4.

Like the human body, any dish is made up of components that work together to produce balance. Compliments offered to cooks remark often on the achievement of balance; perhaps as much as or even more so than ki', declarations of *tun p'iis* or *tiibil* (both of which roughly translate to "balanced" or "just right,") bring pride in one's culinary skills. Ki' tin chi' (tasty to my mouth) is a verbalization of an individual assessment of good taste more than an objective statement on the objective and (ideally) agreed-upon balance of a dish. In contrast, tun p'iis and tiibil embody social expectations for how certain foods ought to taste, look, feel, or smell. That is, food must taste as the eater expects it to taste. Even outside the realm of food, tun p'iis or tiibil are used to describe sensorially experienced qualities that are just right, proportionate, or balanced: a dress that fits well or a framed portrait that hangs straight.

The emphasis on repetition and mastery is central to the reproduction of rural Yucatecan cuisine, and culinary authority in Juubche' is based on preparing correctly a large but discrete repertoire of established dishes. Families may claim different styles of cooking, but there is a general agreement about which women possess the most impressive culinary skills. These culinary experts are those who can perfectly execute an established dish without the benefit of a written recipe (something on which few residents of Juubche' rely). Creativity and experimentation are undesirable and best avoided through careful tinkering based on experienced taste, touch, smell, and sight and, if necessary, through consultation with a more skilled cook. Like Kray (2005), I have argued that this emphasis on culinary standardization is representative of the value placed on consensus in rural indigenous communities in this region (Wynne 2013). As with urban Yucatecan food (Ayora-Diaz 2012), tastes are naturalized, masking the negotiations and transformations that shape what comes to be seen as part of a culinary tradition. While foodways in Juubche' have never been unchanging, exposure and access to nonlocal ingredients has always been more limited than in the largely urban spaces of Ayora-Diaz's work. Since the 1980s, however, exposure and access have greatly increased, as they have throughout rural Mexico (Gálvez 2018), and local experts have mediated the potential disruption this poses for the culinary and gastronomic fields of the community. The critical tasks of these local experts include teaching family and friends to purchase, prepare, and consume novel foods in ways that render them knowable and edible. Getting food "just right" is crucial for the achievement of balance in multiple realms, including that of the body, but it is also matter of maintaining tranquility and achieving pleasure through shared expectations and experiences.

Most residents of Juubche' have discerning palates that seem to be in sync with the tastes of others; typically eaters are in agreement as to whether a dish is too *ch'óoch'* (salty), *paj* (sour), *ch'ujuk* (sweet), or *páap* (spicy), among other taste categories. It would be beyond the scope of this project to measure taste perceptions. Rather I have relied on verbal and nonverbal expressions during direct engagement with food and during interpersonal exchanges around food, evidence of patterns in food use and preparation, and the circulation of normative ideas of food preparation and consumption to identify what I think are not just attempts at agreement or conformity, but rather largely shared ideas about how food should be prepared and consumed.

This emphasis on standardization is evidenced by the use of the very terms for tastes. Ch'óoch' signifies "salty," but not, as the English word implies, "too salty." Rather, ch'óoch' signifies "perfectly salty" or "just right salty"; the response to a question about whether one's food is ch'óoch' is most often those terms that connote balance: tun p'iis or tiibil. *Jach ch'óoch'* signifies "too salty," and *ma' ch'óoch'i'* literally translates to "not salty," though the implication is more often "not salty enough." Other taste words function similarly: for example, páap. My own preference for spicy-hot foods initially led me to proclaim, with pleasure, several dishes *jach páap*. The looks of concern on cooks' faces made it evident to me that jach páap is not preferable and implicates a cook in using too much chile. Instead of marking an individual subjective assessment of food's qualities, such terminology stakes an objective claim to detecting the "just right."

The assumption that one can speak for others' perceptions of food, that is, that one can make objective claims about taste and that this is distinct from individual preferences is naturalized through preparing and consuming food in social settings, rarely alone. Over time and beginning in childhood, everyone in Juubche' develops some sense of what tastes and looks good, and this sense often comes from merely dining with other more expert eaters. Frequent opportunities for commensality, and the incessant food talk that accompanies them, contribute to a degree of consensus on tastes and other material qualities of food. Children hone their palates by observing and mimicking the frequent commentaries of adults. While older women do have the final say at special occasion events, individuals of all ages, male or female, may choose to add some salt or chile to their portions at everyday meals. These actions rarely go unnoticed by the cook. I witnessed one incident in which a ten-year-old girl happened to visit her great-aunt while the latter was doling out *kaabij kaax*, a chicken dish often served in broth. Urged to sit down and eat, the girl dipped a piece of tortilla into the broth, tasted it, and got up to look for something on a nearby table. Her great-aunt watched her and asked, "What are you looking for?" "Salt," the girl responded. "It's not salty?" her great-aunt asked in surprise. The girl replied in the negative and, upon finding the salt jar, threw a bit into her bowl. This ten-year-old was bolder than most for expressing her criticism to an older relative, and that she did so speaks more to their unusually informal relationship than to a cultural norm for intergenerational relations. However, her ability to discern a slight lack of something in her food—salt, sour orange juice, sugar—is not unusual for children her age in rural Yucatán. Seen not as a verbalization of individual taste, her comment was rather accepted as a negative but objective assessment of the dish. Her great-aunt was surprised and perhaps slightly insulted, but she did not counter the girl's critique. Despite a culinary hierarchy that positions the great-aunt higher than her young niece, the latter's ability to taste well cannot be discounted. Even at the age of ten, children are expected to have acquired, through observation, at least some critical tasting skills, especially of more basic dishes like this one.

In another instance I observed collective criticisms of one of the community's most revered dishes. During a meal of relleno negro (pork and chicken or turkey in a blackened chile sauce, served during the annual fiesta and other important events) I heard first the quiet whispers of "jach páap" (very spicy) by younger and middle-aged women and then the more confident, louder "jach páap" declarations by female elders. The hostess and her mother looked stricken. In situations like this one, individual criticisms or compliments often develop into discussions on the (mis)use of ingredients or cooking techniques: Were the chiles too spicy? Was the spice mixture too coarsely ground? Again, such commentaries are rarely attributed to personal tastes. Although criticisms may be challenged, they are generally trusted and, if noted by other eaters, effectively confirmed. Shared tastes are forms of embodied knowledge in and of themselves, acquired over time; but they also expose familiarity with processes of production and consumption, familiarity that, in most cases, grows over the course of individual lives, not only through contact with foodstuffs but through contact with other cooks and eaters.

The relationship between hands-on experience and expertise is clear in the experiences of both men and women. Men who have years of farming and hunting experience demonstrate expertise in matters of plants and meat. In addition to the man who operates the local butcher's shop, there are several middle-aged men who are often hired to slaughter and butcher cattle, pigs, and larger game (women slaughter and butcher poultry). Older children and young men might assist fathers and uncles with these tasks, especially hunting and butchering. Connoisseurship is evident in the critical commentary that accompanies shopping for food, butchering meat, and harvesting crops, and the residents of Juubche' display the ability to make subtle distinctions on matters of food, suggesting that their palates, among other bodily tools for experiencing food, are refined in very particular ways. Some form of this process of socialization, the cultivation of tastes, unfolds everywhere, albeit in varying ways. Still, the degree of agreement in Juubche' is striking. This consensus is not automatic; rather it is an ongoing development dependent upon public displays of connoisseurship through criticism. Connoisseurship in Juubche' develops through the acquisition of expertise, increased familiarity with a given form. Unlike others in their community who might perform such labor only because it is expected of them, for example, as part of their domestic responsibilities, some individuals play particularly important roles in cultivating shared tastes. These culinary connoisseurs in Juubche', some of whom the reader is introduced to in chapter 5, have expertise that begins with an interest or perhaps a "genuine" sensitivity but that evolves into both a concrete skill set and critical taste. This expertise develops through observation and experiential learning rather than through formal instruction and, perhaps in conjunction with natural inclinations, transforms one into a connoisseur. Through criticism connoisseurs cultivate shared tastes among a larger group. According to Eisner (1985), effective criticism is connoisseurship made public, an act of education through "the artful use of critical disclosure" (92–93). Connoisseurs may retain their privileged status and may exert power through critical displays of their expertise, but in Juubche' they are also participating in a larger process of education that supports local ideals of consensus and tranquility. Individual moments of shopping, cooking, and eating are ripe with criticisms that teach the less experienced or gifted how to shop, cook, and taste. Such criticisms draw attention to material qualities of food—as they are perceived by the connoisseur, of course—and school the relative novice both in how to taste and in how to talk about taste.

This is not to minimize the contestations that occur with regard to taste. Rather, such contestations are themselves moments for education and, sometimes, assertions of knowledge and power. During my time in Juubche' I developed friendships with two women, doña Elda and doña Patricia, who lived next door to one another. Like many neighbors in town, they occasionally had conflict with one another: one's dog eating the other's eggs, one building a new outhouse too close to the other's yard, and other neighborly disputes. However, doña Elda frequently complained that doña Patricia did not display enough willingness to resolve these issues, and as a result, the two had a cordial but no longer warm relationship. One day I visited doña Patricia and was sharing atole with her and her daughters when doña Elda walked by. Doña Patricia yelled for her to join us, and doña Elda obliged. One of doña Patricia's daughters offered her a cup of atole, which doña Elda promptly tasted: "It's not salty [enough]," she stated matter-of-factly. Doña Patricia made a face and muttered something softly to one daughter. But perhaps due to doña Elda's more advanced age, doña Patricia quickly added some salt to the large bowl of atole. In this case I suspect each woman thought she was the more skilled taster, but this reinforces the notion that there is a "just right" that ought not be called into question by acknowledging the reality of individual preference. The inability to taste "properly," that is, like others of equal or higher status, in processes of preparation or consumption lowers one's status in the hierarchy of culinary expertise. Consensus does not preclude power differentials but rather is made possible by them here; certain ways of tasting are privileged and become standardized in what is, at once, a moment of both distinction and education.

In the culinary achievement of balance, shared tastes and consensus are reproduced, and desirable bodily sensations, including pleasure, are experienced. Cooking, like eating, is an exercise in care with consequences at the bodily and social level. The balanced use of ingredients and deep attention to process are the foremost ways in which women care for themselves and others. They acquire the expertise to do so through direct bodily encounters during the cooking process: the heat of chile on the tongue, the give of corn dough in the hand, or the visible puff of a tortilla ready to be flipped. The sensory experiences produced in these engagements become naturalized through repetition, creating dispositions and memories.[8] These dispositions and memories are then called forth, consciously and unconsciously, in the practice of care, embodied reminders of how to eat and live well.

CHAPTER 2

Giving Life to Ourselves

Several weeks into my longest stay in Juubche', I developed recurring ear pain and headaches. Within a few hours of waking most days, I would retire to my hammock and lament my lack of productivity. A visit to a doctor in a nearby town and a short treatment with antibiotics proved useless. My condition brought great worry to the people around me. On his occasional trips to a nearby city, my husband fruitlessly searched the internet for the root of my symptoms. Our hosts in Juubche' shared their assessments of my bodily state with friends and relatives, and suggestions regarding treatments began pouring in. The sisters behind the counter at our neighborhood store suggested ear drops made from local oregano, while a young woman strolling by our doorway recommended drops of warm lard. Doña Esmeralda first tried a technique she had learned from her grandmother: she lit a single cigarette and coated the rim around the lit part with VapoRub. She then stuck her mouth around the lit part, blew smoke into my ear two or three times, and plugged my ear with a piece of cotton. I experienced relief but not for long.

Shortly after a course of antibiotics prescribed by a doctor in a neighboring town, I developed painful bumps under my arms and daily fevers. A neighbor, doña Katy, was sure that I had a *xiik'*, a sickness named after the spot where symptoms emerge, the armpit. Doña Katy's mother, whom I had never met, agreed, and before long doña Esmeralda and her husband, don Máximo, were comparing two treatments using resin pulled from the hives of bees. Doña Esmeralda first tried rubbing some of the resin with VapoRub directly on the bumps. When that failed, don Máximo convinced her to try the variation he knew. Soon she was coating the bumps in VapoRub, heating a piece of the hive over a burning hunk of wood, and then applying the warmed resin directly to the bumps. Again, the pain subsided for a brief while. Within hours it had returned, and I was back in my hammock feeling sorry for myself.

After a few visits to doctors in the state capital and many medical misadventures, my symptoms grew worse. I was hospitalized and received intravenous antibiotics, and eventually I recovered. However, during each period of sickness, my awareness of and anxieties about each and every action I took, especially what I ate and drank, grew. I was profoundly attentive to each tingle in my limbs, gurgle in my gut, and hint of tenderness on my flesh. I looked for explanation in every drop of nonpotable water and in every piece of leftover meat. The material conditions of life in Juubche' and the expectations, some my own and some those of generous hosts, that I engage deeply with those conditions seemed to threaten my well-being.[1]

I felt myself growing deeply irrational, even paranoid, but my anxieties seemed, in form at least, normal to my informants. At first I was embarrassed to refuse particular foods at the social gatherings I attended, fearing that I would insult the generosity and culinary pride of each party's hosts. I soon realized that my fear of consuming the "wrong" foods was understood by hosts and other attendees, though our underlying logics were usually distinct. At any given gathering, the woman cooking tortillas on the griddle would avoid a cold drink, a diabetic might decline to grab candy from the piñata, and any individual taking antibiotics was likely to refuse the addition of chile to her food.[2] Food, for all the pleasure it provides in Juubche', also carries risks for the bodies that consume it. Yet, it is not just a matter of the "wrong" foods; rather, there is recognition of the flexibility and fluidity of bodies themselves, necessitating frequently changing engagement with foodstuffs. This chapter considers these bodies, specifically how understandings of them have developed and how they are imagined and experienced in contemporary life.

My own experience of illness led my hosts to test their theories of causality and difference on my body. Together we mapped vulnerabilities and their defenselessness in the face of external entities, questioning my adjustment to local life and implicating all of us—me, them, my husband, and my doctors—in failures of care. Was it the lard perhaps? I rarely consumed it at home; doña Esmeralda wondered if vegetable oil, increasingly popular among young cooks in the community, might better suit my stomach. Or maybe it was my stubborn refusal to wait for heated water to brush my teeth each morning. Doña Esmeralda and don Máximo insisted that my consumption of room temperature bottled water in the mornings was shocking my body, warm from a night's sleep, but, as they wondered, how then could they explain the good health of my husband, who drank the same "cold" water?

It became evident to me that residents of Juubche' too experience acute anxieties about the ways in which the world, especially via food and drink, acts on their bodies, often in very immediate ways. Everyday food practices in this community, and indeed throughout rural Yucatán, reflect naturalized ideas of what foods and drinks are appropriate for what times of day, in what combinations, and for what bodies. To a large degree the choices are not so much choices but rather habits produced out of availability, as determined by the seasons, climate, and, especially post-NAFTA, the global marketplace. Within these limitations, however, people in Juubche' make careful considerations when it comes to food and drink, basing their decisions on such factors as age, gender, illness, and other bodily states. Anxieties about the potential consequences of these choices permeate and, in fact, structure many of the ways in which residents of Juubche' interact with comestibles. My insertion, bodily and socially, into the systems of logic that govern human engagement with food in this community provoked questions about those logics' relevance under contemporary conditions and for certain, different bodies.

Yet while I found the pleasures of eating and drinking slipping away from me in the face of my growing anxieties, I saw that my informants retained a deep passion for food, frequently discussing the pleasures it provided them and waxing over its particular qualities—tastes, odors, textures. Their awareness of the fragility and unruliness of human bodies, accompanied by a respect and fear of the dangers of their world, was far from paralyzing. Residents of Juubche' find great pleasure in food, perhaps more than in any other realm of their lives. They regularly structure their lives—and their meals—in order to maximize that pleasure and minimize a range of risks. Everyday life here is often infused with distrust and social tension, but residents understand themselves to be capable of finding and experiencing pleasure. Furthermore, just as they know that their kin and neighbors often suffer in similar ways to themselves, residents of Juubche' too realize that they may find pleasure in many of the same experiences, whether through the taste of a perfectly hot tortilla, the feeling of retiring to a hammock after work, or the cool of shade on a hot day. Recognition of the collective nature of these anxieties and pleasures strengthens an already rich social life, partially bridging the tensions that suffuse everyday life. Through all this the practice of care is a way for the individual and community to maintain control—bodily, social, and spiritual—and find balance and tranquility.

In this chapter I examine the nature of my informants' bodily anxieties, hypothesize as to why they experience them so acutely and why they so deeply desire balance, and analyze the mechanisms by which the anxieties are mediated, in particular, through this concept of care. I introduce the active yet vulnerable bodies of the people whose stories fill work and discuss those bodies in the sparest sense: their being, as they are thought to live, suffer, and feel pleasure, as they seek to survive and thrive, through and with food. Care is not simply a function of these bodies, however. It is central to the making and remaking of their materiality and to the materiality of food and other elements of the social world. In order to understand the anxieties and pleasures of life in this community, one must first understand the region in which these individuals reside and the historical conditions that have shaped contemporary life and the persistent emphasis on balance.

Balance and Survival

The Yucatán Peninsula has a geological base of limestone with limited elevation and a wide range of soil quality (Barrera-Bassols and Toledo 2005). The climate can be steamy and contributed to a rather unhospitable environment for many European crops and animals. Despite the challenges the peninsula's landscape presents, it had supported human life for tens of thousands of years prior to the arrival of Europeans in the early sixteenth century. Barrera-Bassols and Toledo declare the remarkable adaptive capacity of "Maya culture" in the region to be the product of two factors: the reliance on a multiple-use strategy with regard to natural resources and notions of health that are inclusive of the well-being of the natural world. The brevity of the historical account to follow is a reflection both of the limits of this book and of a deliberately instrumental focus on the persistence of the two factors identified by Barrera-Bassols and Toledo.

The production of maize made the history of this region possible. By 3000 BC humans had begun farming the plant in the Maya lowlands (Lucero 1999), contributing to the eventual development of chiefdoms and then states, and more permanent hierarchies of political power (Ball 1977; Hendon 1999). With widening status distinctions between elites and commoners also came more fixed gender roles, increasingly supporting an ideology of complementariness in which creation and renewal required both male and female actors (Hendon 1999; 2002). Women's roles in material and social reproduction came to be seen as crucial to the fulfillment of spiritual duties; human descendants were valued with the expectation that they would both care for their own human ancestors, including the dead, and worship the gods (Gustafson 2002). The food work of women, especially the grinding of corn, mirrored the ancient Maya's very myth of creation, in which Xmucane, the grandmother and creator in the *Popul Vuh*, grinds the corn form which human flesh was formed (155–56).[3] Reproductive and domestic forms of labor, especially food work, were tied together, inseparable in the perpetuation of cycles of human and nonhuman lives.

The Spanish arrived on the Yucatán Peninsula in 1511 and then again in 1517, but it took decades for the Spanish to even partially wrestle power from indigenous people on the peninsula (Farriss 1984). The process of the decentralization of political and economic power that characterized the years before the arrival of the Spanish continued during the colonial period; ongoing participation in the rituals of milpa production by most indigenous people helped to uphold older belief systems (Farriss 1984; 1987). By the middle of the sixteenth century the Spanish began to develop the *encomienda* system as a way to extract tribute from the natives. The Spanish crown gave rights to the *encomenderos*, the individuals who would receive the tribute, to do so in exchange for the responsibility of caring for their indigenous charges spiritually and materially. The indigenous population, which had been mostly dispersed due to war and famine by the time the Spanish returned in the 1540s, was organized through a policy of *congregación* into tribute-paying units called *repúblicas de indios*, councils that represented each newly formed town (Clendinnen 1987; Farriss 1984). The encomienda system had effects on the material existence on indigenous people, both as individuals and as members of their respective *kaj*, a Yucatec Maya community and geographical entity that comprised its members and their individually and collectively owned properties (Restall 1997). Tribute requirements may have strengthened the central role of corn in agricultural practice for indigenous groups. When stored properly, corn can go months without spoiling, making it well suited for tribute, and this may explain its prominence in precolonial tribute as well (Wilk [1991] 1997). The practice of congregación, which centered indigenous peoples in towns and usually further from their fields, may also have caused them to shift from polyculture to monoculture. In doing so, they could decrease the number of field visits required annually; still the distance of fields from domestic compounds often led farmers to construct a sleeping structure on or near their agricultural fields (Restall 1997; J. E. S. Thompson 1977; Wilk [1991] 1997).

The most dramatic economic and political changes in two centuries began in the eighteenth century when the Bourbon Reforms sought to tighten the power of Spain over its colonies and to encourage free trade. In Yucatán, elite indigenous officials now answered to local agents of the Crown rather than to Spanish or Creole leaders in the capital, Mérida. These local colonial authorities increasingly intervened in the legal and economic matters of indigenous communities.[4] The reorganization of indigenous economic, political, and religious life threatened the principles of corporateness and reciprocity and greatly weakened the social hierarchies that had persisted from precolonial periods. Without access to resources that supported established care practices, the reproduction of the indigenous social worlds seemed imperiled. These challengers were daunting for indigenous communities, but Farriss (1984) argues that they also created conditions in which cooperation become even more essential to cosmological and material survival.

Frustrated by the demands of tribute, church taxes, and forced labor, many indigenous Yucatecans participated in the fight for Mexican independence, but Yucatán's incorporation into the Mexican Republic was a bumpy process. Resentful of the demands of the Mexican state, some Yucatecans staged revolts, encouraging indigenous people to join in with the promise to end church taxes. Yucatán briefly became an independent nation, on and off during the 1840s, but the Yucatec Maya were soon disillusioned by the failure of Creole elites to keep their wartime promises (Rugeley 2001a). Indigenous people still comprised the vast majority of the peninsula's population, about 80 percent, but their access to land and, increasingly, their autonomy was in decline. In the east, home to more fertile land, the elite began to develop more plantations to cultivate cotton, rice, tobacco, and, above all, sugar (Joseph 1986; Remmers 1981). Large numbers of Creoles began migrating to the southeast where land was cheap and fertile, and where the production of sugar was increasingly profitable. In this part of the peninsula, where rural indigenous people had lived more independently during the colonial period, the incorporation of the peasant population into more tightly controlled work regimes threatened milpa production (Joseph 1986). Even in "free villages" indigenous people struggled to maintain access to land, and many rural indigenous farmers were pressured to sell the land their families had cultivated for centuries to Creoles (Joseph 1986; Remmers 1981). Epidemics of smallpox, cholera, and measles occurred during the second quarter of the nineteenth century and contributed to multiple food shortages (Rugeley 2001b). Older residents in Juubche' refer to this period as the beginning of the time of *esclavitud* (slavery), during which their ancestors' labor was exploited, their access to land was endangered, and survival was under threat.

Not surprisingly, indigenous resentment in the region was rising by the late 1840s. In the east, where most rural indigenous peoples still practiced subsistence agriculture, encroachments onto their land were especially threatening. Some peasants fled yet further east, into the jungle of Quintana Roo, but others decided to fight back. In 1847 many of the eastern indigenous people, still armed from their roles in the Yucatecan Army, rebelled against the peninsula's Creole population in what is known as the Caste War. Maya rebels took the colonial city of Valladolid and other Creole strongholds. As they approached the state capital of Mérida, they turned back, and Creoles slowly repopulated eastern towns.[5] The families of the indigenous rebels, who came to be known as the Cruzob (people of the Speaking Cross), fled into the frontier of Quintana Roo in great numbers (Reed 1964).[6]

The next major attempts to address unequal land holdings and debt peonage on the peninsula came after the Mexican Revolution. Yucatán's geographic and cultural distance from central Mexico and the strong hold of its local elite on regional politics delayed most of the Revolution's effects (Joseph 1986, 1988).[7] Disputes between political factions, landowning elites, and corporate representatives continued, and in the decade to come former plantation owners reaccumulated much of the land that had already been distributed to indigenous peasants (Joseph 1988). As the population of indigenous people continued to grow, land shortages grew more acute, often leading men to seek work outside of their own communities. Near the regional center of Tizimín, a small city not far from Juubche', lumber was a booming industry in the early and mid-twentieth century (Steggerda 1943). In the forests of Quintana Roo, rights to cut mahogany and cedar were controlled by the rebel indigenous people for much of the late nineteenth and early twentieth centuries (Juarez 1996). Logging was not the only global industry in which indigenous people in the eastern part of the peninsula participated. Many of my informants recalled their fathers heading to the jungles of Quintana Roo to harvest chicle, resin derived from the chicozapote tree. Chicle had been a source of funding for the rebels for decades, but the market for it was booming by the 1920s. Increasing profits even reached the individual chicleros, who used their earnings to purchase newly available commodities such as liquor and cigarettes. For the most part, their earnings were still not enough to substantially improve their quality of life, and excessive alcohol consumption grew more common with heightened access to cash and mass-produced beverages. The work conditions for many chicleros improved with the development of chicle cooperatives in the 1930s, but in the meantime these laborers had become increasingly dependent on the cash economy (Redcliff 2004). Don Belchor, a Juubche' resident in his eighties, remembered migrating to a chicle camp for six months at a time. He and other men from Juubche' walked for a week to arrive at the camp. According to don Belchor, chicleros had access to guns with which they hunted for deer and smaller forest animals, but that they also each paid fifty centavos (less than five cents today) for meals prepared by the camp's female cook. Isolated in the forest and far from their household care networks and ritual communities, they had few options with regard to daily sustenance.

The chicle industry's movement into previously isolated forests, which came with the construction of roads and the clearing of tall forests, set the stage for new forms of land use, including cattle production and commercial agriculture (Redclift 2004). Once more common in the northwestern part of the region, stock raising became a popular commercial enterprise in the east. The location of Juubche' on the southern border of what is now considered Yucatán's cattle country began providing more wage labor opportunities for men. Since then, boys and men have been hired by wealthy urbanites and, occasionally, better-off neighbors to care for cattle herds. In some cases men may have to sleep at a more distant ranch, but in other cases they return home daily after several trips to closer properties. Years ago men who did this work managed to maintain their milpas in addition to earning wages; close male kin would do agricultural labor, and the fruits of both farming and cattle herding would be shared by a family unit. Prior to the 1970s, both chicle harvesting and cattle herding were supplements, not replacements, for milpa agriculture.

Following the pattern set by the Carnegie Institution in the 1920 and 1930s (Castañeda 1996; Sullivan 1989), archaeological projects also became a source of wage earning for indigenous Yucatecans during the twentieth century. The embrace of Mexico's indigenous history by the state and scholars was part of postrevolutionary efforts to define Mexican identity through idealized notions of indigeneity while simultaneously pursuing assimilation for indigenous Mexicans (Bonfil-Batalla 1987; Fallaw 2004; Knight [1990] 2004; Walker 2009). This tendency and the efforts it employed, particularly in the realm of archaeology, have broadened, though often temporarily, labor opportunities in rural Yucatán. In recent decades the Mexican government and the archeological projects it supports have frequently contracted men in Juubche' to work on excavations of nearby sites. Related to the investment in tourism and to efforts to improve infrastructure more generally, many men in Juubche' have participated in the construction of roads as well. Although many of these men continue to farm milpas, the gender inequalities intensified by men's cash-earning labor in chicle and logging have persisted in these more recent endeavors.

The growing reliance on wage-earning activities like those just described has coincided with other major social changes, many of which were initiated by the Mexican state. In the first half of the twentieth century, the newly established Ministry of Education (SEP) created a Department of Indigenous Cultures, the role of which was to assimilate Mexico's indigenous populations into a modern nation-state. In particular, the public education system sought to introduce peasants, both adults and children, to middle-class values of political democracy, individual property ownership, and entrepreneurship (Vaughn 1982). For Juubche' residents born during this period, public education often remained out of reach. Members of these generations described struggling to afford notebooks and pencils, or having parents unwilling or unable to lessen their children's contributions to domestic and milpa work. Even for those who were able to attend, the education offered was unreliable. According to some of the town's first students, educated in the 1930s and 1940s, teachers often failed to show up, exhausted by the daylong walk to and from Juubche' or unable to travel the unpaved paths, which frequently flooded. The state of Yucatán began officially offering bilingual Spanish–Yucatec Maya education in 1955 (Burns 1998, 382), but it took decades for educational access to become more stable in Juubche'. Over time, according to people in Juubche', teachers stayed for longer stretches and developed close bonds with students and their families. Some residents completed primary school and managed to attend secondary school in the municipal seat, but for most students the acquisition of basic literacy skills was itself a formidable process. Many residents who attended school in the late twentieth century completed just a few years; like students of the previous generations, they could not afford school materials, and their labor was much needed by their households.

Braha-Pfeiler and Franks (1992) found that in the 1980s only about 20 percent of children in bilingual schools in Yucatán completed primary school (187). In the early 1990s, a secondary school opened in Juubche', and for the first time in the town's history, most children were attending school until they reached adolescence. The opening of a preparatory school in the last decade has further expanded educational opportunities. Still, as of 2010, the average resident had fewer than six years of schooling (Instituto Nacional de Estadística y Geografía 2010).

The Mexican state's educational interests were not directed solely at children. During the twentieth century, adult education, sometimes organized by the Department of Cultural Missions, provided brief training on matters of hygiene and health, agriculture, sports, and the arts (Castellanos 2010; Elmendorf [1976] 1978; Vaughn 1982). Government-initiated cultural missions during the mid-twentieth century sent *promotoras* (outreach workers) to instruct women in the preparation of dishes not locally consumed. The cultural missions continued intermittently for decades. For participants in Juubche', memories are vague, but some women embraced these recipes, many of which used locally produced ingredients. Several women recalled learning how to bake and decorate cakes, and a few used their skills to prepare cakes for sale for a short period. Doña Tina, a respected culinary authority in the community, has not worked as a *x-k'uus*, a local culinary expert and community cook, since her conversion to Jehovah's Witnesses about a dozen years ago. However, she often prepares foods for kin and for sale that require specialized knowledge, such as tortilla-like breads made from *sakam* (corn dough), sweet potato, and vanilla, or a savory version made from sakam and *chaya*, a leafy green. Doña Tina was not alone in learning about these foods from a promotora a half-century ago, but she has had the time and interest to continue cooking them.

The nutritional focus of these programs coincided with a broader effort to introduce biomedical concepts and expand access to biomedical care into rural indigenous communities. The post-Revolutionary Constitution of 1917 guaranteed the right of all Mexicans to health, but it took several decades for this guarantee to be even partially fulfilled. Beginning in the 1940s through the 1970s, health care became available to many Mexicans through the Instituto Mexicano del Seguro Social (Mexican Institute of Social Security or IMSS) (IMSS 2018). However, most Juubche' residents worked in subsistence agriculture or informal economies. They were thus excluded from health-care benefits through IMSS during this period. In the 1960s the Secretaría de Salubridad y Asistencia (SSA) began opening health clinics in small rural communities (Stebbins 1993, 221). In the 1970s the Social Security Law was amended to allow IMSS to provide care for marginalized populations, and in 1979 IMSS combined with the SSA program, which had been renamed Coordinación General del Plan Nacional de Zonas Deprimidas y Grupos Marginados (COPLAMAR). The IMSS-COPLAMAR opened more clinics in even smaller villages, reaching several million citizens. Its reach expanded throughout the 1980s, when it was renamed IMSS-SOLIDARIDAD (Stebbins 1993, 221; IMSS 2011). In 1997 it incorporated a conditional cash transfer (CCT) program, Progresa, into its offerings. With a change in the national ruling party, the program was soon renamed Oportunidades (Smith-Oka 2013, 188), its name during most of the time I spent in Juubche'. In 2014 Oportunidades became Prospera. Nearly all of the mothers I know in Juubche' participated in this program during the period of my research, though as I explore later in this chapter, their reactions to it are complex.

Collectively these programs, exemplifying the Mexican state's focus on poor rural and often indigenous communities in the twentieth century, transformed many aspects of everyday life in Juubche'. In doing so they provoked both resistance and appreciation from residents, broadening the systems of knowledge with which people there engaged. More recent biopolitical projects continue to do the same, often challenging how residents think of themselves, their bodies, and their worlds.

Contemporary Imbalance

Of one rural community in late twentieth-century Yucatán, Kray (1997) writes that residents "imagine a community characterized by three adjectives: *tráankiloj* 'tranquil', *tíigual* 'same, equal', and *páarejoj* 'even'" (79). According to Kray, *tráankiloj* in Yucatec Maya is not quite the same as "tranquil" in English; rather than suggesting an idyllic calm, it refers to balance, "the most desirable general state of affairs: the state in which everyone is in agreement, everything is evenly distributed, and respect and respectability characterize human relationships" (80). For the people of Juubche', tranquility and balance evoke freedom from suffering, disturbance, disagreement, and inequality. When they wax poetic about the tráankiloj nature of life in their town, they contrast it not with that of the increasingly sprawling but still provincial city of Valladolid but rather with the rapid growth, visible and vast inequalities, and, as they see it, rampant crime and vice of Cancún. As they frequently told me, in Cancún, neighbors rob neighbors, everything is for sale, and *otsilo'ob* (poor people) like themselves work for a pittance while hotels charge fifty pesos for a Coca-Cola. In Juubche', on the other hand, wealth inequalities are perceptible, but in the end most everyone sees themselves as otsilo'ob. Neighbors and kin can usually be counted on to help prepare tamales, catch an errant domestic animal, and keep an eye on children playing in the street. Social behaviors and bodily practices reflect what Kray (1997) describes as a hexis "built upon principles of tranquility, sameness, and evenness" that "implies a relational model of personhood in that the social body—like the physical body—is most healthy when in balance, when one demonstrates respect and respectability and items are distributed equally" (11).

By the mid-twentieth century, rural communities, large and small, faced social pressures that challenged these ideals. Many ethnographic accounts from this time document changes that threatened values of cooperation and consensus in these communities. In the 1960s in Ticul, a large town in western Yucatán, R. A. Thompson (1974) claimed that a portion of the town's Maya population rejected their "Mayan heritage" in choosing wage labor over agriculture and absolving themselves from the responsibility of organizing religious festivals (13). Press (1975) argued that in the smaller town of Pustunich, also in the 1960s, to not participate in agricultural labor and its attendant ritual activity, as some residents chose to do, was to "stand outside of the tradition and world-view of the majority" (59). In the 1980s Re Cruz (1996) found that new opportunities for migration created ideological and social distance between those who remained in the village of Chan Kom and those who left to work in the growing city of

Cancún. In the second half of the twentieth century, individualized needs and wants became embodied in other new social forms, including consumer identifications and personal tastes (Castellanos 2003; Greene 2002), and religious ideologies of personal salvation (Kray 1997).

In Juubche' such shifts continue to challenge existing mechanisms for maintaining equality and cooperation. Annual fiestas, long opportunities for redistribution and commensality, came to be increasingly commercialized and entirely avoided by new religious minorities, something I explore in chapter 4. Agricultural ceremonies that were once oriented toward collective success in producing food are now carried out by individual households and with far less frequency than in decades past. Compared to their grandparents, most of my older informants noted that they together with other members of their households own significantly more possessions, everything from sewing machines to stereo systems to body lotions. Yet a relative lack of privacy ensures that an individual's consumption patterns can easily become the business of her neighbors, and indeed what others purchase and consume is of great interest to all. In a context of increasing wealth disparities, the exclusion that consumption now enacts more often than not—as it is limited to the household, to the extended family, or to a particular religious group—has the potential to cause social tension and outright conflict.

Still, what Kray (1997) calls the "relational sense of self," a model of personhood she says is shaped by colonial history (4), persists in tying individuals to their households and larger communities through established religious practice, agricultural labor, and domestic life. Within the nuclear family, the bulk of the resources produced or purchased with wages earned are pooled together to meet the basic needs of the family and its members. In most households in Juubche' adult males and females make significant contributions to food production, wage earning, and food preparation. Children make varying contributions depending upon their age and school or work opportunities. Elderly parents may also be included in both the production and distribution of resources, though their contributions may dwindle with age. Thus while some degree of distrust pervades most relationships, it is widely accepted that interpersonal connections are essential to survival, most significantly at this level of the household and in the realm of food. Not surprisingly, childless informants frequently posed the following rhetorical question to me when they discussed their futures: "Who will bring me tortillas?" On a larger level, extended kin or one of the community's religious groups still pool together resources to honor a saint or fund a burial.

Still, even prior to the increasing religious and occupational diversity that threatens established patterns of cooperation, selfishness was not seen as entirely undesirable. In fact, in some forms, it may act as security against disruption. Castellanos (2003) finds great encouragement of the development of personal *gustos* (tastes), to the degree that shy children who refuse to state their wishes are not seen as normal. Like Kray (1997), I found that personality quirks were frequently attributed to the particular *moodo* (way of being) of an individual. Certain qualities were more valued than others though. The ability to defend oneself, to have *na'at* (understanding, reason), is much desired. Na'at aids in protecting one's self from the uncontrolled weaknesses of other, but the aim of this defense is to maintain tranquility. When one's unique traits or acts of self-interest disrupt the household or community, mechanisms of social control such as corporal punishment, gossip, and snubbing work to induce shame and restore order. Common sense and keen observation skills are important traits in learning adult work but also in upholding calm, whether by assertiveness or avoidance. Nurturing individual agentive potential, as it is to be exercised in social contexts, can be essential to the maintenance of balance, not necessarily counter to it, as one might suspect.

The tensions that develop between a seemingly selfish and impulsive human nature and collective expectations of equality and cooperation may be experienced as existential crises of self and community, but these tensions are not entirely new. Well before the roads brought new religions and cash to Juubche', people were screwing each other out of inheritances, spouses, and food. The desire for tranquility itself may have selfish motives; in a universe in which one's well-being depends upon the quality of social relationships and the continuity of life cycles, human and nonhuman, external disruptions usually have consequences for individual bodies as well. The care that one exercises in human relations, and with natural and supernatural entities, aids in both social reproduction and in individual survival. The well-being of the self has been long dependent upon, and crucial to, the well-being of larger social and cosmic worlds. However, the achievement of balance has always been complicated by a diversity of temperaments and motives. Today, the conditions and logics by which humans and nonhumans act for or against balance are yet more intricate in their unfolding in everyday life. Residents of Juubche' manifest multiple and often contradictory desires for and experiences of well-being, some of which posit the self as distinct from or even in opposition to social or cosmic collectives. According to people in the community, existing tensions are magnified, and bodily imbalances become more frequent.

Balance and the Body

Balance is seen as a desirable bodily state or sensation, a social or moral quality, in a wide range of societies (Culhane-Pera, Her, and Her 2007; Daniel 1984; Geurts 2002; Meigs 1984; Saethre 2007; S. J. Thompson and Gifford 2000). As Lakoff and Johnson (1999) point out, however, what balance means, what is in fact being balanced and what this achieves, may differ between cultures. In indigenous American cultures, balance is often enacted and threatened at the level of the body, the social collective, plants and animals, and the cosmos (Lentz 2000; Messer 1987; Parezo 2007; Taussig 1980; Wilson 2003). Of course, all bodily experiences, including the perceptions of corporeal limits and the entities outside them, are mediated by culture (Duden 1991; Mol 2003; Stewart and Strathern 2001). Lived experiences of balance, or imbalance, have not been stable over the course of indigenous history in Yucatán, but at least some of the qualities, something palpable in bodily sensations or social interactions, may have endured, likely due to the centuries-long centrality of certain forms of food production and preparation.

Stewart and Strathern (2001) argue that sensory realms are deeply tied to human relationships with the environment and that for societies in which the natural world is the source of livelihood, humans are "constantly compared with and assimilated into the outside world" (7–8). Humans, plants, and natural features such as earth may be thought to share essential substances and cycles of life (Herdt 1981; Strathern 1982), and scholars suggest that this has been especially true of Mesoamericans (Gustafson 2002; Hanks 1990). Stewart and Strathern (2001) argue that embodiment must take into account the ways in which bodies "embody both individuality and relationality, humanity as separate from other living creatures and as consubstantial with or linked to these others" (8). For rural indigenous Yucatecans, the embodiment of both individuality and relationality is evident in the recognition of omens known as *tamax chi'* (Callahan 2017) and in the ability to identify dozens of kinds of soil (Barrera-Bassols and Toledo 2005), in which the sensory capabilities of the body shape understanding of and engagement with that which is external.

If we understand embodiment as extending outward to the myriad of forces that converge on, create, and demarcate human bodies, then food must be recognized for its primacy in blurring boundaries between bodies and the worlds they inhabit (Meigs 1988; Probyn 2000; Stewart and Strathern 2001). On social and cosmological levels, food fuels much of the interaction between individual humans, and between humans and spiritual entities. Food is at the root of many larger social and spiritual tensions, but its incorporation into the body is one of the most intimate ways in which people in Juubche' exercise care and achieve balance. As ingestible substances, foodstuffs are uniquely situated to make tangible to human bodies their own transformative potential. The processes of assimilation by which food is sensorially experienced and incorporated into human materialities reproduce a relationship of mutual (re)creation. The sensory experiences of eaters become naturalized through repetition, creating bodily dispositions and memories (Bourdieu [1979] 1984; Sutton 2001), or engagement with food can shock bodies for better or worse, creating feelings of intense pleasure or disgust (Haidt et al. 1997; Highmore 2008; Holtzman 2010; Probyn 2000). Vargas and Casillas (2008) argue for food's ability to speak through the body, particularly in contexts of sickness, which for many rural Yucatecans is caused by imbalance. Food acts on their bodies, affecting function and feeling as profoundly as social conflict and spiritual unrest.

In Juubche' discourses of the body reflect this engagement with food and with sensory experience more generally. Speakers of the Yucatec Maya language express their experiences and interpretations of material qualities and sensations through the root verbs *il* (to see) and *u'y* (to feel, hear, taste, smell, sense). Although this categorization might suggest a privileging of sight over other senses, an examination of other words demonstrates implicit references to the full range of sensory experiences. Le Guen (2011) details a series of Yucatec linguistic templates that transform root meanings into adjectives. One template is used largely to describe visually recognizable qualities, but others refer to tactile qualities or to locations in space. Speakers also describe bodily experiences and sensations through reference to their *óol*, the center of consciousness. The most common way to inquire about the well-being of a Yucatec Maya speaker is to ask "*Bix a beel?*" (How are you/How is your road?). Bastarracha Manzano and Canto Rosado (2003) define *beel* as both "road" and "function" (46), synonymous with *bej* (45). Similarly but using a distinct orthography, Bricker, Po'ot Yah, and Dzul de Po'ot (1998) gloss *b'eh* as "road or way" and *b'el* as "road or occupation" (29–30). There is no single word for "balance" in regular usage in the Yucatec Maya language, and the response to "Bix a beel?" does not evoke a direct reference to a road or some variation on that concept. Rather, it is through the use of óol that speakers indicate such a state and variations from it. Kray (1997) describes the óol as "the emotional 'heart'" (93), while Hanks (1990) explains it as "roughly the will and the capacity for involvement and sensate experience" (87).[8] The óol is not an organ so much as a force. According to Bourdin (2007/2008), shamans explain that the óol is obtained through the process of inhaling; the force then moves to the lungs, then to the heart, and finally throughout the body, where it flows with the blood.[9] According to his description, the óol is a centrifugal and ascending force. Not surprisingly, any disturbance of this force upsets the function of the body. This leads to the development of *koja'anilo'ob* (sicknesses), a very general term that transcends the boundaries between what would be, in Western allopathic medicine, mental and physical health.

The significance of the óol is not limited to the corporeal. Rather this force is one that is replicated, metaphorically, on multiple levels. Vogt

(1971) and Villa Rojas (1981) argue that the pre-Hispanic cosmology of the Maya is replicated in the contemporary organization of the milpa, the town, the home, and the body; conceptually, all are divided into quadrants organized in reference to the cardinal directions. Hanks (1990) finds that in ritual discourse the composition of the body too is represented as the same as that of the material world: made up of earth, wind, and heat. In Juubche' the balance or imbalance of the *wíinkil* (body) travels from its center toward the four cardinal directions. This center of the body is both the site of an important organ known as the *tíip'te'* or *cirro* and a crucial point in the movement of the óol. As such, the center both acts and is acted upon in the production of health or suffering. One's óol may be *ki'* (tasty), as in *ki'imak in wóol* (I am happy/joyful).[10] Under great stress or sadness one's óol may *kastal* (go bad). The óol can be shocked (literally, hit) as in *hatsaj óol*. Shocks disrupt the movement of the óol, potentially causing sickness at the óol's point of blockage or at a part of the body to which the óol has now failed to flow. *Sataj óol* (lost óol), also the result of shock, can result in temporary or permanent insanity. *Ná'akal a wóol* signifies that your óol is rising; you are growing annoyed or frustrated. The ideal, and indeed the most common, positive response is that one's óol is *tooj* (straight, even). *Tooj in wóol* indicates both contentedness and good health; I argue that this state is the local form of bodily balance, but that such a state is inextricable from social and cosmological forms of balance.

As it is a central site to and from which the óol moves, the tíip'te', a pulsating organ located just behind the *tuuch* (navel), is considered particularly vulnerable to imbalance. Based on research in several rural communities, Villa Rojas (1981) argues that the tíip'te' is the point of origin for the body's circulatory system. Just as Mayan cosmology imagines the *ya'axche'* (ceiba tree) to be the center of the universe—and in some towns the tree actually marks geographical centers (Guest 1995)—the tíip'te' is the center of the human body, pumping blood to its four quadrants (Jordan 1993). For residents of Juubche' many of the dangers that threaten the óol and tíip'te' revolve around a set of beliefs that may be loosely categorized, following the ethnographic literature, as a hot-cold syndrome. The hot-cold syndrome, common throughout much of Latin America, classifies foods as either "hot" or "cold," sometimes based on literal, or thermal, temperature but often not (Chevalier and Sánchez Bain 2003; Currier 1966; Foster 1994).[11] Callahan (2005) notes that the syndrome in Yucatán increasingly refers to thermal temperature. This is true in Juubche' as well, but many extended classifications persist; thermal temperature in fact often fails to explain classification. My informants, for example, classified citrus fruits as "cold" because they are *pesado* (heavy), while in contrast honey is considered very "hot." To focus on thermal qualities may obscure other qualities that determine any given food's categorization: taste, odor, the feeling it provokes in the mouth or gut, or its growing or cooking environment. The classification of many foods thus depends upon shared knowledge of its production or preparation (and often, along gendered lines, participation in those processes), but it also depends upon some degree of shared sensory fields. Other classifications are more arcane: lingering products of antiquated ideas or projects, or understood only by a select few, such as the local shaman.[12]

The hot-cold syndrome roots individual bodies and their imperative for balance within a larger social order. This order rests upon the maintenance of balance within the multiple cycles—solar, seasonal, and those of life and death—that characterize the existences of living beings, including supernatural forces. In general, balance and imbalance are produced through combinations of "heat" and "cold" found in bodies and their parts, as well as in food, drink, and natural elements; are produced by activities and phases of life; and are caused by emotions such as anger. As in Chevalier and Sánchez Bain's (2003) more general model for indigenous healing beliefs and practices in Latin America, the hot-cold syndrome as articulated and lived in Juubche' relies upon three fundamental principles. First, excessive heat or cold threatens the balance of the human body. Second, the human body is not static on a day-to-day basis; human activities such as work or bathing may change the state of the body. These shifts are a normal part of the body's workings. Lastly, the human life course itself consists of changes in bodily state that may make an individual more vulnerable to various forces at particular moments in his or her life. Chevalier and Sánchez Bain agree with Foster (1994) that sickness is more likely to strike when the bodily state is altered, though the former emphasize, as do I, that these altered states are themselves normal.

For the people of Juubche' the óol is most vulnerable to alteration and, as such, is frequently at the heart (no pun intended) of bodily anxieties. While the ideal for the óol leans more toward "cold," it is normal and natural for the body to "heat" over the day due to work and the consumption of "hot" foods. Dramatic shifts from hot to cold can shock the óol, as can excessive external heat; both can cause sicknesses that affect other organs as well, either via the óol or directly. The most dreaded of sicknesses resulting from such shocks are *pasmo* (chills), *taankas* (evil winds sickness), and *reuma* (rheumatism). Pasmo is a "cold" condition that results from exposure to "cold" foods and natural forces, such as wind and rain, while one's óol is "hot." Pasmo results in a freeze or shock to the body and can affect various organs, including the reproductive organs, the *puksi'ik'al* (heart, often distinguished from the *coorazon* or biomedical heart) and the stomach.[13] Pasmo can cause fatigue, infertility, and loss of appetite. Pasmo is not fatal, but if the sufferer is not cured, he or she may waste away and die of hunger. Doña Graciela, who treats sickness of the tíip'te' through massage, explained: "Because when your óol is hot and you drink water, you get pasmo. Yes, it's possible that you won't eat, you won't breakfast/drink." Pasmo can also cause a shift in the tíip'te' (though the tíip'te' can also move due to pregnancy or a fall). In its ideal state, the tíip'te' is tied to the intestines; the movement of the tíip'te' can shift the intestines or cause them to separate from the tíip'te'. The movement of the tíip'te', up or down, is thought to cause abdominal pain, burping, bloating, and loss of appetite. Doña Cristina, in her seventies, described: "Because when a person's navel rises, it's possible that you won't eat, your stomach will feel full, you won't be able to eat, you'll eat a little bit of beans and after you'll feel you're burping, you're fragile." Doña Paola, in her fifties explained: "Well, when people have gotten ill in the tíip'te', it has on it a sac. You grab it . . . it moves. Tip', tip', tip', tip' tip', it goes. Well, it just gets worse like that. If you don't treat it, you won't get better. It just gets worse for the person: he dies, he stops eating, he wastes away, he vomits. But, it's very bad things he vomits." Doña Graciela, doña Cristina, and doña Paola all emphasize the potentially life-threatening nature of pasmo, especially in its effects on the appetite. Pasmo can be acquired through a lack of care in one's interaction with the world, and it can also jeopardize well-being and even life itself through its interference with eating.

Other conditions similarly reveal the suffering caused by contact between a "hot" óol and "cold" external forces. Reuma (rheumatism) is a "cold" illness that causes pain in the bones and joints. It is especially dreaded because it tends to affect the hands and feet, whose function is essential for both male and female labor. Unlike many of the other ailments resulting from imbalance, the symptoms of reuma can take months or years to appear. Doña Cristina, unmarried until she was middle-aged, often helped her father in his milpa during her youth. On one occasion, "hot" from helping to plant watermelons under a strong sun, she was drenched in an unexpected rainstorm on her way home. Months later she developed reuma, and she, and others, attributed it to this "cold" shock. When preparing food, a woman takes care to cool herself between "hot" and "cold" duties. Should she shred hot chicken meat, thus heating her hands, and then squeeze "cold" orange juice or plunge herbs into cold water for rinsing, she risks developing reuma in her hands. Unavoidable acts require that one must take calculated risks. On one occasion several older adults discussed with me the fear they felt when needing to urinate or defecate during the middle of the night. Though some choose to use chamber pots inside the house, others venture outside. As one man told me, "You're sleeping. Your asshole is hot. When you shit in the solar, there is wind, cold. It gives illness."[14] What these ethnographic anecdotes make clear is that these risks are not aberrations but rather are part and parcel of being in the world. As made evident by the above dilemma of elimination during the night, these sicknesses occur through contact with what are mostly unavoidable forces. Wind, water, and foodstuffs make the world in which the residents of Juubche' live. The impetus is on humans to know their own bodies and any shifts in them—to see them as open and as very much a part of the assemblage that is the world around them. Humans must then care for themselves accordingly with regard to those potentially dangerous but essential forces.

The frequency with which one encounters these forces does not make such risks less frightening. Although neither pasmo nor reuma, for example, is fatal in and of itself, each diminishes human functioning in essential realms of life: food work, including food production (or the wage labor via which one can purchase food) and food preparation, and eating. In this way, the sicknesses also threaten the function of the cycles that reproduce life, human and nonhuman, in the world. Care should then be seen not just as an individual tactic for human well-being but also as a way in which the social value of particular activities and the cosmological roles those activities serve endure. The gendered labor roles by which residents produce and process foodstuffs, the established modes of household production, are reproduced only in that individuals are well enough to carry them out. Domesticated animals and plants, the souls of the dead, and the entities who control life, death, and the weather likewise wither without human care. Again, we see the breadth of self-interest, inclusive of so many interests, human and nonhuman, and yet, to the outsider at least, occasionally precluding other practices of care, suggesting the complicated and utterly contextual ways in which forms of care intersect and diverge.

Difference, Essential and Acquired

According to residents, some bodies are more vulnerable to imbalance and sickness than others, and all bodies change over the course of their lifetimes. Attributions such as gender, age, and race also determine the nature of one's body and its vulnerability to external forces. Age seems to increase one's "heat," and so the elderly must be especially careful around "cold" substances and forces. Infants and young children are "colder," and they must be protected from an excess of "cold." Parents wrap young children in blankets or towels if there is the slightest chill or wind outside, and infants are not given "cold" food or drink. Men's bodies are thought to be "hotter" than those of women, and this classification may reflect the established gender roles they undertake. Men's work in the milpa is considered "hotter" than women's domestic labor, despite the latter including the preparation of food over an open fire. Men's blood is also thought to be "hotter," which is likely linked to the belief that they are more prone to anger and lust than are women.

Older people suggest that "other" people are immune to the hot-cold imbalances of which they are quite fearful. Ts'uulo'ob do not *uk'ul* (drink/ breakfast, always hot beverages) in the morning; they *desayunar* (breakfast), and they are able to eat at that time such "cold" foods as papaya, to no ill effect. They lounge in swimming pools on warm days and chug from bottles of cold water while sweating in the sun during tours of archaeological sites.[15] My and my husband's ignorance of the hot-cold syndrome, and our consequent failures to follow much of the guidelines prescribed by our hosts, led to frequent attempts to trace the causes of both our good and bad health. When we were observed drinking cold water early in the morning—thought to be shocking to our bodies, still warm from sleep—the following week of good health suggested to our hosts that perhaps our bodies were different from theirs.[16] Doña Graciela, an older neighbor with whom I conversed almost daily, asked me one day if, in fact, our bodies, hers and mine, were the same or different inside. The same, I responded, but the observers of our conversation, her similarly aged in-laws, looked unconvinced. Perhaps they were more attuned to the realities of "local biologies," those bodily manifestations of the ongoing interactions between social and biological processes, than I was at the time (Lock 1993). Even more important than the differences in our appearances were the types of labor in which we each engaged. My inability to prepare tortillas over a hot fire or do a decent job washing clothes in the yard by hand also meant that I rarely got "hot" in the ways that local women did. Excluded from the processes of production, my body, in its very workings, was categorized as different.

Beyond assumed differences regarding the hot-cold syndrome, the older residents of Juubche' often looked to racial classification to explain the relationship between the labor activities between themselves and ts'uu-lo'ob and related dietary distinctions. Many residents explained to me that ts'uulo'ob have more delicate constitutions that require finer food. Furthermore, the hearty foods of rural peasants do not suit ts'uulo'ob and their largely sedentary labor practices. During our extended stay in Juub-che' my and my husband's frequent illnesses led some well-meaning kin to urge our hosts to prepare foods such as quesadillas that they had been exposed to in urban areas and saw as representative of the typical cuisine of Americans. Many older women, all of whom raised children before infant formula was widely available, were surprised by the breastfeeding of *xunáano'ob* (feminine equivalent of ts'uulo'ob), as they perceived formula to be "finer" than breast milk. While Juubche' residents of all ages believe that one can sometimes *suuktal* (grow accustomed) to different foods and environments, older informants frequently impressed upon me their belief that the foods that they were accustomed to eating and their care strategies were uniquely suited for their bodies and lifestyles and, as such, characteristic of their place in one of a limited number of racial categories. Furthermore, though bodies might adjust to new circumstances, the initial change can be shocking and cause sickness.

External transformations are complicated by the stubborn nature of those bodies and their dispositions. Quite often, the habits and tastes of the body linger, stubbornly, even when one's world rapidly changes. The failure of the body or collective bodies to adapt easily to changing conditions is what Bourdieu (1977) calls the "hysteresis effect." Farquhar (2002) explains it as "a kind of historical, bodily stutter marking the impossibility of feeling comfortable in the present" (17). During one interview I conducted in Juubche', doña Paola, a woman in her midfifties, begin to detail a long trajectory of suffering and failed healing. Most recently, she explained, an urban doctor had diagnosed her with acute gastritis and put her on a liquid diet. Since then, she had subsisted largely on cow's milk and pureed fruits and vegetables. She lamented: "Yesterday the doctor told me that I will survive with just milk, but meanwhile I am hungry every hour. Whatever the hour I'm hungry because there's nothing in my stomach . . . I say to them, my children, I really wanna eat holy tortillas. . . . Meanwhile, when I get up like this, I don't have an óol. When I get up, I feel like I'm going to die. I have no strength. Oh God, I really don't have strength."

Doña Paola's body needed tortillas; she could not adapt to the forms of sustenance promoted by a biomedical practitioner and experienced suffering as a result. Such "stutters" are clear in the experiences of many residents of Juubche', where forms of care can collide with locally constituted biologies.

Other individuals seem to adjust more easily to changes in their lives and communities. How people interpret responses to changing conditions varies as well. Younger women and men often question the racialized notions of care and food requirements posed by their elders. In challenging established ideas of racial difference through practice, however, young people have actually contributed to the development of an alternate theory of bodily difference: younger generations, some elderly residents posit, are growing more like those of ts'uulo'ob. The changing lifestyles of the young, as well as selective evidence of phenotypic change, especially with regard to height and skin color, reinforce this theory for some older people. Doña Susana, a woman in her fifties, noted how her younger neighbor gave her children "cold" drinks with "hot" food in the cool evenings. Doña Susana explained that she wouldn't have dared do that with her children a few decades earlier, but she then concluded that it didn't seem to do as much harm to children today. Conflicting understandings of the nature of bodies and variations between them, provoked by shifting external conditions, make somewhat unpredictable how one ought to engage with the world and with which modes of care.

Contested Waters

During my time in Juubche', nearly all adult women I met participated in the federal program then known as Oportunidades, described earlier in this chapter. The program was what is known as a conditional cash transfer, or CCT, program. Increasingly common across the globe, CCT programs are antipoverty efforts designed to offer cash incentives to promote health and education among economically marginalized populations. The focus and scale of CCT programs vary globally, but Oportunidades was one of the larger efforts, reaching approximately 20–25 percent of the Mexican population. Cash was distributed to female heads of household, as with most CCT programs. The payments received every two months by Mexican participants included up to four types of assistance, with a combined limit of about U.S.$300 in 2009 (Fiszbein and Schady 2009).[17] In order to receive their funds, women had to meet certain conditions, including making twice-annual visits to the federally funded health clinic in their community, obtaining immunizations for their children, and participating in regular *pláticas* (lectures) and in the shared maintenance of clinics. Failure to comply with any of the requirements resulted in a reduction or eventual termination of cash transfers.[18]

Doña Patricia recounted the happenings of one two-hour plática for me. About one hundred women attended the talk on financial responsibility, which began with an icebreaker game. The speaker discussed the economic crisis; this was 2009, and the global recession had hit the region's tourist industry hard, leaving many residents deeply concerned. The speaker told the women not to fear dying of hunger; they would survive even if they had to survive on beans for days at a time. She encouraged thrift, telling the women to eat leftovers until they were gone, instead of throwing them out to dogs or chickens. The speaker then asked the women who was responsible for various matters in their lives. A few women responded with God or their husbands or themselves. The speaker then impressed upon them the significance of their own action, telling them that it's up to them, not God, to care for themselves and their families, to not waste the money they receive from Oportunidades, and to fulfill their responsibilities to the program: going to checkups and sending their children to school well dressed and on time. Such rhetoric is characteristic of the program as it operated as Oportunidades and in its next iteration as Prospera (Gálvez 2018; Smith-Oka 2013), as it reinforced the expectation for individual responsibility for well-being, after several decades of federal policies that have negatively impacted the health of poor and rural people in Mexico. Doña Patricia's retelling of the speaker's emphasis on thrift struck me as especially tone-deaf. In kitchens throughout Juubche' I observed women making use of everything they could, from plastic bags to moldy tortillas.

Nevertheless, women sometimes found the information acquired from pláticas valuable, even if only as a way to present themselves as urbane. I often heard doña Katy, in her fifties, reminding other women of information she had acquired through the pláticas, and she sometimes nodded knowingly when I begged off food or drink that I feared might be unsafe for me. Within her own household, however, she expressed confidence in many of her own habits, some of which conflicted with the information

4. Mural outside the health clinic in Juubche'. Courtesy of author.

disseminated in the pláticas of Oportunidades. For example, doña Katy's daughter Rebecca had begun purchasing purified water for her own toddler daughter. I occasionally witnessed Rebecca reminding her mother to serve the child purified water in place of the water piped into some homes in the community. Doña Katy always obliged, but on one occasion, after handing the child a cup of purified water, she looked at me and sighed, "My children didn't drink this water, and they survived." The privileging of something in strange packaging and of strange origins seemed illogical to doña Katy. She had lived with local water for her entire life; it was familiar, and its potential dangers, as articulated mostly through the hot-cold syndrome, were clear and thus manageable. Even its "bacteria," a term she had acquired from Oportunidades pláticas and explained to others as "very little things," were local, part of the ecosystem in which human bodies lived, ate, and drank.

Mexico's CCT programs have relied on women to spread new information to other members of their households and the larger community. The development of women as local authorities on biomedicine, education, and home economics widens their sphere of influence, rendering them as more than just keepers of tradition.[19] Many of the program's participants interpret the information they receive through the lens of care, and they must then decide if and how to integrate this information into their own daily practices. Participants in Oportunidades become the gatekeepers for this new knowledge, often acting as decision makers in matters of multiple care logics. At times the lecture speakers, many of whom grew up in communities similar to Juubche' (or, in the case of one nurse, in Juubche' itself), may actually use the terms *kalan* and *kanan* to encourage particular practices. Other times the content of the lectures, which often promote human, especially women's, action in the face of external dangers, evoke responses that conceptually reference habits of care. For many women the lectures help them to adapt their care tactics to the changing circumstances of their lives: husbands who are absent for longer periods of time and thus thought more likely to stray, children who are more vulnerable to impurities in food and water than were earlier generations, and the women's own bodies, subject to novel diseases and unfamiliar measures of well-being. Quite often then, the information women absorb through these lectures does not strike them as an inherent challenge to existing systems of knowledge but instead as a toolkit for living well in changing bodies in a changing world. Moreover, the conflation of care with public education, community participation, and state intervention via programs such as Oportunidades reinforces for women the significance of care as a crucial, and in fact modern, tactic in twenty-first-century living.

Nonetheless, women do not always integrate the information they have received into their own practices. As Smith-Oka (2013) finds in another indigenous community in Mexico, Oportunidades often devalues the existing expertise of mothers. In Juubche' the information relayed through Oportunidades does sometimes conflict with the habits and assumptions they have acquired through experience, as evidenced by doña Katy's ambivalence toward her daughter's preference for purified water. During a discussion with doña Esmeralda about the qualities of certain foods, I mentioned the healthfulness of oranges. They are rich in vitamin C, I said, and so are good to eat when one has a cold. Doña Esmeralda shook her head. The clinic had told her the same thing, she explained, but she didn't believe it. After all, she continued, oranges are "cold"; consuming something cold when one has a cold will only make the situation worse. What might be perceived in the biomedical world as noncompliance is rather a careful calculation of the worth of different forms of knowledge. Doña Esmeralda respects the knowledge of the clinic staff and her resident anthropologist, but she knows through experience the "cold" of oranges and its effects on a cold. While "cold" oranges and purified water should not be thought of as fixtures in stable webs of ideas about the world, such ways of categorizing and engaging with these objects are bound to other, also deeply felt ideas about bodies and the worlds they inhabit. What I attempt to do throughout this work is not to suggest a fixed indigenous worldview that is fractured by contemporary happenings but rather to analyze how care is a prominent mode through which residents of Juubche' constitute themselves and their worlds, as they have done in the past. Still, the late twentieth century was a period of radical change for people in this community and one during which people's tactics for living well were tested and, quite often, revised. The place of food as both an object of and force for change here, in a context in which its centrality is strongly evidenced, suggests that food practices cannot just tell us what has happened but may also hint at what is to come.

My older informants often lamented that they held only a fraction of the culinary and healing knowledge of their ancestors, but the residents of Juubche' have adapted their everyday practices to shifting circumstances. They act with expectations for how they will fare in the world, and their constant attention to care reflects deeply felt assumptions about human anatomy and nature, often rooted in their own experiences. As discussed in the next chapter, the shifting circumstances of life in Juubche' have in some cases created and intensified divides between individuals and groups, shaping complicated logics of care and diverse bodily experiences. In a context of dramatic economic and social change, care enacts new values and tests established hexeis. The possibilities for pleasure expand, though often selectively and sometimes at the expense of collective processes of social reproduction.

CHAPTER 3

If It Tastes Good

During the week of Finados in 2007, doña Katy asked to purchase banana leaves from her sister-in-law, doña Susana, who had a number of trees full of the leaves in her yard. The banana leaves were to be used to prepare tamales for a *reza* (memorial prayer session) in honor of doña Katy's deceased daughter. Doña Katy inquired about payment as a matter of course, but she was surprised and angered that doña Susana did not brush off the offer immediately. Instead doña Susana set a price, which doña Katy dutifully paid. Later, doña Katy explained to me that she was displeased with what she saw as stinginess on the part of her sister-in-law. Doña Susana's decision to charge for the banana leaves upset doña Katy for a few reasons: their relationship as close kin and neighbors, the purpose for which the leaves were to be used (a reza; held in sharp contrast to, say, the preparation of tamales for sale), and the large quantity of leaves doña Susana had hanging from the trees in her yard. I did not have an opportunity to inquire of doña Susana how she set a price for the leaves and how she rationalized charging for them. Given my understanding of their relationship and of the complicated nature of exchange in the community more generally, I can only hypothesize as to the logic behind doña Susana's decision to charge for the leaves. She would likely have pointed, first, to the fact that doña Katy has cash to spare, and, second, to the fact that, in contrast, she and her husband lack such resources.

Such a scene might appear to unfold like a mid-twentieth-century portrayal of life in a typical "folk" community (Redfield 1941), replete with homogeneous cultural practices and barely-under-the-surface peasant tensions. Yet in fact this interaction is very much a product of dispersed and complex forces, as the later work of Redfield (1950) and Wolf ([1982] 2010; 1986) better recognizes, exerted from both within out and outside of this geographic community. By and large doña Susana's family has suffered under the recent economic and social changes. Her husband is too old to migrate any longer so he farms and occasionally does odd jobs for neighbors and kin. The couple is frequently in debt to others, often to pay for medical care. While one of their adult children is economically stable, the others are not. Excessive drinking and domestic violence plague the relationships of their adult children; all of the male partners migrate. In contrast, although doña Katy and her husband suffered the incredible tragedy of the loss of their daughter, she does a brisk business in handicrafts. As two elderly and childless individuals, their government assistance remains with them. Their expenses are minimal, and they have been lucky to have few medical issues.

Value is not fixed, nor is it a mere matter of supply and demand; it is carefully and often contentiously calculated based on numerous factors. In these processes of calculation, the care that goes into determining cash value manifests other care imperatives, working to reconcile desires for profit or savings with those for tranquil and reciprocal relationships. Frequently these imperatives cannot be neatly bound together, either in individual reckoning nor in interpersonal negotiations. Nor can such processes be avoided if one is to survive: rural Yucatecans have long sustained life, their own and that of the community, through acts of reciprocity, especially through the exchange of food. This reciprocity, in a variety of potential forms, is embedded in long-standing practices of care that attempt to maintain balance within a web of interrelated interests. Gifts, as Mauss (2000 [1950]) most famously theorized, are never free, and this is certainly the case in Juubche'. Milpa farmers offer *sa'* or *atole* (a corn-based drink) to the guardians of their fields in hopes that they will receive a bountiful harvest. Women prepare ornate tables full of fresh flowers, handmade tortillas, soft drinks, and tamales for the *pixaan* (souls of the dead) so that they will achieve salvation and not haunt the living. Girls and young women "give themselves" to their husbands in marriage but in turn expect their husbands to provide food and cash for them.[1]

In fact, it is this last mode of "gift giving"—marriage—that forms the most basic unit of exchange in Juubche', and it is deeply connected to food.

Marriage initiates fresh cycles of care at the level of the household that, ideally, provide material and social support for its members. Only through the smooth functioning of the household can its members enact care and maintain balance outside of domestic space. A man must be well fed and healthy to labor effectively in his milpa or be emotionally healthy to represent himself well at a meeting of *ejido* (collective land ownership) members. A woman must have the money to purchase flowers for the *Santa Cruz* (Holy Cross) or to purchase a prepared meal of *panuchos* (tortilla-based fast food) for her family on the day she must attend a lecture at the clinic. Transformations in the modes of exchange, most markedly the increase in commodity exchanges, reverberate throughout the nesting realms sustained through care: household, community, and the larger world. In particular, the disruption of the tight links maintained through sex and food at that basic unit of the marital relationship suggests the gradual loosening of the webs that once tied not only households but also communities and ecosystems together.

This is not to suggest an idyllic and stable past, lacking in inequalities and tensions. Scholars have challenged Robert Redfield's view of a homogenous rural community, based on his fieldwork conducted in the 1930s and 1940s (e.g., Castañeda 1996; Goldkind 1965). In subsequent research Redfield (1950) himself noted the presence of a few Protestant families and the use of Western clothing and housewares by some more affluent villagers, but he continued to argue that distinct social classes had not yet developed and that social cohesion persisted. In another, smaller town a few decades later, Rivera (1976) linked a lack of distinct social classes to the near-universality of agricultural subsistence. Ethnographic accounts from elsewhere in the region, described in earlier chapters, noted increases in occupational and religious diversity that threatened collective participation in Catholicism, milpa agriculture, and related rituals in the second half of the twentieth century (Press 1975; Re Cruz 1996; R. A. Thompson 1974). Many older informants in Juubche' remarked on the evident wealth disparities they recalled witnessing as children in the 1920s, 1930s, and 1940s: while some families struggled to feed themselves, others possessed large herds of cattle and gold jewelry. Girls and young women traveled to regional cities to work as domestic servants in middle- and upper-class households. However, Roman Catholicism and milpa agriculture still organized the routines and rituals of every household in the community itself. Some men worked as bakers or prepared candy from sugarcane, but they still produced corn and other staple crops to feed their families. Some families were more active in religious activities—they were more likely to act as sponsors for the annual fiesta or for the feast of the Virgin of Guadalupe—but everyone prepared offerings for the souls of the dead, baptized their children in the Catholic Church, and sought the favor of the lords of the forest and animals. Collective ownership of much of the land helped to maintain an ideology of social balance and equality, despite existing inequalities. Processes of production and consumption held in common marked human engagement with food and drink throughout the community, reinforced by the rituals that emerged through a history of shared economic and religious activity. Doña Feliciana recounted of her childhood in the 1920s and 1930s: "Well, as for life then, nowhere was it different. Nowhere would you say, 'Ah, you're the atole drinkers.' Everyone was the same."

Since doña Feliciana's youth, and especially since the 1970s, the shift from agricultural subsistence to wage labor and the conversion of some residents to non-Catholic religions has resulted in greater occupational and religious diversity in rural indigenous communities (Press 1975; Re Cruz 1996; R. A. Thompson 1974). The population increases of the twentieth century transformed many rural settlements into more bustling towns, as in Juubche', where one older informant remarked, "Today I don't recognize everybody. Back then I did." The consequent alterations in everyday routine and discourse manifest a changing bodily hexis, intimate new formations of practice that represent and produce how individuals see themselves as members of generational and gendered cohorts. Additionally some residents of Juubche' have found success in new industries, while others have made almost no economic gains through agricultural or wage labor. The broadening of potential economic pursuits and increasing specialization bring new modes of class difference, made visible by novel consumption practices that bind together markers of gender, religion, and ethnicity.

Recent economic and social changes have complicated already gendered processes of production and consumption, reflecting the nuanced effects of commodification in Juubche' more generally. The influx of cash into rural communities in this region in the late twentieth century inspired new ways of caring, as consumers or as guardians of wealth, that conflicted with earlier practices of redistribution and ideologies of equality. Some of these conflicts may be rooted in ideological dissonance between a more influential ethic of individualism, supported by consumerism and religious conversion, and more established values of equality, balance, and tranquility (Castellanos 2003; Greene 2002; Kray 1997). Other conflicts are evidence of the intensification of long-standing social tensions resulting from more visible wealth disparities; divergent experiences along lines of gender, generation, and economic status; and, quite simply, an increase in the very number of exchanges happening on any given day. Economic and social changes such as an unprecedented influx of cash, occupational diversity, and encounters with novel cultural forms only exacerbate what residents assume to be the weaknesses of human nature. As in other rural indigenous communities in this region (Callahan 2005; Juarez 1996; Kray 1997), many people in Juubche' express the belief that the natural emotional and moral state of humans is weak and prone to temptation. They are wary of the behavior of others because they regularly experience what they presume to be the same challenges in resisting selfishness. This exercise of self-control is a struggle, yet it is thought to be essential to the maintenance of tranquility. For example, in other communities in the region, anxieties about "natural" sexual urges structure gender relations (Callahan 2005; Juarez 1996), and certain social relationships, especially between genders, are based on benevolent avoidance (Hanks 1990). Even in a nonsexual context, individuals are thought to want to *toop* (screw, fuck, bother) each other, out of self-interest, and the suspicion and caution this inspires mar many intimate relationships. Woodrick (1995) argues that the mother-daughter relationship is the only one usually free of such tensions; the very strength of that relationship is only reinforced by the lack of trust in others, especially in those relationships between men and women. Rugeley (2001b) suggests that, more generally, relatives pose a conundrum for the rural inhabitants of this region: they are crucial to one's survival but are also a source of frequent tensions. On one hand, survival has historically been a collective endeavor. Kin and often neighbors as well help to maintain balance through reciprocity, shared labor, and collective rites of renewal. On the other hand the maintenance of such balance must contend with what are thought to be natural and thoroughly human qualities.

Still, the need for balance and all it embodies persists, despite a new proliferation of desires. Balance is, after all, seen by residents of Juubche' as the most crucial means and end in the maintenance of well-being, and commodities and their exchange may be manipulated to achieve this condition. A New Year's Eve party, with its extravagant spread of grapes, roasted goat, bakery cake, imported chocolates, and sparkling wine, would have been unimaginable to the residents of Juubche' a half-century ago, and yet in recent years it has become a tradition for some upwardly mobile local families. The prestige it earns for them as hosts, with their access to nonlocal and relatively expensive foods, and their knowledge of how and when one ought to consume them during the course of the night, is substantial. Just as significant is the way such a party can cement bonds between them and their extended kin, who feel honored to be included in the feast. Without this invitation to commensality, the wealth of the hosts might have been more likely to foment animosity than good favor in their kin. Such tricky maneuvering around consumption is a classic object of ethnographic analysis, but in Juubche' so much of this negotiation of values and desires occur through food. Evident when doña Feliciana waxed about the past, that all were atole drinkers in her youth, food is held to be a visible and meaning marker of sameness but also one of difference.

In Juubche', differential access to commodities reproduces inequalities and strains already fractured ideals of cooperation and consensus. Networks of exchange may themselves depend upon concurrent successes and misfortunes. A destitute woman sells her gold jewelry to a sister-in-law or her husband sells his cattle to a neighbor, but these are not practices of reciprocity that necessarily enhance positive social bonds. In both the domestic and the public realms, commodities are often seen to embody some dark assumptions about human nature. As material extensions of selfishness and a lack of self-control, commodities may become emblematic of uncaring natures, manifestations of human weakness and prostheses for shameful behavior. Moral and sexual differences are increasingly expressed by objects and services that call into question established modes of caring. Or the perceived dangers commodities bring inspire an increased fervor for care as a strategy for achieving well-being. As objects and services are commodified in different ways at different moments, so too do they reshape bodies and make them capable of new appetites and pleasures. Old distinctions— between male and female, old and young, rich and poor—emerge anew, at the sites of the bodies and the commoditized sensory fields in which they experience the world. In this chapter the focus is on how these experiences emerge through exchange, at the level of the marital pair, larger kin group, and the community, in the first part of the chapter more generally and then with a focus on gender. Collectively, these cases demonstrate how food's potential as a source of both balance and disruption positions it, symbolically and practically, as a critical site of negotiating the transformation of contemporary life.

Social Life and Surveillance

While living in Juubche', I shared a small three-room home and an outdoor latrine with my hosts and, along with them, constantly entertained impromptu visits. My occasional discomfort with the spatial and social intimacy of life here obscured the more complex nature of privacy in the community, where practices such as bathing, sex, urination, and defecation are closely guarded.[2] Although at times doña Esmeralda would dissolve into laughter when either she or I would nearly intrude on the other in the latrine, had the incident been a cross-gender one, it would have been immensely awkward. Likewise, my husband's discomfort with having a room full of guests conversing while he bathed in an enclosed area only a few feet away was eased only by his realization that no one ever dared pass the curtained opening during his showers. Perhaps the most notable display of respect for privacy is the highly formalized way in which visitors approach a home. Doors are often swung wide open and a home's residents may be visible either in the house or out in the solar, but a guest is not to enter the yard without yelling a "Días" (Good day), "Tardes" (Good afternoon), or "Noches" (Good evening) and being invited inside.[3] This is effective in preventing awkward interruptions of intimate activities and in giving homeowners a chance to hide from unwelcome guests.

Yet privacy is rare outside of domestic spaces and, among kin, rare even within those more intimate spheres. Many homes are close to streets, and doors and windows are almost always left open during daylight hours. Women often choose to move their sewing machines or hammock looms to an open door both for the breeze and for the opportunity to watch happenings on the street. Residents are highly aware of the domestic disputes and drunken antics of their neighbors, and news of major purchases or interesting visitors make their way down a street at rapid paces. Children playing in the street can be counted on to relay to their parents those occurrences that the adults themselves did not see or hear. Similarly, physical proximity between households in the community helps to spread new of events on the other side of the nation or world, as those watching televised news or scrolling through social media on their phones share happenings with family and neighbors. Residents returning from visits to nearby cities report back on happenings there, updating neighbors on everything from power outages to wait times at the regional hospital.

Beyond small spaces and open doors, the rhythms of daily life in the community preclude much time alone. With the notable exception of men who work alone in their milpas, time alone is rare for residents of Juubche', especially women. Women's social networks are comprised mostly of kin and, to a lesser degree, neighbors. Even in the case of girls, most of whom now attend school much longer than women in previous generations, school friends are often cousins or neighbors first. Those who are not may quickly grow apart when school ends and girls marry and begin their own families. The home-based labor activities of women do not encourage friendships far beyond the neighborhood. Socializing occurs primarily with those with whom one has a clear relationship and pattern of exchange: first, other women in the nuclear family, and second, extended female kin such as sisters-in-law and nieces. A woman may have a friendly rapport with a neighbor, but visits between the two are rarely just social. Such visits usually serve a practical and often economic function: the purchase of some eggs or the sharing of the latest cosmetics catalog circulating the neighborhood. Purely social interactions between nonkin are largely relegated to the public realm: in the town center during school or other community events, in the town's stores, and through participation in government programs. Still, male migration has made it easier, and perhaps more necessary, for migrants' wives to strengthen relationships with other women. These migrants' wives are able to move more freely through town while their husbands are away, and they often make frequent visits to female kin for company and to share meals.[4]

For men, male migration in groups encourages camaraderie between kin and nonkin alike, and nonkin friendships for men tend to be more intimate than those between nonkin women. The amount of time many men spend together is greater than in previous generations, when agricultural labor was solitary or limited to close kin for much of the annual cycle. Just as shared experiences in the male space of the milpa might have once encouraged a gendered solidarity, the migratory experience connects men to a gendered cohort. Yet in contrast to the solidarity produced through participation in farming, in which men worked in the same ways but often on an individual basis, returning home to family homes at the end of most days, today's migrants often work and live with their male peers while away from Juubche'. For migrants who spend much of the week with male companions in large urban areas, a return to the domestic routines maintained by women, children, and older men can feel strange or unfamiliar. To be on the street back in the village, drinking and talking with the same men with whom one shares these migratory experiences, helps some men bridge the gap between these rural and urban worlds. Groups of young men share the pleasures and trials of urban life, while most women, children, and older people are embedded in the routines and rhythms of rural life.

Even prior to the development of regional tourism, most women did not spend much time in milpas. However, nearly all occasionally helped their husbands there, and a few widows told tales of doing the bulk of the farming after their husbands' deaths. Still, for the vast majority of women who did not work regularly in the milpa, they understood the kind of work that occurred in that space. In contrast, few women I interviewed could provide details on what work their husbands performed during migratory periods. Some women struggled for the words to describe the labor itself—ironworker, construction worker, gardener—relying on a child or other relative to suggest a job title, while other women were unsure of whether their husbands actually worked in Cancún or another coastal community. In one less common case Cristiano, a young man in his twenties, migrated to Puerto Vallarta, on the other side of Mexico, with two friends from Juubche'. "What work is he doing, and when will be back?" I asked his wife Dalia. "Who knows," she responded matter-of-factly. The less stable, and often less lucrative and prestigious, a man's job, the less his wife seemed to know about it. In part, this is a practical matter: construction workers, often the most poorly paid among the common migrant professions in the region, move between jobs with great frequency. Offers for work can be vague, with men only learning details upon their arrival on the coast each Monday. The small minority of women whose husbands worked in more lucrative and, one assumes, more stable professions, as tour guides or waiters, seemed to know more about their husbands' labor activities; some had even met their husbands' employers or visited their work sites.

Circular male migration from this region is not new, but its scale in the last three decades is unprecedented. During my visits from 2006 to the spring of 2008, prior to the global economic crisis that grew dire later in 2008, few men under the age of fifty were present in town on an average weekday. Furthermore, the encounters migrants have with the world outside of Juubche' encompass a broader range of experiences than those of past migrant laborers. As opposed to the chicle camps and isolated ranches where men worked in the mid-twentieth century, the urban spaces of Cancún and Playa del Carmen expose migrant men to diverse national and global cultural forms: everything from big box stores to Chinese restaurants to internet cafés. These men build hotels and office buildings, often in the wealthiest neighborhoods, or they serve tourists or local elites in restaurants or hotels. Additionally, an increased flow of cash between these urban centers and rural communities like Juubche', the product of relatively greater wages than in the past, enables the movement of new commodities, between urban and rural spheres and within the rural sphere itself. As in other rural communities in the region (Greene 2002; Heusinkveld 2008), residents of Juubche' use these cash earnings to start businesses (that then produce more cash) and to purchase everything from tortillas to bicycles.

Men and women alike adapt to this new proliferation of commodities, but concurrent transformations in other aspects of their daily lives, like the prevalence of male migration, produce differential access to commodities. Later in this chapter I track the ways in which men and women's adaptations to social changes such as increased commodification reflect and reproduce notions of gender difference and shape distinctive subjectivities. Given the centrality of food to social reproduction and to collective and individual well-being in Juubche', it is critical to recognize its historically inextricable ties to sex and the processes by which those ties are loosened in contemporary life. Commodification in particular reconfigures the nature of marital and sexual relationships and shapes real and novel gaps between male and female experience. The shifts that unfold through these processes do not only alter domestic relationships between men and women. They also infuse public life—its mundane exchanges, displays of power and desire, and scandalous gossip—with the possibilities of pleasure and the threat of imbalance. Before examining issues of gender and how they structure intimate exchanges within and outside of the household, I first detail the expectations that permeate any sale, trade, or gift interaction and the sometimes contradictory logics of care that infuses almost every exchange. Such expectations and logics, I argue, reveal exchange as a complex site of negotiation, negotiation that is not just economic but about value *and values* in a much broader sense, especially when it comes to food.

Rules of Exchange

Wealth disparities among rural Yucatecans and in the larger societies they inhabit are not new phenomena. However, the transition from agricultural subsistence to wage labor produced economic and cosmological shifts that have deepened old tensions and created others anew. In Juubche', commodities increasingly flow into and out of the community: the factory-made Lycra clothing worn by most young women, the locally woven hammocks destined for tourist markets, and the ubiquitous chips and soft drinks sold in most every place of business. These objects and the labor that produces them are already deeply rooted in the anxieties and perceived vulnerabilities that infuse human interactions with the material world. Socially, contemporary exchanges enact an array of tensions between capitalist models for economic self-care, including the values of thrift and profit, and cooperative ideologies of equality and interdependence, with their expectations for reciprocity and sound moral judgment. Notions of collective caregiving and relational wellness were embedded in older values of cooperation and consensus, but today they coexist uneasily with capitalistic imperatives and consumer culture.

On any given day the average Juubche' resident engages in multiple exchanges of objects and services. Migrant men sell their labor daily in Cancún or Playa del Carmen. Other men might work in the milpa of a neighbor or on a state-funded road project for wages. Women pay a few pesos for a packet of instant coffee or to have the day's corn dough ground. Children are sent out to buy a small bunch of cilantro or a couple of habanero chiles from a neighbor, and they demand some change from their parents to buy a snack during school recess. The town's seamstresses check the final fit of made-to-order dresses and collect their fees. A girl might care for her young cousins or a mother might wash her adult daughter's dirty laundry, both for a few pesos. Yet even today cash does not mediate every exchange. Small pots of broths and beans circulate between households of kin.[5] Hosts distribute sandwiches and ensalada at birthday parties, and thick stews and hot tortillas at christening celebrations. A *x-k'uus* (expert cook) oversees the preparation of relleno negro for the annual fiesta in exchange for a few servings and some laundry soap to clean her cooking clothes. Male migrants treat each other to beers on Saturday evenings as they drink in cantinas or on park benches.

The goods passed along in any exchange are mostly small and inexpensive. Based on my observations in stores and homes, on an average day, a woman in Juubche' will herself or with a child as a proxy make multiple small purchases, most of which cost less than an American dollar. Of course, residents do sell house lots, stereos, and cars, exchanging the equivalent of hundreds or thousands of American dollars, but such exchanges are far less frequent. Several practical explanations might account for frequent and low-expenditure shopping trips, but small shopping trips can also serve as strategies for maintaining positive relationships with vendors.[6] Women tend to be picky about where they purchase any item: one store might have fresher eggs, but another sells crackers at a lower price. Making those purchases on separate trips out of the house will draw less attention to a woman's "shopping around" than would carrying a bag from one store into a competing store. Shopping trips are also an opportunity for women and children to walk around town, stop and chat with neighbors and relatives, and check out happenings in the square.

Despite the frequency with which objects, services, and cash pass through multiple hands, some of these exchanges produce anxieties and tensions. Although cash has been in daily use for generations, its growing dominance as *the* way in which one obtains goods and services, and the very increase in those goods and services available, has complicated older habits of exchange. A few general rules seem to apply. Within the nuclear family in each household, generalized reciprocity is common: most items are freely exchanged; indeed they are hardly thought of as individually possessed at all.[7] In many households the presence of teenaged wage laborers complicates this; they may own smart phones or gold jewelry that they see as well-deserved products of their own labor. Outside of the household, exchange is yet more complicated. Gifting rarely occurs when the object has already been marked a commodity in a previous exchange (e.g., a television, a kilo of tomatoes from the corner store). Likewise, gifting is less common when the recipient herself makes the request for the item. Home-cooked foods are almost always exchanged as gifts between kin, particularly in the case of ki' waaj, the savory dishes that are often exchanged in pots or on plates. Homemade foodstuffs that can be exchanged more easily in discrete units, such as tamales, discs of drinking chocolate, or small bags of spice mixtures, may be exchanged for cash between kin and nonkin alike, but they too are sometimes gifted.

In the case of other items that are homegrown or homemade, such as garden products, the line grows blurrier. Nonkin will almost always be charged cash for such items unless they have recently done one a favor or paid a special visit (or are a visiting anthropologist; in fact, the frequency with which I was gifted objects, even those that my hostess had sent me to purchase, often made me uncomfortable). Women selling cilantro or habanero chiles will charge most buyers for what they sell, usually, at a rate of just a few pesos. Close relatives may be charged only for larger quantities, or if the seller is particularly needy. Again though, blurriness persists. The degree of kinship between two individuals or any perceived tension between them will often complicate the nature of any exchange. Outside of settings in which gift giving is the norm (e.g., a wedding or a child's birthday party), a polite formality is used to clear up any uncertainty as to whether something is a gift: it is customary to ask the price of any object offered. During my first few months in Juubche', many residents would give me a few eggs or a small bag of dried squash seeds after I visited their homes. Upon my arrival back to my hosts' home, doña Esmeralda, always mindful of how I represented her in town, would ask me to repeat the dialogue involving the exchange of the gift. She did this largely to ensure that I had asked "How much?" even though I expected full well to be told, "Nothing." Such is the care one must take to avoid being labeled stingy or ungrateful. Of course, one risks being asked a fee for what is, in many cases, an unintended or unneeded purchase, but this outcome is rare and reflects poorly on the gift giver or seller.

When items are to be sold or traded, bargaining is not unheard of, particularly in informal contexts (e.g., outside of clear commercial spheres, such as stores). Disagreements over value rarely escalate into full-scale arguments; the signs of tension tend to be subtle. Residents are acutely aware of the tones of each other's voices and disparities, minute and substantial, in the quality of objects: a less choice cut of meat, a hasty exit, and an unchilled drink can all indicate or produce discord. For this reason residents take great care to consider how any item or service might be perceived. On one occasion I watched doña Esmeralda thoughtfully dole out servings of an elaborate stew for a number of her sisters. She consulted with her mother on each portion—was it too much, not enough, the right cuts of meat—and made sure her young niece, the appointed delivery person, knew to say it was from her. Usually all parties sense any tension and may even seek to interpret the exchange through a retelling of the encounter in the audience of trusted kin.

Although the parties in each exchange may come to different conclusions regarding the value of goods, participants in socially normative exchanges seek to achieve similar aims. Each exchange must accomplish three things to preserve individual and social balance and tranquility: first, each individual must avoid insulting the other participant in the exchange, both to prevent the development of social tensions and to begin or maintain a valuable relationship of exchange; second, each individual must protect his or her own reputation, both as a fair participant in exchanges but also as a moral and reasonable community member (as, that is, someone who cares in socially acceptable ways); and lastly each individual must guard her own financial interests. Most daily exchanges in Juubche' often occurs between individuals who enjoy kin or neighborly relationships. Even those who have the luxury of buying many goods from relatively anonymous sources in nearby cities may resell such goods within the village, and they too are not exempt from the need to purchase the occasional good or service locally. Preexisting relationships, based on kinship and contiguity, color the particularities of all exchanges. Positive relationships are perceived as both socially and economically beneficial. The decision to risk a relationship over a financial quibble must be weighed carefully. For close kin to fracture a relationship over the price of a plot of land is not unheard of. To do so over the price of a bunch of cilantro would be unthinkable. Doña Katy did not dissolve her relationship with her sister-in-law over banana leaves; they are practically next-door neighbors and rely upon each other for favors on a regular basis. Their neighbor doña Teresa, on the other hand, has not spoken to her brother, don Mauro, in almost a decade, since he failed to contribute to medical costs for their dying mother. Doña Teresa and don Mauro, both in their seventies, live several blocks from each other with their respective large families and follow different religions; for years they managed to avoid each other with few negative consequences for their material well-being. The seeming ease with which their social distance endures is itself a function of contemporary life in

Juubche', made possible by the town's large population (compared to a half century ago) and the religious diversity that frees them from shared worship. The lack of social bonds between the nuclear families of doña Teresa and don Mauro does not entail the risks to material survival that such fractures might have threatened in the past, when bonds of reciprocity tied together most households in one way or another.

Still, participants in exchanges understand that their reputations as buyers, sellers, and community members are at stake, and few are willing to abandon most or all social relationships for what might seem narrow self-interests. Residents of Juubche' make a distinction between those who are thrifty with their own household economies, an admired quality, and those who are stingy in their exchanges with others.[8] To be stingy is to be one who is willing to screw others financially, by, for example, charging too much or paying too little. Practically speaking, those thought to be stingy may be excluded from future exchanges, but they may also be subject to other social punishments. They may be the targets of gossip, shamed, or, in more serious cases, shunned by others. Their *moodos* (ways of being in the world) will be questioned. In the most egregious case an individual may simply be declared *k'asa'an* (bad), a very harsh commentary on one's moral fiber and basic nature. In conversations with me, a number of women accused their neighbor doña Elda of overcharging them for corn dough in her small corner store. They gradually took their business elsewhere, and doña Elda's store stood empty most of the time, leading its proprietress to focus on other cash-earning endeavors. Doña Elda's perceived stinginess did not have merely economic consequences; few of her neighbors made social visits to her home.

Buyers and sellers must balance their desire and need to behave in acceptable and moral manners with the personal or familial responsibility to take great care with money, down to each *centavo*. There are instances in which to be exceedingly generous, to gift an item or service when unexpected, to pay too much for something, or to ask too little in payment, is socially admirable, but to do so repeatedly may open one to criticism, especially if one does not necessarily have the money or time to spare. One elderly husband and wife in Juubche' are characterized as particularly *siij óol* (generous;

having a giving óol). They were generous with their time and food in my presence and, more importantly, to others in the community. They were known to feed a poor and lonely older woman in their neighborhood, and when they hired neighbors to help with work on their property, they paid fair wages and offered generous helpings of good food. However, public admiration of their generosity was tempered by the acknowledgment of their relative financial security: they were, by local standards, comfortable; both worked to earn cash, but they were not known to struggle and had support from some of their grown children. In other cases in families that faced greater financial challenges, one member's generosity could provoke tension and criticism. Women might chastise their husbands for charging too little for a good or service. When this behavior is often repeated, as in the case of a man who rarely charged local children for the fruit from one of his trees, a wife or other family member may question the giver's dedication to caring for his own family. To be too generous in cases of limited resources can signal to close kin the neglect of primary responsibilities, which as nearly everyone in Juubche' now recognizes, are in large part tied to the successful navigation of commodity exchanges. Such tensions are not necessarily new, but the people of Juubche' encounter them more frequently, as they engage in more commodity exchanges than in the past.

In such exchanges both buyers and sellers must be on the alert to avoid getting screwed, and this is itself a process of careful negotiation designed to balance individual and collective needs. The deliberate distinction made by two terms suggests the delicate nature of this balancing act. Bastarracha Manzano and Canto Rosado (2003) cite the Spanish *chingar* as a synonym for the Yucatec Maya *toop* (or *top*) (233). Castellanos (2003) defines *toop* as "to fuck, to screw, but also to harm, to bother" (248). *Chingar* is often defined similarly, yet as Octavio Paz notes (Castellanos 2003, 249), it is a flexible word whose meanings, depending on tone and context, can range from aggressive to frustrated to merry. In Juubche' the word *toop* is narrowly used, rarely spoken with a playful edge; as such it generally serves most speakers' purposes fairly well when it comes to expressing a sense of having been screwed.[9] Sullivan (1989) finds that many Maya speakers use *toop* in the context of exploitative encounters with foreigners (176).

Though one at times hears *toop* in that context in Juubche', I was more often privy to its use with regard to relationships within the community, especially with family and neighbors.[10] In the late 1990s don Erasmo had worked with his neighbor and fellow Jehovah's Witness, don Umberto, to cultivate watermelons for sale. Don Erasmo recalled laboring more hours than don Umberto, but don Umberto, who took the watermelons to sell in an urban market, "screwed" him (using *toop*), giving him less than his share of the profits. Similarly, doña Ana declined to join her sister-in-law in selling her handicrafts at a local tourist market, fearful that her relative would "screw" (*toop*) her out of her profits.[11] In a community in which many households increasingly desire accumulations of wealth and material objects, the line between screwing and success blurs. In the case of individuals who screw others, caring for themselves and their families trumps other forms of caregiving.

Those who are known to screw others are engaged with caution. Not surprisingly then, language use reveals emphasis on such caution. In Juubche' *chingar* is less commonly used in verb form; one hears the active noun *chingón* (fucker) much more often. More importantly, as Castellanos (2011) found in her research as well, *chingón* often signifies, first, the quality that keeps one from getting *toop*-ed, rather than the inclination to do the screwing, and, second, a sense of defiance. When children manage to get their way or beat the odds in a situation that doesn't risk their parents' anger, they may be subtly praised with a "Chingónech!" (You're a fucker!).[12] On one occasion doña Cristina stopped by to see my hostess and found me repairing by hand a torn piece of clothing, she exclaimed, "Jach chingónaech!" (You're such a fucker!). My ability and willingness to do this work, a task that many residents doubt an American could or would ever do, and the thriftiness it implied defied doña Cristina's expectations and suggested an active and thus desirable quality to my character. To be a chingón is to be an active and careful participant in a capitalist economy that, like some kin, can be set on screwing a person.

The frequency with which individuals feel themselves to be getting screwed or being at risk of getting screwed speaks to the opportunistic tendencies attributed to human nature, to what some people in Juubche' see as a decline in the local controls that discouraged narrow self-interest in the past, and to the unequal and exploitative conditions they face regionally and nationally. To resist the "natural" urge to screw others is to position oneself within a relationship that will be, ideally, mutually beneficial and to maintain the social balance through which a tranquil life is achieved. Again, we see the breadth of self-interest in Juubche'. The practice of care as enacted during and through exchange is twofold: first, out of long(er)-term self-interest and in deference to social norms and tranquility, what Fischer and Benson (2006) describe as "communalistic moral orientations" (119), one must provide goods in an acceptable fashion, not too stingy nor too generous; and second, as recipient, one must care for oneself and one's family's economic well-being by, again, walking the line between generosity and stinginess. However, ambiguities surrounding both the value of new commodities and the meaning of the exchanges through which they are circulated generate persistent anxieties about screwing and getting screwed. As a recognized means for both independent survival and interdependence between and within households, food and food practices are thus delicate sites of negotiation.

Food and Tension

Food production has been an organizing structure in the routines and rituals of rural Yucatecans for centuries. Historical accounts emphasize gender complementarity at the level of the household: men and women relied on each other for material sustenance; with men growing crops in the milpa and women processing these crops into tortillas and other staple foods (Faust 1998; Kintz 1998; O'Connor 2010). In Juubche', food exchanges are also an important way in which a woman maintains relationships with other women and, by extension, entire families outside of her own household. These exchanges are crucial in the development of associations within the neighborhood and with extended kin. Women who desire the social benefits of having allies in their neighborhoods—and most women do—build bonds with in-laws or neighbors by sending over gifts of a pot of beans or a bag of tamales. In turn, women must accept the food gifts offered to them, either food sent to their homes or received as guests in others' homes.

Doña Maritza recalled that, as a teenager, she visited relatives who were eating a simple meal of tortillas and chile. Her hosts offered her some, and she declined. On her next two visits, they again offered her food, and she declined. During a fourth visit, she was actually hungry and noticed that her hosts were dining on a particularly delicious chicken dish. On this occasion she was not offered any food. As doña Maritza interpreted it, unwillingness to try the simple but nourishing food offered on her earlier visits offended her hosts and threatened the generous bonds between them. Since then, she told me, she never refuses offers of food, understanding them to be not just displays of generosity but also building blocks in the development of reciprocity and social support. Like doña Maritza, few older people do not accept food gifts. In contrast, younger people more easily refuse food, perhaps because they have had less personal experience with hunger and because they tend to be pickier eaters (a luxury itself, to a large degree). Of course, such refusals are also linked to larger changes in economic and social conditions, the tightening of bodily boundaries hastened by individual wage earning and wealth accumulation, and less relational notions of well-being. Older people typically respond to the food refusals of young people in two ways: first, by taking it as a personal insult to one's cooking or housekeeping, and, second, as resistance on the part of the young person to build a social relationship through exchange.[13] For doña Tina, who often had conflicts with her siblings, the occasional reluctance of her nieces and nephews to sit down for a meal at her home suggested to her that their parents harbored unresolved animosity. Their food refusals challenged her desire to care for them and also reopened old wounds, new disruptions of tranquility, that bring her fresh *yaj* (pain).

Sometimes social expectations for generosity conflict with what are seen as stingy natures, thus producing new tensions. Doña Graciela bitterly reminisced about her miserly mother-in-law. Doña Graciela and her husband, don Pablo, married very young and built their own house when they were still teenagers. During this time, in the 1950s, don Pablo struggled to make his milpa, and they often went without food. Upon visits to don Pablo's parents, his mother sometimes would be patting out tortillas and greet them with an unenthusiastic "Come eat." Her offer was clearly not genuine, claimed doña Graciela; she didn't urge them to come closer, nor did she begin setting out portions for them. Her bodily movements (or lack thereof) and terse verbal offerings made evident the half-heartedness of her invitation. Doña Graciela and don Pablo would respond that they had already eaten, and the mother, even knowing full well that they had little food, easily accepted this falsehood.

The desire and indeed the social pressure to share food is complicated by a history of food scarcity. I heard many tales of hunger and of making do with very limited food resources.[14] During a conversation about a transient who moves between several local communities (highly unusual for rural Yucatán, where homelessness is largely unheard of), doña Ana recounted the family strife caused when her stepfather invited this transient in for a meal. Her mother, doña Lupita, who had eight children still at home, served him a portion roughly equivalent to her husband's and then began to dole out the children's servings. The transient quickly devoured his helping and asked for more. Doña Lupita protested that she had many mouths to feed, but her husband interrupted, ordering her to give the man a second helping. She did so but not without a visible sign of protest: she gave the transient a serving of broth, minus the meat. Despite the high value long placed on reciprocity and redistribution, daily food practices, particularly during periods of scarcity, prioritized the well-being of the household over the larger community. During such periods even collective rituals such as the annual fiesta in honor of the patron saint and agricultural ceremonies were threatened by difficult conditions, unhappily abandoned, or held on far-smaller scales.

As in the past, trying economic times provoke greater anxieties about feeding and being fed, particularly for those individuals who have tense relationships with kin. Unmarried and childless adults also express concern about a potentially hungry and lonely old age. Even when such a person has perfectly amiable relationships with his or her siblings and their children, these kin are not socially obligated to provide for anyone outside of their nuclear families. Doña Esmeralda often pointed out thin elderly people to me, noting how their extended families were failing to care for them; in some cases she even described these people as having been cheated, stripped of land rights or homes, by greedy nephews and nieces. Though particularly egregious cases often earned offending parties the descriptors of "evil" or "bad," it was generally understood that to provide for the extended family was kind and admirable but not obligatory. However, as occupational and religious diversity limits opportunities for collective ritual and redistribution, such forms of caring no longer fit within the functions of some community institutions and grow more dependent upon the actions of individuals or the state. When those individuals, such as the nieces and nephews of childless individuals, prioritize the needs of their own nuclear families, some residents fall through the cracks, becoming skinny and lonely.

While food scarcity can provoke anxieties about getting fed and feeding others, the contemporary proliferation of new food products also intensifies desires for recognition. Based on her research in one rural Yucatecan community, Holmes (1978) maintains that the realm of food is one in which women, especially kin with tense relationships, can best compete with one another as well (137). In Juubche' some women attempt to outdo each other in the quality and variety of foods prepared, make or interpret minor slights—late or nonexistent invitations to events, less-prime pieces of meat—and tempt members of their competitors' households to eat their food. In these ways established caregiving practices can manifest desires for recognition and power, challenging some of the effects, equality and balance, that they might have otherwise sought to achieve. The women I discuss in chapter 5, who have fashioned themselves into local experts on novel foods, use their knowledge about these foods to wield power both over their elders and over their less cosmopolitan peers. Traditions of reciprocity can be disentangled to reveal competing forms of embodied knowledge and strategic care practices—for example, feeding the local gringa a fancy meal. Culinary expertise itself becomes a source of tension, as it can reproduce inequalities linked to differential access to new foodstuffs and knowledge. The status one gains with such expertise might reflect long-standing expectations for caregiving: for example, food work as women's primary way to care for their families. Still, it bristles against other forms of caring, especially those embedded in local agricultural production and ritual commensality.

5. Vendor at the annual fiesta in Juubche'. Courtesy of Justin Nevin.

Commodification and the expanded availability of manufactured goods have complicated exchanges not only in the ambiguities of value these processes sometimes produce but also in relation to a growing desire for ever more goods. The promise of a good life is increasingly inclusive of commodities that necessitate yet more economic relationships. At the same time, however, the desire for goods and the goods themselves can appear to threaten well-being. After a conversation in which doña Esmeralda and I discussed soft drink consumption, she calculated her annual soft drink expenditures. Shocked by the high total, she exclaimed, "That Coca, it's making us poor!"[15] For most families, though, such commodities are now seen as essentials. The average household purchases a number of edible products almost every day; even in families that grow their own corn, beans, and other crops, women and children make at least a few shopping trips a day to purchase small amounts of items such as salt, Coca-Cola, and onions. Each neighborhood has several small stores selling food and household items, and two larger stores attract shoppers from all of Juubche'. Specialty establishments, such as *tortillerías* (tortilla stores), butchers, and cantinas also dot the town. Many households offer products and services on a less formal basis, everything from jars of honey to the administration of injectable medications to haircuts.

Few, if any, of these exchanges feature the anonymity common in many urban or suburban settings in the United States. Almost all Juubche' households have large numbers of kin within the town's borders, and between nonkin households there may exist fictive kin, friendship, or neighborly bonds. Even some of the itinerant vendors who visit town weekly or monthly become familiar faces; in some cases they themselves may have kin in the community or live just a town or two away. As evidenced by the tensions produced through any exchange, as discussed earlier in this chapter, familiarity between parties does not necessarily bring a sense of trust. Rather, it can magnify the implications of any negative interactions. In some cases individual tensions may dissolve once-close relationships but not necessarily the need or desire for a good or service once supplied through that relationship. With the increasing availability of a wider range of goods, Juubche' residents sometimes have both the option and the notion of entitlement to "shop around." Doña Elda, whose perceived stinginess negatively affected her sales of corn dough, now does much of her own shopping in a nearby city, perhaps because of conflicts arising from doing business in Juubche'. More anonymous venues offer her settings in which she can bargain with fewer consequences for her reputation in Juubche'. The ability to do this, however, is dependent on her ability to travel with ease, made possible by her husband's ownership of a car. Other consumers in Juubche' may be dependent on just one individual to obtain a particular product. The desire for specific goods can itself become a motive for exercising care and maintaining positive relationships with the individual who provides that item. Differences in access to resources can determine the spheres in which one must exercise this form of care. Those without cars or taxi fare may find themselves vulnerable to the whims of local storekeepers who are well known to them; thus, attempts to maintain good relationships with fellow townspeople can sometimes reflect more limited economic power as much as it arises from adherence to ideals of cooperation and consensus. As we will soon see, economic privilege, particularly as made possible by gender and sexual inequalities, also reshapes other social relationships and experiences, with consequences for the ways in which people care for themselves and others.

Sex, Love, and Exchange

Social and economic changes of the late twentieth century, especially male migration out of Juubche' and the increasing commodification of food and labor, have altered social lives and sensory experiences in a multitude of ways, all of which are experienced through gendered subjectivities *and* are productive in reshaping those subjectivities (Boehm 2012; Jansen 2008; Liebelt 2011). Men's migratory experiences frequently create in them a keen awareness of regional and global inequalities. This awareness, and in most cases the fact that those at home may not fully share it, force many men to negotiate a set of contradictions that center around their own bodily experiences of food and sex, particularly as mediated by local and nonlocal notions of ethnicity and class. They gain economic power through participation in wage labor, and their cash earnings permit them to participate in exchanges of money, food, and sometimes sex beyond the boundaries of their rural households. Young men in particular consume mass media that normalizes machismo and hypersexual masculinity. At the same time, their new labor experiences often come to mirror the histories of exploitation that have shaped their home communities. Just as farmers in Juubche' might recognize the agency of the lords of the milpa, the guardians of animals, or the powers that be at PROCAMPO, the agricultural subsidy program upon which many of them depend, young migrants develop an understanding of themselves and their labor as constrained by the global economy. They come to know this economy as replete with inequalities that seem to affect them, as rural indigenous men, disproportionately. Despite what is for many migrants a palpable sense of marginality in the socioeconomic hierarchies of the region, their individual roles in the maintenance of their communities, clearer for generations of milpa farmers before, are obscured, drawing into question how these men ought to care for themselves and others. Other social changes made possible by and through male migration and other features of late capitalism in rural Yucatán can reverberate in the spaces of bodies and social collectives.

Although her case study focuses on a young woman who was born in a rural community and moved to Mérida as a child, Reyes-Foster (2012) explores the experience of alterity, existence outside of the accepted categories of identity. Other scholars have suggested that men's migration experiences and continued economic marginalization, themselves forms of alterity, may encourage alienation, increased alcohol consumption, and domestic violence (Holmes 1978; Leatherman and Goodman 2005). In her analysis of the effects of wage labor in one indigenous Yucatecan community, Greenberg (1996) sees a loss of the rural knowledge and authority that enriched men's value in their home communities. In Juubche' the value of men's work is increasingly aligned with economic value, wages earned, but women's labor, especially the unpaid work of food preparation and childcare, is still highly esteemed. The labor that has eased some residents close to middle class, such as nursing or education, is not gendered labor in Juubche', but few residents have made their way into those fields.

Despite what are usually low wages, men's participation in migration carries social and economic benefits. Back in Juubche', migrant men accrue authority as liaisons, however marginalized, with urbanites and tourists.[16] Women usually report a strong reliance on migrant husbands' wages, and the economic and social power that accompanies the migratory experience tends to intensify existing male privilege in matters of consumption, sex, and violence. This power and the access to commodities it subsumes challenge the established relationship between food and sex, a pairing long legitimized in marriage in Juubche'. On the other hand, men's migration can expand the realms in which women exercise power at home: in the absence of their husbands, women may become primary decision makers and money managers within the household. Their own participation in cash-earning activities can also position them to contribute to their household incomes to a degree that sometimes exceeds the contributions of their husbands and sons. These roles acquire political recognition through federal assistance programs that appoint women financial guardians of their households and, implicitly and explicitly, cast doubts on men's fiscal responsibility.[17] At the same time, however, rural girls and women may be held to even more rigid sexual norms, particularly if they appear to stray from established modes of caring. Although the cultural forces of Mexican and international mass media may try to persuade them otherwise, women and girls still often face social condemnation for engaging in sexual and gustatory practices that are deemed deviant in some way. In short, contemporary gender politics reveal the persistence of food as a force for care by women and men, but migration and wage labor often unravel the ties between sexual activity and local social and material reproduction for migrant men. For women, on the other hand, these ties seem unyielding, creating experiential gaps between the genders that expose the divergent spheres—bodies, kin networks, geographies, economies—in which and on which care acts.

Among the women in one small Yucatecan town, Woodrick (1995) finds the desire for a tranquil life: "a life that is free from suffering" (231). Women in Woodrick's research site suffer most in their relationships with men and as a result of gossip; women in Juubche' report similar stresses. Problematic male-female relationships typically revolve around one or more of three types of conflict: those regarding work, alcohol use, and infidelity. Residents of Juubche' speak of such conflicts as threats to bodily and social well-being, damaging reputations and causing conditions like *nervios*. Furthermore, such conflicts are often directly linked to the gossip that Woodrick finds to be a cause of shame and suffering. In Juubche' both male-female conflicts and the gossip that circulates knowledge about them reflect, in part, recent shifts in the life of the community: physical and emotional distance between spouses, magnified tensions within and between households, and the partial replacement of locally produced foods with commodities from distant places. As I argue earlier in this chapter, the proliferation of new commodities in Juubche' has destabilized the values of objects and of the relationships forged through their exchange. Through ever more frequent exchanges, the residents of Juubche' negotiate these values and the new conditions that increasingly complicate their relationships with one another. In doing so, they reassess their own care strategies and come to know the caregiving—or threatening—potential of novel commodities.

Conditions within the household, where exchange relies far less on cash, are similarly complex. Transformations in the established patterns of household production, particularly in the complementary gendered activities of farming and cooking that for much of the last century materially sustained nuclear families, disrupt established exchanges of food and sex on an intimate level. Complaints of infidelity are common, and rumors about illicit sexual behavior characterize many a casual conversation and heated domestic dispute. The two, complaints and rumors, converge to create an environment of marital distrust and a social climate in which sexual practices, and, in fact, most any male-female interactions, are closely monitored. According to many residents in Juubche', this is not a recent development. Extramarital sexual activity and concerns about it are not new. However, the ways in which this kind of distrust and the surveillance around it unfold, and the manner in which residents speak of these things, signal the manner in which recent economic and social changes help to frame deviance as such.

The Place of Pleasure

Such anxieties and tensions should not suggest an entirely "sex-negative" environment (Bullough 1976). Food and sex are, in many ways, democratic pleasures for people in Juubche'. If one has access to food and sex, and most adults in Juubche' do, one has access to what are seen as particularly reliable forms of pleasure. Like food, sexual activity is seen as a socially acceptable medium for experiencing pleasure, provided the conditions are proper.[18] Food and sex frequently appear together in popular discourse reflecting, first, the significance of both in everyday life and, second, a presumed natural linkage between the two, rooted in the household as a site of material and sexual reproduction. Sexual jokes and puns, often in the form of *báaxal t'aan* (play-talk) and frequently using metaphors of food, are an oft-noted part of Yucatec Maya linguistic practices (Holmes 1978; Sigal 2000; Sullivan 1989). Faust (1998) finds that in a rural indigenous community in the state of Campeche, chile peppers are often used as metaphors for penises in jokes, referencing the similarities of heat associated with both the consumption of peppers and the arousal of sexual contact (616). Faust (1998, 621) and Holmes (1978, 242) note the usage of *queso* (cheese) as a metaphor for the vagina. In Juubche' to say that a woman makes tortillas for a man is to imply a sexual relationship between the two.

Discussion of one's own sexual practices are closely guarded though, almost always taking place with others of the same sex. In these more intimate and trusted settings people in Juubche' use few veils to disguise sexual meanings. In referring to sexual satisfaction and orgasm, my informants always used the Spanish *conformar* (to be satisfied). On occasion *conformar* is also used to refer to the sense of satisfaction one feels after eating or drinking a particularly pleasurable meal or beverage. Such usage implies more than mere tastiness or a feeling or fullness; rather it suggests that one has engaged in a well-rounded and deeply pleasing act of consumption. While discussing the questionable nutritional qualities of Coca-Cola with a group of woman, one protested that she could never eat a meal without drinking Coke. When she tries to do so, she explained, "Min conformar" (I don't get satisfied). More rarely, *conformar* refers to satisfaction in both nonsexual and nongustatory matters, as when a woman whose fussy baby finally settled down to sleep told me, "Saam conformnak" (She's just become satisfied). Much more frequently, however, *conformar* is relegated to the realms of sex and food talk, as when a woman relayed a rumor about her aging neighbors having sexual intercourse multiple times a night, until the female partner *ku conformar* (is satisfied/reaches orgasm). Such linguistic usage hints that Yucatec Maya speakers in Juubche' do not see pleasure, from eating or sex, in opposition to or as mere by-product of these actions. Rather, pleasure as it is produced in normative eating and sex is desirable and representative of restorative and productive practices.

Juarez (1996, 2001) argues that historically, indigenous Yucatecans made few distinctions between the sexual appetites of men and women despite a tendency toward reserve in discussing such matters. By the middle of the twentieth century, however, marital relations had been complicated by the sexual opportunities presented by more frequent male migration, experiences that were not available to the women who remained at home in their rural communities. During periods of migration during the chicle boom of the mid-twentieth century, many rural men engaged in relationships with sex workers. Given that many rural migrants now work in large urban centers such as Cancún and Playa del Carmen, opportunities to pursue sex with sex workers as well as with residents in and visitors to these cities have increased (Hirsch et al. 2007; Quintal López and Vera Gamboa 2014). Aside from actual sexual encounters, the voyeuristic possibilities provided by an urban and touristic environment and access to this particular sexual geography have altered the possibilities for sexual pleasure perceived by many men. Given the historical significance of the rural marital relationship in indigenous forms of social reproduction, such possibilities loosen the ties between food (i.e., family feeding) and sex (i.e., marital relations) in rural communities. The differences between male and female experience are, according to my informants in Juubche', greater than in the past. With a widening in the experiential gap between the sexes, the imperatives and desires that often motivate care become more rigidly gendered but also less predictable. Long-standing gendered care practices, seen as complementary to one another, are partially displaced as, together, the most basic forces for material and social reproduction.

Rugeley (2001b) finds evidence of anxieties about adultery in nineteenth-century Yucatán and attributes the prominence of such anxieties to the material interdependence between husbands and wives. Juarez (2001) argues that, more recently, increased emphasis on romantic love as the basis for marriage led to more tension and jealousy in modern marriages, rendering infidelity a greater threat. Furthermore, young women must balance their interest in notions of what Juarez terms "eroticized romance," developed through practices such as dating and through consuming romanticized entertainment, with cultural norms that condemn premarital sex and unmarried motherhood (147). At the same time, women must also negotiate their male partners' and potential partners' shifting sexual values, expectations, and desires, dealing in particular with increasingly naturalized notions of male hypersexuality and the behaviors it promotes.

Local attitudes toward and rumors about adultery reveal the complicated and often contradictory expectations of modern marriage in Juubche'. Spousal and community views on the infidelities of men depend upon the circumstances of the dalliance; if the adulterous affair leads to fewer resources making their way to the man's wife and children, it becomes cause for justified retribution, anything from a wife's refusal to cook for her husband to a formal separation between the couple.[19] Religious leaders in the area condemn adultery, but standards are looser on the ground. The standards are also more forgiving for men than women, as they are more generally with regard to sex, as in other rural communities in the region (Castellanos 2010; Guzmán Medina 2010). However, for both men and women, allegations of adultery invite community interest and judgment, often expressed through the rhetoric of care. In the case of a young migrant man from Juubche' whom I'll call Teo, several members of his extended family took it upon themselves to be quite vocal in their disapproval of his economic neglect of his first partner, a young woman living in the community. Teo had stopped returning home on the weekends from the coastal city where he worked and, according to many in Juubche', had formed a household with another woman, with whom he now had two children. His first partner, with whom he had one child, was now pregnant with a second, conceived on one of his rare trips home. That partner was struggling to feed herself and her child, as Teo had failed to send money to her in months. In one particularly tense moment, one of Teo's aunts held the floor during a weekend lunch attended by numerous relatives, including Teo's parents. Mincing no words, the aunt condemned Teo for his failure to financially care for his first partner and child. Other relatives looked down or chuckled nervously, but some of them had expressed similar feelings to me in private.

Extramarital sex more generally and adultery especially challenge long-standing expectations for exchange within the household. As the most basic practice of care in which the men and women of Juubche' engage, the production and preparation of food unfold with expectations for reciprocity, for active participation in complementary labor that ensures that the maintenance of the household. Following that, sexual activity in Juubche' is expected to begin only with marriage, usually by age twenty for girls and a few years later for boys.[20] Some girls "escape" to the homes of their boyfriends without their own parents' permission when they finish secondary school (at age fifteen or sixteen).[21] The parents of these girls and their boyfriends are rarely willing to arrange church weddings following such an "escape," and some of these couples never pursue civil recognition of their relationships.[22]

The practice of elopement, which many informants claim has increased since the late 1990s, stands in contrast to the formal engagement and wedding rituals that characterized most of the twentieth century. These rituals began after a meeting between the future spouses, which, in most cases, occurred without family interventions. Many residents recounted meeting their spouses as children or teenagers on the street or at a dance, striking up a conversation, and then relaying their interest to their parents. Following this, the parents of the groom-to-be would gather gifts of foods that they would then deliver to the parents of the prospective bride and give in exchange for the promise of her hand in marriage. For couples that meet early in adolescence, courtships are often extended to allow both young people to learn how to perform adult labor or, increasingly, to finish secondary school. Since most families encourage their children to court for several years before marriage, the bride's interest in the groom is usually assured by the time a formal engagement is sought. The "asking of the hand" ceremony, which formalizes the engagement, has become a larger affair, to which extended kin are invited and at which a large meal is served. During one such ceremony I attended in 2007, the bride's family served beef tacos, sandwiches, soft drinks, and beer. After guests had eaten, the couple's parents and grandparents gathered in the center of the room to offer the young man and woman advice and to formalize their engagement, with the groom's paternal grandfather issuing the most advice, emphasizing the couple's responsibilities to each other and to their respective families. For example, he reminded them that they were now expected to greet the other's kin properly and as though they were their own (i.e., as "mother," "father," etc.). The couple showed their agreement by shaking hands with their parents and grandparents and then with all adult guests. Finally, the groom's family presented to the bride's family large quantities of Coca-Cola, pastries, tablets of drinking chocolate, and cigarettes.[23] Several months later the couple married in a Catholic Church ceremony and celebrated at the groom's home with *relleno negro*, a wedding cake, and an abundance of beer. Such events are elaborate and expensive, and, it appears, they are becoming increasingly so.

Following these usually happy celebrations, tensions sometimes arise. This is not new, though there are distinct qualities to these contemporary tensions. Residents of Juubche' recounted that prior to the 1970s, most adulterous relationships in and around the community followed one of three patterns. First, some married men took on lovers as second or even third wives; such behavior was more common in isolated settlements outside of the town itself. Second, some married individuals carried on long-term affairs with other townspeople, married or unmarried. When these relationships were discovered, spouses often reacted harshly—one man remembered his father attacking his mother's lover with a machete— but in other cases marital relations continued peacefully. Third, men who migrated for short periods, as chicle harvesters or loggers, occasionally had brief relationships with sex workers or women living near their worksites, but these relationships ended when these men returned to Juubche'. In all three cases, household activities were rarely disrupted by adultery; men's participation in milpa agriculture and women's role in processing and preparing food for consumption still ordered daily routines and maintained connections between food and the marital unit, what we might consider the most fundamental form of exchange in the community, as least for as long as current residents can remember.

Since this time, the rapid growth of tourist-oriented urban centers like Cancún and Playa del Carmen and the corresponding availability of sexualized media have dramatically expanded the erotic worlds of men in the last few decades. In the tourist neighborhoods and beaches of coastal cities, Yucatec Maya men mingle with crowds of visitors and migrants from throughout Mexico and the world. In the roughly constructed urban neighborhoods where many migrants head to find affordable housing outside of the tourist zones, there exist opportunities for relatively cheap services provided by female and, less frequently, male sex workers from throughout Mexico (Arroyo and Amador 2015; Hirsch et al. 2007; Juarez 1996; Quintal López and Vera Gamboa 2014). According to many residents of Juubche', migrant men may meet female residents or migrants from other rural communities and take them on as girlfriends or wives. Several qualities of these sexual or romantic relationships differentiate them from those that men may have at home. First, these relationships are, for many men, in addition to primary commitments to women in their rural home. Second, that these women are living and working in urban areas, often away from their own families, sometimes marks them, at least for people in Juubche', as socially or morally distinct from women who remain in rural areas. Female migrants to coastal cities themselves may feel freed from the sexual norms of their home communities, or in the case of permanent female residents, they may more deeply assimilate into the more liberal sexual norms of urban life.[24] Thus, the nature of the longer-term relationships in cities may be more eroticized, at least initially. Don Pablo frequently joked about the urban girlfriends of some younger migrants in town, but when commenting on the extramarital relationship of one man, David, he became serious: David's urban lover had given birth to their son, and David was now obligated to offer her financial support. Until such a situation occurs, fewer familial and financial obligations accompany extramarital pairings; such a relationship often begins and may continue with few expectations or intrusions on the part of either partner's kin group (in many cases, because the relationship itself may be a secret or because kin may be distant). Such relationships lack many of the characteristics of rural marriage, with its many, widely dispersed duties of care. Rooted in the established routines of domestic life, including food production and consumption, rural marriages also function under and through close observation by extended families and joint participation in religious rituals. With migration, it has thus become not only conceptually imaginable but practically feasible to decouple food from sex.

Recent economic and social change has impacted the sexual possibilities and imaginaries available to women in Juubche'. Few women from Juubche' migrate to urban areas for work, and those who do rarely live independently, but rather with aunts, uncles, cousins, or older, often male, siblings. Male and female migrants thus inhabit what Hirsch (2010) calls "two parallel dimensions of the local sexual geography" (294). Even within the rural community, expectations for romantic and sexual relationships—and for women these are often the same—have changed. Over the last half century, exposure to media such as pop music, television, and film has shaped the desires of younger generations in Juubche'.[25] Women must also balance suggestions of the erotic, such as more provocative styles of dress and *tele-novelas* (television soap operas) that stop just short of showing sex acts, with an equally, if not more, powerful media emphasis on romance. The pop songs beloved by many young rural women almost always detach abstract notions of love and romance—care as thought, affection, consumption—from the realities of domestic life with its messy care networks of marital pair *plus* children, parents, domestic animals, and deities. These songs and other media also make vague, if any, references to actual sexual practices, thus further distancing the romantic fantasies of young women from the desires of increasingly sexually informed young men. The greatest challenges for young women come in balancing their own expectations and wishes with those of the men they get to know and with the entrenched sexual norms of their communities.

Women negotiate these contradictions through a variety of means. Some use certain kinds of comportment and dress to tighten the borders between themselves and morally questionable externalities. In doing so, they fashion themselves as individuals in ways that reinforce existing assumptions about human weakness while making visible their own moral superiority. Most notably, young evangelical and Pentecostal women resist the changing fashions that most of their Catholic counterparts have embraced. The use of long skirts, modest tops, and little to no makeup is thought to temper both their own desires and those of the men around them. Likewise, they, and men of their faith, are supposed to abstain from listening to and watching nonreligious music, films, and television. Although in private this abstinence is by no means uniformly practiced, it does somewhat limit exposure to romantic and sexual images. Perhaps what most leads *hermanas* (evangelical and Pentecostal women) and their male peers to struggle less with social changes surrounding sexuality than other young people is that, by most accounts, young hermanos often continue to adhere to religious proscriptions when they work away from Juubche'. They may choose to room with other hermanos or older relatives to resist temptations, continue to abstain from alcohol use, and remain active in their home congregations. Though sexual transgressions on the part of young hermanos do occur, they seem to be fewer and farther between compared to those of young Catholic men. Ironically, in light of the clear gendered hierarchy of their faiths' doctrines, for young hermanos this appears to produce more closely aligned expectations for sex, romance, and marriage between hermanos and hermanas than between Catholic males and females.[26]

For Catholic women recent social changes present greater challenges for their romantic and marital relationships. Some may choose to dress conservatively (though rarely as conservatively as hermanas), but many enjoy wearing the less conservative clothes they see modeled on television and on visits to urban areas. New consumption-oriented care practices, intended to make one feel and look attractive through grooming and dress, pose two dilemmas for these women. First, they require funds so women must earn the cash themselves or convince husbands to give them cash for these purposes (and some husbands may be suspicious of their wives' attention to physical appearance).[27] Perhaps more importantly, such grooming and dress, in the eyes of most younger community members, do in fact make these women more attractive to local men. Young Catholic women also indulge more readily and publicly in highly romantic products than their evangelical and Pentecostal peers, and they may dip their toes into sexual encounters condemned by the community at large. For those who take such measures too far by local standards, the end result can be, at best, a quick elopement, or "escape," in which a young woman moves into her boyfriend's home with no ceremony or, at worst, social ostracization, to the point where a woman may choose to leave the community for good. If marital relationships prior to the middle of last century were marked by established exchanges between women and men, required for subsistence, today's marriages are strained by the competing demands of domestic and wage labor, and sexual and romantic ideals (Castellanos 2010; Juarez 1996). Ideas of machismo that naturalize and valorize male hypersexuality have further complicated gender interactions.[28] Men's increasing participation in cash economies and labor migration also disrupts the ideal of balance many once sought in marital relationships. Social expectations for hetero-sexual marriage and the economic dependence of women on male partners persists, but the stresses of migration and the experiential gaps it produces are often at odds with shifting ideals for marriage: relationships comprised of emotional and physical intimacy.

Men engaged in wage labor have a variety of ways of managing family cash, but typically they exercise total control over their spending while away from home. The amount of remaining cash they hand over to their wives upon their return to Juubche' depends very much upon the degree to which they indulge desires for food, alcohol, and other commodified goods and services while away. This consumer power exercised by men is not fully available to women. That is, while women's networks of exchange, though altered in ways soon addressed, remain largely reliant on men's contributions, men can meet their sexual and gustatory needs independent of their wives. Just as men must purchase prepared foods during their time outside of Juubche', so they can use their consumer power, however limited, to purchase sex. While unmarried women who earn cash may have more discretionary income than those who do not, they usually earn less than migrant men. Even those married women who earn decent wages sewing or selling prepared foods are more likely to use those funds for household expenses rather than things such as clothes and beauty products. Although women's roles as consumers have clearly increased, men are often the first to be exposed to the commodification of various food products and, by all accounts, the commodification of sex. Both contributing to and aggra-vating these issues is the fact that the regional expansion of the capitalist market and the increased earning opportunities presented by migration have created and reinforced structural inequalities in which women are less employable and less valued as employees. The gendered demands of domestic life and questions about the safety and propriety of women who occupy public spaces have restricted the labor potential and financial value of rural females. Second, even when earning opportunities do come to women, such work tends to be in lower-paying and less visible positions such as those of domestic servants and hotel chambermaids. The result is that women are often further marginalized in Yucatecan gender regimes by their participation in new economies (Castellanos 2007; Juarez 2001).

For many migrant men from Juubche', their gender privilege is relative, tempered by the discrimination they may face on the basis of appearance, language use, and economic status. The new diversity of sexual and gustatory experiences visible to them creates disconnects that, despite the pleasures these experiences may bring, cannot be integrated into their rural realities. Equally, if not more important, is the likelihood that poverty and racism may restrict their access to these experiences. Cristiano told me: "The life of the poor is not the same as the life of a person with money because the people with money, they walk well. They use nice things. Their lives are relaxed. Their clothes and shoes are nice. They go sightseeing. And you, you don't have time to go sightseeing because if you go sightseeing, how are you going to make a living?"

Migrant men are aware of the conditions of inequality and difference that keep them from fully embracing the pleasures that they see available to economically and ethnically distinct groups, and these pleasures may nonetheless provoke desire. Castellanos (2010) argues that migrant men's wage labor is feminized, leading consumption to become the space in which such men can assert virility. New practices of masculine consumption take various forms in Juubche', but, in general, they tend to be more conspicuous than the consumption practices of women. Unlike women, men wear clothes and accessories with prominent labels, drive cars and motorcycles, and drink to excess in public spaces. One man in his sixties commented, "The men today, they know how to earn money, but they don't know how to care for it." On another occasion, a woman in her fifties remarked to me, "There are no men today. Just boys." Just as highly gendered experiences of migration bond men to their male peers, these experiences also distance them from the women in their rural lives and thus from their families. Regardless of the attempts of some women to adopt new culinary and erotic practices, intended both to please their husbands and to fashion themselves in particular ways, the distance between men's and women's subjectivities cannot be fully bridged.

Deviant Food, Deviant Sex

As Juarez (2001) points out, men are no longer dependent on women for domestic and sexual services, whereas women's sexual needs, if they are to be socially legitimate, must be met within the limits of marriage. Despite the introduction of increasingly processed foods, the role of women as, above all, transformers of raw foodstuffs into consumables persists. There are exceptions to this: many women earn much-needed cash through the cultivation of foodstuffs in their solares and through raising domestic animals for meat and eggs. However, the most productive and lucrative food work is typically undertaken by men.[29] A critical distinction between men's and women's food work is also the domestic caregiving aspect: the food prepared by women is not for the consumption of cook alone, but for an attendant male partner and, in most cases, children and other kin. Both normative food and normative sex, for women, is inextricably linked to their responsibilities for the care of others. In contrast, deviant sexual behaviors on the part of girls and women are often discursively linked to individualized and commodified eating, morally suspect and counter to women's established roles as family cooks.

Although extramarital sex has the potential to disrupt the exchange of food and sex within a marital relationship, certain forms of extramarital sex, especially adultery, are seen as more threatening to the social order than others. As explained in the previous section, some people in Juubche' accept men's sexual indiscretions as natural and normal. However, wives are thought to have the right to protest if their husbands are sharing resources such as cash, food, or other goods with their mistresses. It is not just the *distribution* of these resources that invokes the ire of wronged wives and other members of the community though; it is the fact and the forms of *consumption* of these resources that also violate the norms that govern caring. Witnessing how care is neglected in these situations, we can again see revealed the assumed weaknesses of human nature and the manner in which those weaknesses are gendered and often made material by engagement with food.

During a discussion of premarital sex, doña Graciela compared girls to *k'óol*, a soupy mixture of ground corn and lard that forms the base of certain tamales and is sometimes eaten on its own: "If you see that someone dipped his finger in the k'óol, are you going to want to eat it?" Reputation, as Hirsch (2010) also finds in rural Jalisco, is a critical part of sexual identity *and* a family characteristic. In Juubche', given the expectation that adult children will care for their elderly parents, especially through the gifting of food, it is not surprising that encouraging "good" marriages for their daughters is of great interest to parents.[30] Yet, the anxieties are rooted not just in distrust of the "someone" who might dip his finger in the k'óol but also in distrust of girls and women themselves. If women's greatest responsibility for care is to feed their families, it is the failure to do so, or the failure to treat eating as, above all, a collective act, that threatens their moral standing in the community. In the following accounts of sexual indiscretions that, real or imagined, circulate in gossip, the sexuality of women remains linked to their role in the family as providers of food. When their sexual activity diverges from this role—that is, it transgresses the boundaries of the marital relationship—it calls into question their dedication or ability to fulfill their gendered care roles. Likewise, their indulgence in commodity consumption is, for other members of their community, a mark of immorality and selfishness. Unlike for men, for whom participation in wage labor has broadened the possibilities for gustatory and sexual pleasures, the appetites of women must remain within the confines of the family.

Most gossip about rumored sexual activities originates from two sources: from neighbors and others party to the actual sexual liaisons or suspicious behaviors that indicate them or from the wives of men thought to be involved in extramarital affairs. In this section I compare two cases of women's participation in adultery to examine the ways in which women's caring roles, especially in the realm of food, shape community response to their sexual behaviors. I heard many stories like the ones I present here, that is, gossip centered on similar exchanges of sex and cash or food commodities. I cannot say whether the rumors I have chosen to analyze are true, untrue, or highly embellished. It is, however, the narrative account of each rumored relationship that interests me most, in particular the careful details and moral judgments of several exchanges: not merely of sex but also of food or money. These anecdotes and rumors demonstrate the threats that excessive appetites for food or sex pose for established modes of care, weakening the economic solvency of households and the marital relationships on which they are based, enabling conspicuous consumption, and challenging ideals of equality and cooperation. The desires enacted in these displays of excess are facilitated by participation in the capitalist economy, both practically, with increased access to cash and commodities, and affectively, in the production of new desires. According to local gossip, girls and women may be tempted by the cash and commodities that now circulate in their community, and men's access to that cash and those commodities makes them more attractive to such women.

Rumors abound of women engaging in illicit sexual relationships with men, sometimes for money. One rumor recounted strange behavior on the part of two village women, a mother and her unmarried daughter, several years ago. As doña Ana told me, the two women would bathe and perfume themselves, dress in their best iipiles, freshly ironed, of course, and walk off into the brush. To those they encountered along the way, the women explained that they were going to work in their milpa. Though residents pride themselves on dressing well for special outings and even afternoon visits, dressing up to work in the milpa is certainly not the norm. According to doña Ana, the women would meet two men there and pair off to engage in sex. Upon their return to the village, the mother and daughter would stop at a store, and each would enjoy a bag of chips and a cold soft drink. The daughter, doña Ana argued, had learned this "bad" behavior from the mother and would likely pass it on to the next generation in turn. In the meantime, doña Ana lamented, even after marrying the daughter continued to engage in such activities, doing so while her husband labored in his milpa, unaware of his wife's daytime activities. The stability of the marital relationship and the centrality of care to its material survival are threatened by the wife's gustatory and erotic selfishness. Her husband works to feed the family, fulfilling his marital and cosmologically ordained role, but she has strayed from her hearth, perhaps neglecting her own duties of food preparation while indulging in the consumption of commodities.

The narrative convergence of deviant appetites, both sexual and gustatory, is no mere coincidence. Except when they have pregnancy cravings, few women justify the expenditure of precious funds on snack foods for themselves. The individual consumption of store-bought snack foods is largely limited to children who are indulged in numerous ways, especially in their younger years. These children are often allowed to eat what and when they choose, provided the food is deemed safe by their mothers. Of the dozens of mothers I interviewed during my research, only one claimed that she would let her picky children go hungry rather than prepare them special food. In contrast, women rarely buy soft drinks for themselves; it is far more common to purchase them just before a meal or for visiting guests. Likewise, when women initiate the purchase of snack foods such as chips or cookies, they almost always share them, usually with everyone present: adult kin, children, and any guests (even if it means that everyone eats just one chip). As with the novel foods discussed in chapter 5, chips, cookies, and other purchased snacks are luxury foods. They are too expensive to be shared in great quantity, but women rarely buy them just for themselves. These products are not the stuff of survival nor are they the food of caring, and yet their consumption by adults must be treated in the same way of that as of homemade foods: offering food is an expected display of hospitality and an important means of maintaining mutually beneficial relationships and preserving at least the appearance of social balance and equality. Like that of more established foods, the shared consumption of newer commodities is important to the maintenance of social relationships. Indeed, when an unexpected guest arrives, the first thing a hostess usually does is send a child out for a cold bottle of Coca-Cola.

It is not then the mere exchange of food for sex that offends many residents of Juubche'. When food earned through sex is consumed individually, withheld from hardworking husbands and hungry children, public opinion is different. Such indulgences are unquestioned evidence for storytellers of a pattern of excess. Although excessive appetites for home-cooked food and marital sex may not go unremarked and may, under certain conditions, affect one's bodily balance, individualized eating and adulterous sex immediately threaten the balance of both the bodily and the social worlds. It is the wanton desire for illicit sex, and the chips and cold drinks one might gain, that most often earn the condemnation of others. Accounts of antisocial eating and illicit sex reveal the tenuous pull thought to exist between individual desires and social expectations. Moreover, these narratives suggest a breakdown in the idealized and gendered economic exchanges that should take place in the household. The materialities of the foods themselves—indulgent, sweeter or saltier than locally produced foods, appealingly and individually packaged—and the conditions of their production—unknown, distant, unattached to local cosmology—are important here. These foods are not by nature of such qualities inherently embedded in the local economy of care. They must made be made to be a part of it, as soft drinks have, appearing on ceremonial tables for the spirits of the dead and during feasts for weddings and baptisms. Such work, as performed, for example, by the young culinary authorities I introduce in chapter 5, can gain human actors prestige and can legitimate such commodities as tools for and agents in care. Yet, when such foods simply linger outside this care economy, when they are consumed alone or paired, in actual exchange or merely in discourse, with extramarital sex, they suggest the neglect of care, the displacement of consumption from its role in human and cosmic reproduction.

Doña Ana's story of the two women and their postcoital chips and soft drinks is especially interesting when held in contrast to another story she recounted to me. Given the practical requirements for daily shopping, trips to purchase food give women and children frequent opportunities to observe the happenings in their neighborhood, as they walk along the road with casual peeks into the yards of others and once they reach their destinations. Furthermore, many residents sell goods in an informal fashion; although they do not have stores, they may invite customers into their homes to purchase eggs, herbs, and other foods produced by the household. Doña Ana recounted a shopping trip she made years ago to a neighbor's home, where she discovered the neighbor's wife, doña Ursulina, engaging in sexual intercourse with her own brother-in-law. Doña Ana quickly ducked out before her presence was noticed. This occurred again on a second occasion, at which time doña Ursulina was, much to doña Ana's amusement, kneading tortilla dough while being penetrated from behind, or "in the manner of dogs," as doña Ana recalled. Doña Ana voiced no criticism of doña Ursulina and only made note of her lover's disloyalty to his own brother. Doña Ana had no particular fondness for doña Ursulina nor any dislike for her ignorant husband, who was off working in his milpa, so I wondered about her lack of judgment. Perhaps, it occurred to me later, she was struck by doña Ursulina's insistence on making tortillas in the midst of a sexual liaison. Although doña Ursulina's sexual behavior might threaten her own and her husband's honor, she remained dedicated to her most significant duty. In Juubche' the importance of a woman's sexual fidelity is perhaps only matched, if not exceeded, by the centrality of the care she exercises in feeding her husband and children.

In rural Yucatán as elsewhere, gossip can both discourage deviant behavior and reaffirm the moral righteousness of the speaker and her listeners (Callahan 2005; Kray 1997; Rivera 1976). In Juubche' this moral righteousness valorizes both sexual and gustatory restraint, as well as a commitment to the social order and the modes of caring by which it is reproduced, in spite of what are taken to be natural urges. Sex is thought to be a normal and pleasurable part of adult life in Juubche'. Both men and women are considered capable and worthy of attaining pleasure through sexual activity. As with eating in the legitimized settings of the home or special occasion outings, marital sex is understood as an equal opportunity joy from which rural indigenous Yucatecans are not excluded (in contrast to such perceived pleasures as fancy cars and mansions, largely the domain of ts'uulo'ob). Even when practiced in excess and with the wrong people, sex and eating are thought to be no less gratifying than in more socially acceptable situations, and both men and women are thought to be tempted by such (Callahan 2005; Kray 2007). As doña Katy once told me, using the common metaphor of food to talk about sex, "Of course, if you try it, if it tastes good, you are going to want to eat it whenever you can."

However, extramarital sex and eating threaten household stability and the peace of the larger community. The task for the moral-minded resident of Juubche' is to balance natural and understandable desires with the demands of the existing social order.[31] This dilemma reflects the larger assumptions residents make about human nature and the need for self-control. Gossip about deviant sex and eating also underscores the anxieties residents feel in their dependence on each other, within and outside of the household, and the ways in which commodification—and the new appetites and consumption practices it has brought with it—can challenge established ideologies of balance and tranquility. Care becomes a strategy not for resisting new pleasures but rather for successfully integrating them into normative practices, that is, practices that maintain balance and tranquility on multiple levels.

In the past, people in Juubche' lived with conflict, frequent scarcity, and marginalization and shared often-unattainable ideals of cooperation and equality, but common modes of production and consumption supported ideas of difference predicated upon complementariness, fair exchange and reciprocity, and redistribution. Today residents must negotiate more and frequently contradictory ways of caring, of making the lives they want for themselves, enacted at and through bodies that no longer fit within the imagined boundaries of the home and milpa.

CHAPTER 4

So That We Won't Die

On October 31, 2007, a group of women, including myself, prepared tamales for the janal pixaan reza for doña Esmeralda's son Samuel. Luz, a daughter of doña Esmeralda's sister Fabiola, came over early. I went with Luz to grind the corn, and doña Esmeralda killed and cleaned the chicken. She cooked it with *xak*, a local spice mixture carefully ground and mixed by another one of her sisters, and cleaned all the banana leaves. She prepared k'óol, a liquidy corn dough flavored with lard, tomato, chile, and salt. Fabiola came over to help along with their mother, Anastasia, and sister-in-law doña Patricia. The three of them sat in the center of the room at a low table and assembled the tamales, placing hard-boiled eggs, ground chile, and meat on top of a few spoonfuls of k'óol in each banana leaf. For several hours, they assembled tamales. Don Máximo and I (and another niece, Dalia, who stopped by briefly) helped to tie them with doña Esmeralda. Doña Esmeralda tied the ones for the prayer with special strings. Afterward tamales were sent home with those who had helped.

On the following day doña Esmeralda hosted the reza for her son at 6:30 a.m. She set up an altar on the table that usually held the television. The table held platters of tamales, pan dulce, and chocolate tablets, as well as candles, fresh flowers, a photo of her son, and a Jehovah's Witness Bible. The candles were lit, and doña Berta, a neighbor, led the prayers. She stood directly in front of the altar with her shawl over her head. She would sit periodically, and the other women would sit and stand in turn. After the prayers, everyone greeted each other with "Buenos días." Doña Patricia told Dalia to pass out the bread from in front of the altar. When the plate was empty, more was taken out of a box. Hot chocolate was passed around too, to the oldest women first. Some ate their bread while others took it home. Everyone took home tamales.

Doña Esmeralda converted with her family to become Jehovah's Witnesses over a decade before I met her. During Finados, the eight days of mourning activity that begin on October 31 and include All Saints' Day (Todos los Santos) and All Souls' Day (Día de los Muertos), doña Esmeralda explained to me that she could not risk failing to care for her son's pixaan (soul).[1] Admittedly, she stated, she was probably half-Catholic and half-hermana, but she asked, "How could I not do the reza?" She enlisted the help of Catholic kin to prepare food and pray for her son's pixaan. While she made no obvious efforts to conceal her participation in Finados from her former co-worshippers at the Jehovah's Witness temple, some of them neighbors, she did not invite them to attend her reza. During later conversations doña Esmeralda expanded on other factors that contributed to her declining participation in the temple she had attended for years. Yet it was clear to me that the restrictions that faith placed on her care for her son's pixaan were among the most crucial. His death, it became evident, led her to question the transformation that her conversion had required in her caregiving practices. The deaths of loved ones create spiritual crises in which new religious teachings conflict with a deep sense of responsibility for the care of pixaan and with a particular kind of relationship with the material world.

For many people in Juubche' the significance of food extends well beyond the seeming confines of the physical body. Practices of care that are enacted through food can define an individual's moral and social status in the eyes of the community. However, the stakes are also high because care requires attention to a broad network of relations upon which one's well-being depends. This includes the living and the dead, the human and the nonhuman. What specifically comprises that network of relations is shifting, however, and during the rapid social, economic, and ecological change of the late twentieth century, new modes of and new needs for caring emerged. Shifting care practices created and intensified social divisions, and many of these shifts reflect and incrementally construct new subjectivities.

Food is an integral part of care practices in Juubche': food serves as a more-than-object that circulates between humans, and between humans and nonhumans, even as agent itself. Chapter 3 focuses on the former, exploring how processes of commodification have challenged human interactions and affective bonds. In this chapter I consider how concurrent transformations in labor and religious practices have the potential to radically reshape how individuals and communities think of themselves and their world. Of course, such shifts are not entirely new in Juubche' or elsewhere in the region, but as this chapter explores, the contemporary convergence of these shifts within the context of the economic and social conditions of the last half century have expanded the possibilities for experience and modified residents' understandings of their own roles and responsibilities. I argue throughout this book for recognition of the prominence of food, in its many stages and forms, as an organizing force in daily life and as an agent and motive in the practice of care in rural Yucatán. This chapter acknowledges that while this is still very much the case, food's continued centrality—its infusion into most every realm of life here—and the depth of meaning that makes this possible are not necessarily givens.

Care and the (Super)natural

Most residents of Juubche' identify themselves as Roman Catholics, but in recent decades a sizable minority, at least 10 percent, has converted to non-Catholic faiths, such as Jehovah's Witnesses and the Seventh Day Adventist Church. Such converts to evangelical and Pentecostal religions are known as *hermanos/as* (brothers/sisters). Of the residents I formally interviewed, roughly eight-five percent identified as Catholic, with most of the remaining identifying as Jehovah's Witnesses. One informant was a Seventh-day Adventist. Most of the non-Catholics converted in the 1990s, thus during the period of my research only their children, at that time young adults and youth, had spent their entire lives outside of Catholicism. For most non-Catholic residents, then, religious conversion was a pivotal point in their lives, one that they themselves spoke of as transforming how they saw themselves and the world around them. Conversion, by their accounts, was remarkable by virtue of that transformative nature, of the clear differences between life as a Catholic and as a believer of their new faith.

For Catholics in Juubche', spiritual life is centered on two often-intersecting realms: the Roman Catholic Church itself—the doctrine but even more so the saints, prayers, and other rituals—and what I imperfectly call the (super)natural world and its rituals—the cornfields and forest; the animals, plants, and other entities that inhabit them; and the elements that sustain all of these life forms. As Kray (2007) argues, religious rituals are not just representations of social life, but rather "ritual is the actual stage for social life" (532). In their daily and special occasion practices many Catholics in Juubche' display respect, fear, and gratitude for the (super) natural world around them. They know this world to be full of spirits with potential to affect human life in profound ways; it is through practice that they acknowledge and nurture the world as they know it. Indeed, the (super)natural world, along with kin and ritual activity, are central to the construction of the selves of Catholics, for whom identity and everyday existence is highly relational. That being said, the degrees to which the two realms matter vary even among Catholics. For those who work in the milpa, the (super)natural world is more tangible and meaningful. For a migrant constructing condominiums in Playa del Carmen, other actors, from the fluctuating tourist industry to labor contractors, may hold more day-to-day importance.

Colonial-era indigenous populations in this region adopted many of the symbols and rituals of Roman Catholicism, often through coercion. As Rivera (1976) points out, Catholicism offered little doctrine or practice that was relevant enough to agricultural life to supplant indigenous activity in that realm. Over time, however, elements of Catholic religious practice gradually influenced agricultural rituals. Farriss (1984) and Early (2006) argue that for indigenous people of the colonial era, the fixed prayers of the priests, the rituals of masses, and the collection of saints were also likely to have provided a sense of familiarity. In private and on far smaller scale, indigenous people continued to perform precolonial rituals; the continuity in agricultural practice ensured that many such rituals remained relevant. In both lowland and highland Maya regions, the centrality of food in

6. Shaman at an altar. Courtesy of author.

indigenous ritual extended to Christian rites as well. The ritual food practices of indigenous people had long sustained their relationships with the natural and spiritual world, including deceased ancestors who were subsumed under the Roman Catholic category of "souls." These ritual food practices came to be seen as ways of caring for the saints and Virgin Mary as well, particularly through the Maya populations' embrace of saints' days fiestas. As they did with their pre-Columbian deities, indigenous peoples in this region endowed the saints with human attributes, including tendencies toward fickleness and capriciousness. Like those deities and humans, the saints, along with the Virgin Mary, also needed to be cared for, with food offerings and regularly laundered clothes (Farriss 1984; Watanabe 1990). Restall (1997) claims that the saints came to embody the centrality of the kaj and that the possession of individual saints by individual kajo'ob created a means for each kaj to accrue social prestige.[2] The saints were sometimes opulently adorned, lavished with attention and care, and often had material value themselves. Farriss (1984) argues that despite a lack of documentation attesting to the purpose of food offerings during fiestas, prestige was not the primary motive of the saints' caregivers. According to her, there is no explanation that makes sense of the practice other than that, like indigenous ceremonies for rain and harvest, food sacrifices to the saints and Virgin gained their favor and helped to ensure the human food supply.

The incorporation of the Catholic deities into food-based care practices, like those offerings intended for indigenous deities, worked to sustain a multiplicity of life forms: humans and maize, among others. Catholic concepts became infused in practices outside of standard doctrinally sanctioned worship. In Juubche' this is evident in references to corn as *sáantoj xi'im* (sacred corn) and in the use of Catholic prayers in the rain ceremonies held deep in the cornfields by the few remaining shamans. Catholic deities took on the agentive potential of precolonial supernatural agents, becoming comparably powerful forces in the pursuit of balance and survival. The cyclical nature of the agricultural calendar paralleled the Catholic sacraments that marked life, death, and the transitory phases in between, and together the two structured the rhythms of rural life. However, with the relative absence of the Catholic clergy, most notably a priest who generally comes only weekly to give mass, this system of beliefs and practices can be characterized as "popular" religion, what Norget (2006) describes as stemming "not from a shared set of doctrines, but from a certain configuration of the social world" (70).

Catholics in Juubche' see themselves as forming, together with God, the saints, and other supernatural agents, what Early (2006) calls "a sacred covenant of mutual support" (69), and this covenant is rooted more in practice than in doctrine. When I asked doña Angelica, in her fifties, which religion she adhered to, she responded: "I go to church . . . I'm Catholic. If I feel like it, I go to holy mass. We go to the fiesta. We don't like the ways of the hermanos. If there are dances, we go to them. If there are fiestas, we go to them . . . we're not hermanos because I have my little saint for whom I light a candle. If I converted to become a hermana, maybe I would be dead already. I don't understand it [non-Catholic religion]. I don't have any use for it." To be Catholic in Juubche' is to engage in practices that affirm the presence of the material in the spiritual and the spiritual in the material. As they unfold through objects like candles, a bottle of Coca-Cola on an altar, and a framed image of a loved one, Catholic rituals and related social events are life-sustaining and affirming, according to followers in Juubche'. Such activities fulfill cosmogonic duties while also sanctioning (moderate) pleasures such as dancing and drinking.

Although the decline in agricultural subsistence and the decline in Catholic religiosity have been parallel and often intertwined processes, in other ways the economic changes of recent decades have enhanced some Catholic ritual activity.[3] Participation in wage labor can enable Catholics to better invest in material displays of care and reproduce social bonds and networks of reciprocity in doing so. The ability of one woman, Elena, to fund an elaborate celebration of the Virgin of Guadalupe, complete with a mariachi band and abundant food, renewed her relationship with the kin and neighbors she invited to join her, some of whom had earlier criticized other individualized consumption practices in which she engaged.

In contrast, converts to evangelical and Pentecostal faiths reject the body as a meaningful site of spiritual activity and see Catholic practices as rooted in a belief in false idols and false gods. Faith for them is more purely immaterial. Doña Fernanda said of the worship practices of the Jehovah's Witnesses: "We don't light candles for idols. We don't have masses for idols because God doesn't want us to. God is just one, but for Catholics, in the Church, there is San Roman, there is Augustine, there is the Sacred Heart, there are Jesus's women [the virgins].... We don't light candles to the idols because they're like a piece of wood, but Lord Jesus, he is alive, his glory lives." For converts like doña Fernanda, the spiritual core of the individual exists in spite of and often at risk from the material world. Each human exists as part of his or her own progression toward salvation, not as part of a larger cycle that deeply intertwines human lives and nature. Furthermore, such doctrines significantly narrow the field of actors in the universe; a Jehovah's Witness might care for a more limited range of nonhuman entities because he or she recognizes them as creations of God, not because they themselves hold life—and power—that sustains the universe. Similarly, evil is the work of the Devil alone, not a larger pantheon of deities. Doña Tina criticized the Catholic practice of praying to saints for health and said of the attribution of cures to saints, "The saint doesn't do it because the saint is just an idol. It can strike you, but if it strikes you, it's not its power that does it. It's evil. It's the Devil that gives sickness, not the idols." In contrast, Catholics see their relationships with the saints as reciprocal, to a large degree because the saints are, like them, capable of agency and characterized by many of the same strengths and weaknesses as humans, a pattern of personification that has been noted in other communities in Mexico and in Guatemala (González 2001; Kapusta 2016; Norget 2006; Watanabe 1990).

Several centuries of the weaving together of Catholic concepts and symbols with those of precolonial belief systems coincided with the growing importance of milpa production during the colonial era (Restall 1997; J. E. S. Thompson 1977; Wilk [1991] 1997). The incorporation of Catholicism into agricultural production and attendant rituals, while never static or bounded, created a seemingly coherent set of principles and practices; incorporated into one another, especially the Catholic into the indigenous, agricultural practice became Catholicized. For these reasons foodstuffs and the processes by which they are produced and prepared, including established agricultural practices, are not imbued with the same sense of importance for evangelicals and Pentecostals that they hold for Catholics. The shedding of the more relational understanding of self that accompanies Catholicism may be a gradual process for many, but it is made easier by the decline in agriculture, increased reliance on cash, and greater access to commercial goods, a precipitous convergence of social, economic, and ecological transformations. Kray (1997) argues that the oppositional pull indigenous people in this region feel between divergent conceptions of personhood, the more recent of which develops out of participation in capitalist endeavors, results in alienation that, for some, may be eased through conversion, thus more fully individuating their sense of self. As for Taussig's (1980) informants who work in the mines and cane fields of South America, for Catholics in Juubche' "the revolution in the mode of production" is not complete (38). Relational selves that ought to fulfill cosmogonic duties are alienated through participation in an economy that discourages this relationality and, in some ways, limits the ability to fulfill those duties.

Religious conversion can hasten the completion of the revolution. Joining evangelical and Pentecostal churches allows converts to more easily abandon corporate activities such as the annual fiesta or agricultural ceremonies. The rejection of milpa agriculture helps these individuals avoid physical and conceptual spaces that might provoke dispositions and anxieties contrary to the doctrines to which they now adhere. Although some older evangelicals and Pentecostal men do farm, younger men of these faiths often find alternative work; the opportunity to pursue wage labor means that they do not have to worry about controlling the fate of their crops.[4] Free from constant concern about food production, these men no longer have any use for many of the care practices that shaped the lives of their fathers and grandfathers and defined their very purpose as rural indigenous men. They see little sense in the logic behind those very care practices and their promises of reciprocity, having embraced a faith that challenges older assumptions about the agentive potential of a pantheon of deities and forces in the world. For them, food may be a product of the grace of God, but it is disentangled from a web of activity, physical and spiritual, that connects food producers and consumers to the nonhuman.

Religious Diversity and Cooperative Care

New religious diversity has posed fundamental challenges for communities such as Juubche' for that reason. For centuries, popular Catholicism was tightly tied to both material production and collective rituals. During the colonial period and up until at least the mid-twentieth century in Juubche', organized village life featured several community-wide religious practices, most importantly certain agricultural ceremonies and the annual fiesta in honor of each village's patron saint. On a smaller level the tradition of *compadrazgo* (godparenthood), along with exchanges of labor and spiritual attentions during mourning and other rituals, has created networks that strengthen and establish relationships in ways that were long reliant upon religious homogeneity. Together, community members exercised care for supernatural and natural beings, and in doing so they also ensured the regular redistribution of resources, appropriate outlets for both grief and pleasure, and the maintenance of both kin and nonkin relationships. According to residents of Juubche', shared experience, epitomized by religious practice and gendered labor, mediated wealth disparities and other sources of tensions to maintain a sense of community.

Locally meaningful practices featuring Catholic elements developed in response to colonial and then nationalist ideologies, as well as in relation to participation in agricultural subsistence and the changing conditions under which it has been practiced in rural indigenous communities. During the colonial period in Yucatán, many ceremonies transformed from community-wide events to private, household-based activities in order to avoid punishment from religious or political authorities (Early 2006; Farriss 1984). For Catholics in Juubche' during the twentieth century, these spiritual care practices ranged from annual occasions such as the town fiesta to making regular offerings to the spirits of the milpa or the souls of the deceased. Such practices were deeply intertwined with the material conditions of everyday life and the persistent emphasis on cooperation and consensus, despite the existence of economic inequalities.

However, over the course of that century, increasing religious diversity challenged collective ritual life. Beginning in the early twentieth century, the arrival of missionaries to rural Yucatán created and exacerbated social tensions. Protestant prohibitions against the worship of saints and natural spirits, alcohol consumption, and dancing restricted the participation of converted non-Catholics in established community practices (Re Cruz 1996; R. A. Thompson 1974). Residents spoke little of the kinds of tensions and even violence that plagued some communities during the earliest conversions.[5] Similarly, I never witnessed any major conflicts between religious groups in Juubche'. However, the 2010 census notes the presence of religious tensions (Instituto Nacional de Estadística y Geografía 2010), and effects of the social changes spurred by religious diversity are felt in communities throughout rural Yucatán, even in what, from an outsider's perspective, seem like unrelated spheres. Taxi drivers in Juubche', for example, are organized into two different groups, replete with distinct communication systems and signage. The fracture, residents explain, derives from the financial support Catholic taxi drivers provide for the annual fiesta, support that non-Catholic taxi drivers do not wish to give. In Juubche', social fractures resulting from conversion became apparent in the 1980s and 1990s, when more and more residents left the Catholic Church. Individuals and families also grapple with fundamental spiritual debates on a regular basis, as conversion can challenge the most valued of relationships, such as those created through marriage or godparenthood.

Still, while fundamental doctrinal differences and the abandonment of rituals can strain relations between Catholics and non-Catholics, there exists a good deal of fluidity and movement between the groups in Juubche'. Although the non-Catholic denominations in town profess to avoid moral judgments and are generally quite welcoming to both new and returning worshippers, the regularity with which some converts move between their new faiths and Catholic-influenced traditions creates religious hierarchies within each group. Those who consider themselves to be entirely faithful to one denomination may blame the misfortunes of others on a lack of complete dedication. Leaders of one temple visited a couple after the death of their child, remarking to them that the tragedy was likely related to the family's sporadic attendance at temple in recent months. Though these suggestions angered the grieving parents and convinced them to permanently leave the temple, the deceased's mother struggled with the less-than-subtle accusations of blame and often wondered if they held any truth. In another instance, a non-Catholic family suggested that their neighbor's regression into drunken behavior was a result of his failure to participate in temple activities. Still, relations among families of different faiths are usually amicable, and if they are not, it is rarely for religious reasons. As one non-Catholic woman noted, her Catholic kin still visited her, and she them. One older non-Catholic man complained that he was no longer invited to the weddings of his Catholic kin, but he interpreted this to be a function of his abstinence from alcohol consumption. He saw his exclusion as an indirect result of his conversion, rather than a result of his shift in religious beliefs. By most accounts, even the early days of conversion were not as contentious in Juubche' as they were in other rural communities (Armstrong-Fumero 2013; Re Cruz 1996; Redfield 1950), and reaction to conversions has likely been further tempered by a general decline in Catholic religiosity during recent years. In fact, for many younger Catholics, it is the intensity of non-Catholics' beliefs, rather than the beliefs themselves, that they find notable or even strange.

However, whether out of genuine concern or out of self-righteousness, kin and neighbors may express worry for the spiritual well-being of those of other faiths. Non-Catholics frequently express pity for the pain that drinking and the domestic violence linked to it brings to Catholic families, while Catholics feel badly for non-Catholics and the loss of pleasure they are thought to suffer through their abstinence from alcohol, dancing, and secular entertainment.[6] Individuals may have reservations about what they cannot attain or enjoy through their chosen faith, and this surely contributes to occasional movement between the groups. One woman who left the Jehovah's Witnesses told me that she was happy to be able to watch telenovelas again: "I like them. I don't think they're bad. It's not like I'm doing the things they [the characters] are doing." However, those who resist converting from one faith to another can be presumed to weigh the risks and benefits, both social and individual, that accompany religious practice with some confidence in their choice and in the cosmological implications it may carry. Among the young in particular, these choices appear less burdensome, as they often understand their actions within broader and more complex trajectories of causality. In many cases their reluctance to farm has already weakened their attachment to a worldview in which religion is inextricably tied to labor and food. For older Catholics for whom the current heterogeneity of belief and practice has not always been a given, serious concern is sometimes expressed about the implications of religious diversity for community life, individual well-being, and cosmic order.

The Fiesta

Among the many established rituals that characterize Catholic and milpa-based ritual life in rural Yucatán are a few that are considered especially crucial. No event holds a greater degree of significance for community cohesion than the annual festivities held for patron saints. Unlike other spirits who are assigned to protect particular elements, patron saints are thought of as guardians of the entire communities who worship them; they can bestow favor on individuals and groups alike. According to Nutini (1976) and Saldaña Oropesa (1952), during the early colonial period Roman Catholic friars often assigned patron saints to indigenous communities based on some economic or environmental quality that would more greatly endear the saints to their respective communities. Over time these patron saints have become deeply meaningful guardians for communities across Mexico.

In Juubche' doña Katy explained the premise of reciprocity at work in the relationship between community and patron saint: "Well, he's the patron of the town. In church, it is said that he [the saint] brings miracles so we should adore him. I'm telling you, it's a tradition, a tradition because he's said to be miraculous so we make promises to make a procession with *ramilletes*, music, and us following behind." Juubche's annual fiesta celebrates both the town's patron saint and the Holy Cross. The ten-day event was once funded entirely by a rotating group of residents and attended by all in the community. Over the last few decades a system has developed by which the sources of funding and intensity of religiosity of the fiesta alternate depending upon the year. Every other year Catholic taxi drivers pay for some of the operating expenses, but attendees must pay admission to enter the bullfight. A group of households known as *diputados* (deputies or sponsors, though the term usually more specifically refers to the male household head in each family), prepare food, including the head of a pig to be included in the festival procession, and the ramilletes, tall posts that are decorated with paper flowers and sweet breads baked in the shape of birds. The ramilletes and pigs' heads represent the *kuch* (burden) taken on by the diputados.

In May 2008 I joined the preparations in a diputado's household for that year's fiesta. About ten girls and women were already hard at work when I entered doña Susana's kitchen. Three nieces were patting out tortillas with their mother while their grandmother was chopping green onions, chiles, and mint. Another older woman joined her to cut the already butchered portions of pork (the tongue and many other parts) into small pieces. These were then mixed with the chopped ingredients, xak, salt, and the pig's blood to fill the tripe. Meanwhile another shift of women, mostly young, began patting out tortillas. Doña Susana's daughters mostly ran around fetching things and sending children to the store. The men were busy cutting up the remainder of the carcass and frying *chicharrón* (pork rinds) outside. Once the chicharrón was done, doña Susana and her daughters began serving it to the men with beans, followed by cups of cold Pepsi. Then doña Susana and her daughters began serving the women beans, and doña Susana snapped at her oldest daughter, who was trying to feed her own kids and failed to put out chicharrón for the women. Other women continued making tortillas to feed the new arrivals. A few of the older women moved into the back room to begin preparing the relleno. They had two big metal tubs that would eventually go into the píib. In them they piled parts of the pig, including the head. They added epazote, tomato, and the chile sauce. By the time I left, the tubs were being placed in the píib and being stirred by the men. In another room young women, led by doña Susana's sister-in-law doña Katy, were preparing the ramillete, a moveable wood altarpiece to be decorated and brought to the church. Doña Katy began stringing together sweet breads in the shape of birds, five little birds and one or two bigger birds on each of the levels. Then she and her nieces glued colored paper flags (*flores*) to each stick until all were full.

During years like this one, the diputados take on more fully the event's expenses; during such years there is no charge for admission to the bullfight,

7. Men roasting *chachak waj* in a *píib*. Courtesy of Justin Nevin.

and locally prepared foods are distributed free of charge to those who visit the homes of diputados. Regardless of the year, some changes from the recent past persist annually, such as the sale of food by small vendors and the highly lucrative sale of beer by national manufacturers, both of which were unheard of half a century ago. In 2008 a major beer company hired a dancer in skimpy clothing to perform in their tent, where many men from Juubche' and neighboring communities had gathered. Much to the dismay of some older residents, the fiesta is highly commercialized, particularly during those alternating years when the taxi drivers sponsor it. The alternating funding structure provides consistent opportunities for residents to compare degrees of commercialization, rendering their critiques especially powerful; though there may be nostalgia at work in those critiques, comparative models are always also recent. According to those who are most critical of the commercialization of the fiesta, the worship of the patron saint seems to have become an afterthought.[7]

Still, the fiesta is nonetheless a decidedly Catholic affair. It begins with an evening novena (a special mass), the first of nine, held in honor of the saint at the Catholic church. Even many of Juubche's Catholic residents do not attend all of the masses. Near the end of the fiesta period, during what is termed the kuch ceremony, the diputados deliver the ramilletes and pigs' heads to the front of the church, where they dance with them. The year I attended, I entered the church with doña Susana and her family, watching as the ramillete was rested against a beam near the door, later to be joined by other ramilletes prepared by other diputados. After sitting briefly, doña Susana, her husband, and one of their grandsons carried flowers to the altar as gifts to the Holy Cross, placing them down before kneeling to light candles and pray.

In recent years this ceremony occurs during that day's bullfight, and many residents, especially the young, choose to attend the bullfight rather than witness the kuch ceremony. Changes in the religiosity of the fiesta are evidence of the dual challenges facing Roman Catholic rituals in the region: first, processes of commodification that increasingly mark many ritual celebrations, and second, a lack of community-wide support, largely a product of non-Catholics' refusals to participate but also linked by some elders to declining religiosity among young Catholics. For some Catholic residents the contemporary fiesta reveals a double lack of care: a failure by non-Catholics to participate in a centuries-old community ritual and a failure by many Catholics to prioritize the religious aspect of the fiesta over the commercialized consumption that now characterizes the event. Those older Catholics who worry deeply over transformations in the fiesta are quite often those who are still engaged in milpa agriculture; it is not surprising then that they are especially concerned with earning the favor of the patron saint. In the views of these individuals, the community is not just failing its own interests and those of the saint; it is jeopardizing their own material well-being. Such worries expose generational and religious rifts within the community but also threaten trust in kin and neighbors, revealing the new and often narrower self-interests that are emerging.

Given that this ten-day event is the most-anticipated event of the year, as it has been for as long as residents can remember, the voluntary self-exclusion of a portion of the community is significant.[8] Not only do hermanos abstain from the beef that comes from a butchered bull after the bullfight, citing its "hot" blood, but many avoid even passing through the town center once each day's fiesta activities are in full swing. One afternoon I visited a family of Jehovah's Witnesses as festivities were beginning several blocks away. We could hear the loud music being pumped out in the town square, and the middle-aged doña Fernanda, who had converted from Catholicism over twenty years earlier, called out the names of each song as she patted out tortillas. She still remembered them, she told me, because they were old songs from her youth, when she was an avid dancer. The moment of nostalgia passed quickly though, as she told me how pleased she was that her daughters did not attend the fiesta. Young female attendees, doña Fernanda explained, wear barely any clothes and dance wildly; to do so, she emphasized, is *k'eban* (sinful). Yet while the family did not attend the fiesta and disapproved of some of the behaviors that occurred during it, they profited financially by renting out elaborate iipiles to young women dancing the *jarana*, the much-loved dance performed by young women and men in the community. In the case of this particular family of Jehovah's Witnesses, a narrower, capitalistic mode of caring—accumulating profit for one's own family—inadvertently supports the much larger, cosmologically oriented project of Catholic members of the community (some of whom, it should be made clear, also profit financially from the commodification of the fiesta). These forms of care intersect despite what seem to be ideological differences in the caregiving parties, one example of the complexity of ideologically inspired care practices in this community.

Still, hermanos do avoid contributing directly to any individual or community funding for the fiesta, and they are not asked to assist in the preparation of food or ramilletes. For Catholics, the withdrawal of a segment of the community from fiesta activities threatens the well-being of the entire community; while the diputados may take on the burden of much of the festival labor and funding, the attendance of all is, in many Catholics' viewpoints, a crucial part of the demonstration of care made to the saint. The implications of a lack of cohesion, what might occur if the community falls out of the saint's favor, ought to be of concern to all, according to Catholics. Yet it is clear that some Catholics feel the dangers more intensely than others, and, again, these tend to be those for whom survival and success is a local matter, usually tied to subsistence agriculture and dependent on local deities.

The Milpa and the Forest

Also troubling to many of these Catholics are the changes in subsistence farming that have occurred over the last century. The correspondence of new religious practices with a decline of agricultural productivity has shaped for some Catholics a theory of causality that roots this decline in a collective lack of care. As with ceremonies related to hunts, cattle, and bees, most duties associated with collective agricultural ceremonies are carried out by men. In Juubche' during the twentieth century, all adult males who farmed, as members of the ejido system, were expected to sponsor *ch'a-chak*, a ritual intended to bring rain. Don Uribe detailed the practice as it was performed before the conversion of many of the town's men: "When the time came, you would make the ch'a-chak. We would bring chicken. We would bring corn dough. We would bring squash seeds. We would pay whoever was performing it, the shaman. Well, then beginning in the afternoon men would come, until the middle of the next day when they leave. So it gets dark, then nighttime is ending, and when the light comes you make the ceremonial breads, you make the corn gruel, and you boil the chicken, if you haven't found venison."[9] In the past, the ch'a-chak lasted as long as three days, and in between the men's preparation of the sacred foodstuffs the shaman offered prayers to the *chaaks*, the rain god and related deities, requesting that they send rain from all four corners of the universe to every parcel of land belonging to the ejido. As in other communities in the region (Hanks 1990; Redfield and Villa Rojas [1934] 1962; Rivera 1976), a ch'a-chak in Juubche' often included large groups of men from the ejido. The event has become a more individualized activity, with just a small group of farmers or members of an extended family organizing the event. It is the not merely the scale that has changed, however, but also the frequency: many farmers admit to not performing ch'a-chaks at all. Today, as don Belchor explained to me, "There are men who don't do it. They say that you don't need it, but we do it. . . . If you don't, the sáantoj [holy] rain will not fall." Doña Ana compared her father's agricultural practices to those of many farmers today:

> At times, during the rainy season, if God gave rain, even if you had planted late, you would get a good harvest. But it all depends on God. He doesn't forget the old ways. What the hermanos say is that it's not true. But it's not like that. Not here. But my father he didn't forget. He didn't forget the old ways where you put out your atole. Now they're forgetting these things, what the great ancient men did, and for this God doesn't give them their harvests. . . . Now there's none of this. When there is a harvest it's only for eating. They don't make offerings or even say the rosary.

Doña Ana's words stress the reciprocal relations underlying agricultural production, relations that render the harvest more than "only for eating." In order to receive food, one must also share food. In her critique of the beliefs of non-Catholics, doña Ana declares, "But it's not like that. Not here." Situating the practices of offerings within a clear place—"here"—she reminds us of how such practices have developed in response to the conditions of life in this community, a contrast to the conversions, initially prompted by visiting missionaries, not from "here."

While the chaaks and the Christian God exercise control over the universe as a whole, they are not the only supernatural agents at work in the milpa or forest. The *yuumtsilo'ob* are another category of spirits, each of whom guards a portion of the forest or an individual milpa. The milpa yuumtsilo'ob are known as *aluxo'ob* and are often compared to gnomes. Although they are often spoken of regionally as the stuff of folklore, many farmers believe enough in their existence to make offerings to them. Don Valentino, a farmer in his thirties, told me: "It's necessary to offer atole in the milpa. When you look, it seems like it's just forest, but there are lords of the forest. There are little gnomes. If you are accustomed to offering atole in the forest, when you go to make your milpa, of course there are times they frighten you. You'll hear, "Bojon!" The trees rustle, but you see nothing. If you enter forest where atole has been offered, you whistle before entering . . . because they were sent there to care." For don Valentino, the lens of

Catholicism does not preclude and perhaps even permits the possibility of other life forms, even those that may not be visible. Don Teo, a farmer in his seventies, captured the ways in which multiple lives are intertwined in the work of the milpa: "But there are men who don't do it [make offerings], and then the plants die, and pigs can die too. If you're accustomed to doing it [making offerings], they won't die so easily. Well, God will help you. If we hear that plants are dying, we quickly take some atole out there, we kill a chicken, and we offer it to the guardians so that they help us and so that we won't die." These guardians of natural elements can be counted on to perform their own acts of caring, provided that humans care for them in turn. Above all, offerings of food embody the productivity of care and its reciprocal nature within this realm; without these acts of mutual caring, there would be little food for humans and nonhumans to share. For many farmers the frequent failures they have experienced in recent years from droughts to hurricanes to pests are evidence of the displeasure of the gods, or the Christian God, and of the fact that, in the (super)natural realm, the failure to care has consequences far beyond individual bodies.

Nonhuman animals, like nearly everything else in the milpa and forest (k'ax), also have guardians from whom humans may receive supernatural punishments. The residents of Juubche' articulate respect for and sometimes fear of wild animals, and thus they must carefully weigh the benefits and dangers of killing them. To hunt excessively or to hunt the wrong animals is likely to anger those animals' guardians. This may lead to sickness or even death for hunters, or to the absence of prey during future hunts.[10] Don Tino explained to me what and why he hunts, "Well, it's only badgers, raccoons, those that get away with all the corn. And if I don't care for it [the milpa], I won't have any [corn] left." Many indigenous farmers see milpa production and the processes of human and social reproduction it makes possible as their primary responsibilities. Although wild animals are certainly a part of the universe that these processes should always re-create, their deaths, even at the hands of humans, are sometimes understood as necessities in the practice of care. In an essay on farming in the Netherlands, Harbers (2010) writes of "animals as partners and animals as enemies. Care was devoted to both, although care was of a completely different nature—both between categories (positive and negative care) and within categories (the intensity and individuality of the care taken)" (155). Similarly, in Juubche' it is understood that some life forms must die so that others must live, but this must be done carefully and with close attention to reciprocity. As Nadasdy (2007) writes of indigenous hunting practices in the North American Artic and Subarctic, "'Even the spiritual sanctions that animals impose on hunters . . . can be seen as consistent with a system of reciprocal relations" (28).

Among non-Catholics, such recognition of agency outside that of humans and the Christian God challenges the tenets of their faiths. The conception of a relational human self that must both ask favors and give thanks to deities through material offerings is counter to the doctrines of the non-Catholic faiths practiced in Juubche'. Kray (1997) describes such faiths as reliant on "a spiritual core within the individual, its rejection of the social and physical world outside of the individual, and its rejection of what links the spiritual core to the outer world: the body" (297). In Juubche' the Jehovah's Witnesses with whom I spoke drew explicit links between immateriality and spiritual life. The food work of men and women alike loses the sacred qualities they held as central components in cosmological cycles, and the role of food in religious practice becomes peripheral, even counter to the spiritual essence of their faith. Doña Fernanda compared Catholic worship practices to those of her current faith: "In the past, people liked to go [to special Catholic masses] because they were given roasted corn. We went because they gave it to us. When we stopped going, we started attending where we go now. There is not one image, nothing. It's well, you are praising God. We don't eat there. We don't go there so that they give us food. When you hear the word of God, it lingers in your soul and your heart. We don't go only to eat. Food passes through you. What we go to hear is for the spirit." Unlike the rituals of local Roman Catholicism with its deep ties to agricultural production, those of the Jehovah's Witnesses separate the physiological need for food from spiritual processes. Food's life-sustaining properties are more bounded, in a spatiotemporal sense: for converts, food is a gift from God that sustains human life physiologically—"Food passes through you"—but there is no generativity beyond this, no notion of cycles that propel these life forces forward back into the world. Rather than a marker of human interdependence with the natural world and the cosmos, food for Jehovah's Witnesses can be a reminder of the dangers of earthly temptations. It may be pleasurable, but it ought not distract from more serious matters, such as salvation.

The necessity of eating is visibly marginalized in the religious rituals of Jehovah's Witnesses. In contrast to Catholic baptisms and saints' days, during which at least some women stay home from the formal religious festivities to prepare food for larger groups of kin and neighbors, doña Fernanda explained that all Jehovah's Witnesses must attend temple. The food they share there, she told me, is either prepared well in advance or the worshippers hire Catholics to prepare it while they are at temple. Food preparation itself is not part of the ritual. Commensality persists, albeit in often altered forms; habits of joining together to eat are perhaps even more important for sustaining camaraderie among members of what is a minority group. Rather than have a priest come to bless a new house, Jehovah's Witnesses will invite their pastor and other members of the congregation to their new home for prayer, followed by the sharing of soft drinks together. Events like this, often between nonkin, replace the food-centered rituals of Catholic extended families. Yet food also remains conceptually peripheral at the non-Catholic gatherings. While it offers sustenance and an opportunity for conviviality, food lacks any tethers to the supernatural, rendering its materiality a weakness. That which makes it so saturated with life for Catholics is that which forces it into the mundane and even threatening category of object for non-Catholics.

Rezas

In contrast, without the insertion of the body and the materials that feed it into spiritual practice, older Catholics sense a disruption of the principles and practices that make human life possible. They question the disavowal of the care work that ties human well-being, in all of its corporeality, to the well-being of the larger material world. This attention of care is not limited, however, to matters of earthly survival. Not all Catholics attend mass regularly in Juubche' anymore, but most are dedicated to carrying out mourning rituals, including the domestic rituals associated with Finados, anniversaries of loved ones' deaths, and sometimes the birthdays of the deceased. Although I focus here on Finados, Catholic residents commemorate the deceased at regular intervals. As doña Daniela told me:

> It must be celebrated. It is also done three days, eight days later, the three weeks, the four weeks, the six weeks, and also the celebration of the seven months. So, when they do the seven months, they wait until one year to make another one, as it happens with my sister who is already one year old. . . . That's right, because they say that at seven months their soul has not yet gone, until they are one year old. At seven months, when the celebration ends, the people gather again, the guests and the relatives, so when it gets close, you have a little time to collect a little money, because after a year again you have to make the celebration and you have to make the food again.

The first year offers kin an opportunity to pray for the release of the deceased's sins (those who died as children are believed to have died without sin). After the first anniversary of the death, Finados is one's chance to reconnect with the deceased; during that time, it is thought, the dead are able to visit the living.

Catholic residents see these rezas as the primary manner by which one cares for the pixaan, the souls of the dead, thus ensuring their well-being and sustaining connections between them and the living. On these occasions, offerings of food on a carefully decorated table nourishes the pixaan, providing them the earthly pleasures to which they no longer have regular access, and help maintain a positive relationship between the living and dead. As in other rituals occurring in domestic spaces, women do much of the food preparation and perform the *rezas* (prayer sessions) of Finados. Doña Cristina, who had once recounted to me an incident in which the soul of her deceased sister visited her, described the offerings: "When I do the reza, I put some sweet bread and a tablet of drinking chocolate for breakfast. For midday, *espelon* [a tamale filled with espelon beans]. That is for the children. . . . For the adults, for breakfast you will have *chachak waj* [a tamale filled with chicken, tomato, and hard-boiled egg] and *xboj* [a large hunk of corn dough with espelon beans].... We do the reza so that the souls never leave us. If they go, that's it."

Connections between the living and the dead must be actively maintained, and the offering of food is arguably the most vital part of caring for the pixaan.[11] Doña Oliva noted that if the souls are not fed upon their visit to the living, they will cry; they must, she stressed, "go to heaven full, without hunger." That the food remains visibly untouched does not provoke skepticism so much as it reaffirms the otherworldliness of these reciprocal relations. Don Crisanto, a widower in his sixties, explained that each human has a spirit, and "for this they put out the food, though it's not actually eaten." As with food offerings for the deceased elsewhere in Mexico and in Guatemala (Brandes 2006; Faust 1998; Kray 2007; Watanabe 1990), it is the essence of the food that is consumed by the spirits.

The moral impetus is not just on the surviving kin to feed the pixaan; there are expectations that others in the community actively pray for the deceased. Rezas are family affairs, but neighbors may be included as well. Select attendees are invited to help prepare food in advance; women prepare food inside the home, while men dig the píib, the underground pit in which many of the foods will be roasted. The *maestra*, one of the local women who lead prayer sessions, arrives and begins the ceremony as other guests arrive as well. The reza is a solemn event in many ways, but its domestic familiarity lends it a sense of informality. Women fill the room, and most recite the prayers along with the maestra. Men tend to linger outside. Children filter in and out of the room, and both men and women often engage in conversation during the recitation of prayers. Despite these informal qualities, concerns about pleasing the pixaan are evident. Just before one reza in Juubche', the last-minute realization that she had forgotten a floral bouquet for the offering table led a hostess to frantically send a child off with some coins to purchase flowers from a neighbor's yard. Maestras may lead multiple prayer sessions a day during Finados and might reject a request if they have multiple obligations. For this reason households planning to host rezas must maintain good relationships with at least one maestra in town and give her sufficient notice. Should any part of the prayer session or its planning go wrong, a pixaan may be left hungry, haunting her surviving kin and threatening their well-being.

Through their participation in the preparation of food and the recitation of prayers at rezas, attendees assist in the attainment of salvation and well-being of the deceased. Non-Catholics exclude themselves from this long-valued act of care. For them, the rituals are characterized by idolatrous practices: the display of prominent images of the deceased and saints and an abundance of material offerings in the form of food, drink, and flowers to the pixaan. Catholics often see non-Catholics' abandonment of this ritual as an act of neglect with regard to one's kin, but the failure to participate in the rezas of extended kin and neighbors also weakens spiritual ties between Catholics and non-Catholics. For most Catholics, to choose not to take responsibility for the dead is as serious as the failure to care for the living, for the pixaan too are part of the community. As Kray (1997) explains, the distribution of food among both the pixaan and living guests reflects "the essence of idealized social relationships, the ideal that people are supposed to feed one another" (154). Similarly, Norget (2006) describes death rituals among working-class urban Oaxacans as having "an overarching ritual script [that] allowed mourners to display to one another their personal commitment to a given set of ideals" (165). In Juubche', at times, people fail in their caring; doña Oliva, noting that her brother's refusal to visit for a reza for their deceased parents, concluded, "It's not caring of him. He doesn't have affection." Still, as Kray and Norget claim, the ritual itself is structured to enact care, through its thoughtful offerings, most evident in the presentation of food that suits the tastes of the deceased.

The ideals epitomized in these rituals recognize the centrality of food as a medium of care in what has long been a subsistence-oriented economy, and these rituals exist as part of a larger experience of bereavement in everyday life (Rosaldo [1989] 1993). Those with whom I was close in Juubche' who had suffered the loss of loved ones often expressed tremendous grief. The most powerful statement of grief came from don Máximo, who, while speaking of the death of his only son, told me, "Kaschaj in wóol" (My óol [life force] went bad). Women spoke of the pain of losing children they nursed or mothers who nursed them. Their expressions of loss were often rooted in the material: attachment to objects that belonged to the deceased, sensory memories provoked by tastes or smells, or visions of the birds that had foretold the deaths. Mourning rituals failed to eradicate their suffering but rather reinforced the bonds of caring that sustained their relationships with the dead and the living. For this reason, religious diversity and the abandonment of such rituals provokes not just questions about individual and community responsibilities but also about the very nature of life and death.

Evangelical and Pentecostal Christian Care Practices

For evangelicals and Pentecostals, care often takes on very different meanings and functions in a world that is ordered differently than that of the Catholics. Among Jehovah's Witnesses in particular, care practices are directed, primarily, at God and Christ and, secondarily, at human relationships, especially those within the nuclear family. Just as the failure to care might have personal repercussions for Catholics—not performing a rain ceremony might leave one without food—Jehovah's Witnesses too might have seemingly self-interested motives. The most pressing of care imperatives for them revolve around individual salvation. The greatest repercussions of a failure to care are thus other-worldly, distant from the very present disruptions that the failure to care brings to Catholics.

This does not mean, however, that care is not enacted in concrete ways for Jehovah's Witnesses nor that it lacks lived consequences in this world. A failure to care is seen as a failure to perform the duties with which God has entrusted each individual, and these duties apply to self-care as well as the care of certain other humans. These duties include keeping oneself physiologically and morally healthy and encouraging one's spouse and children to do the same. Doña Nieves explained her own logic of care: "As for me, I have to care for myself because if you don't care for yourself, God won't care for you either. And children who are not fully grown, you have to care for them too." Still, while care, or a lack thereof, may hold consequences for life on earth, this causal relationship always extends even further to life after death. Importantly, death comprises an alternate world; the dead do not circulate in *this* world the way that the dead do for

Catholics. For Jehovah's Witnesses there is a world beyond the material. Doña Tina shared her vision of salvation with me:

> There will come a time when money is not accepted, when nothing will be sold. But we are not afraid because God says that whatever he does, he will care for us. He will care for us. He will not leave us to suffer. God says do not be afraid of the knife, do not be afraid of the gun, do not be afraid of punches. . . . He will return again. As for what we believe, it's that he is there in heaven [the sky]. He will come to grab me when he rises. He is preparing a place for us, for those who believe in him, those who love him. If you don't believe the word of God . . . you will not achieve salvation.

According to doña Tina, God has ways of knowing if one ought to be saved: "Well, there are tests. There are tests and battles, but those God will save are those who continue, who are not frightened by the tests. Because there are people, there are people, they get a little sick and say, 'I'm not going to templo. I'm still sick. I'm not going again.' That's not good. It's not good because you should go even more if you're sick to ask pardon from God, that he cures you. Yes, God, he will cure you. He will cure many people." The networks that matter most to Jehovah's Witnesses and other non-Catholics are those comprising the individual believers and their God. Stripped of the many interdependent agents who inhabit the social worlds of local Catholics, the lives of non-Catholics are imagined as more linear, on a path toward salvation, with only God and the Devil along the way.

In contrast to many Catholics, Jehovah's Witnesses more explicitly couple care with morality, especially with regard to human relationships. The exercise of care in human relationships enacts the fulfillment of the duties, often highly gendered, that God has entrusted to people. Jehovah's Witnesses express strong disapproval of domestic violence and frequently draw connections between it and alcohol consumption, which they also condemn. Many followers in Juubche' criticized these activities as damaging to the bodies with which God had endowed them. According to adherents, these activities also compromise men's ability to care for their families and, in doing so, threaten their individual salvation.[12] Doña Fernanda, who converted along with her husband while she was in her early twenties, compared his behavior before and after conversion: "He began to go to templo and left this vice [drinking]. . . . It's nice because he doesn't get drunk. Today he doesn't bother me. He doesn't get angry." Don Erasmo, who admitted drinking to excess and fighting with other men prior to his conversion, was grateful for the similar transformation in his son after conversion: "Starting at eighteen he got drunk. He was a bad drunk. . . . Thanks to God, he's done with getting drunk. It's all finished. Now he works. Even on Sundays he works. He has four children, and he's good with them." For many of these men, abstinence from alcohol is a crucial part of the fulfillment of their caregiving duties. Avoiding ritual activities such as the annual fiesta and Catholic weddings makes it easier for many men to abstain, and Jehovah's Witnesses instead spend much of their time with their nuclear families and fellow worshippers, some of whom live outside of Juubche'.

For Jehovah's Witnesses, religious faith is defined almost as much by practice, even if that practice is abstention, as for Catholics. Doña Celia depicted her conversion in terms of behavioral modifications that matched the gendered ideals of her new faith: "In the past, well, I was a little worldly. I walked on the roads, to fiestas, to dances. Today I don't." Doña Elda once waved her hands over her ears and neck as the recounted to me exactly how much gold jewelry (a lot) she had worn prior to her conversion. I had seen her adolescent daughters smoothing pomade into their hair and spraying themselves with perfume, but she proudly declared to me how they did not wear makeup. Women's faces, she explained, ought to remain as God made them. The practices of Jehovah's Witnesses are a marker of detachment from the material world, rather than attachment as for Catholics. The sphere of worship itself is grounded less in the geopolitical boundaries of the material world. Unlike Catholics, for whom the village church is the site for formal worship, Jehovah's Witnesses can choose from a range of temples within Juubche' and in neighboring communities. Their choices often depend on a range of factors, including access to transportation, relationships with fellow worshippers, or attachment to a particular pastor. For them, then, collective ritual life is potentially extended beyond the community in two ways: first, geographically, with worship sometimes occurring outside the community, and second, with recognition of another, immaterial world. For Catholics in Juubche', ritual life remains bound to the town and milpa as components of a single social world, one in which both dead and living circulate and in which God is not the only force for action. Even when Catholicism draws its faithful outside of the physical or affective limits of the community—for a visit to a neighboring city for a fiesta or, virtually, via televised footage of the pope's visit to Mexico City—the circles of connection overlap or are even nested within one another. Juubche' is the spiritual and geographic center for its Catholic residents.

The decline of agricultural sustainability, the growth of religious minorities, and the expansion of mass media and education have increased ideological and material diversity in Juubche'. With these changes have come new anxieties and even conflicts that reflect concerns about the places of the body and soul in the world. Care continues to be a force for managing these anxieties and achieving desired states, yet it does so on a widening set of terms, drawing into question who should care for whom and how. For religious converts in Juubche', established patterns of care threaten their chances for salvation from a new God. For those residents who continue to embrace Catholicism, these patterns of care are essential to their own survival as well as to that of the many other agents with which they interact. Modes of caring, such as feeding in particular ways, become tactics for self-fashioning with consequences that may, intentionally or unintentionally, expand possibilities for sensory experience and perhaps radically alter subjectivities. When squash seeds become something that is thought to be inanimate, this suggests profound transformations in the ways in which people understand themselves, their roles in the world, and the very composition of those worlds.

That's not to say the collective ritual life is absent or relegated to distinct religious groups. Residents of Juubche' mark time according to secular rituals as well, rituals that bind them to each other and to the state. During my time in the community, the bimonthly distribution of Oportunidades funds lent a festival-like feeling to the community, with vendors setting up stands selling everything from undergarments to pots and pans. The *clausuras* of each school, end-of-the-year ceremonies that feature student dance performances, are attended by families from across the town and are much anticipated (though still not as much as the fiesta). The reification and commodification of some older practices, categorized collectively as "Maya culture" by the government, has even led to more secular takes on religious ritual. In 2017 I viewed pictures of janal pixaan altars from Juubche' on the social media account of a friend in the community. The altars had been constructed by children in the local elementary school and were displayed in front of the school building, in the space used for recess games and clausura rehearsals. The tables were decorated with hollow halved gourds filled with atole, chachak waj, pan dulce, fruit, and flours. The children were dressed in "traditional" clothing, the boys in white shirts and pants, and the girls in iipiles. I don't know if non-Catholic parents permitted their children to participate; perhaps the event was sufficiently stripped of overtly religious references to make participation palatable for them. Or perhaps in a nation-state that has embraced neoliberalism and multiculturalism in recent decades, they have come to embrace such rituals as markers of indigenous culture rather than as material expressions of faith. The aging out of the small-scale farmer in rural Yucatán suggests a continued decline in milpa agriculture (Ebel and Castillo Cocom 2012), loosening the ties between food production and ritual life. Yet this occurs as rituals become increasingly important in claims to indigenous identity and in the marketing of that identity amid tremendous economic dependence on tourism.

This chapter began with an account of a reza organized by the still-grieving doña Esmeralda who had lost her only child several years earlier. The day of the reza, All Souls' Day, was also her birthday. The day did not end when the reza's attendees dispersed. Doña Esmeralda suggested that we buy some beer. We patted out tortillas as we drank, and she added two new bottles of Coke, fresh tortillas, and some chicken to the altar. Four of us ended up drinking six *caguamas* (each about forty ounces), taking a break only to eat some chicken *salpicón*, shredded cooked chicken, freshly mixed with finely diced tomato, onion, chile, and lime juice. Doña Esmeralda and I patted out some more tortillas, and then she invited her brother, his wife, and one of their daughters to join us for tacos filled with salpicón. A few hours after they left, the itinerant baker who drove through town selling his goods each evening arrived with a birthday cake my husband and I had ordered. We had wondered about whether ordering the cake was a good idea; the cruel irony of celebrating a birthday on a day in which one is ritually obligated to be reminded of a tremendous loss was clear to us, but doña Esmeralda was becoming like a mother to me, and we wanted to acknowledge her in some way. Although even now I wonder if we made the right decision, she seemed pleasantly surprised by the colorful frosted cake and invited the kin who had joined us earlier, Eliecer, Patricia, and Dalia, back over again. Before we cut the cake, doña Esmeralda placed it on the altar and posed for photos with it, having made sure the framed picture of Samuel was included in the shot. At that moment Samuel was both present and absent. My eyes were drawn to the photo of him, but for doña Esmeralda, her attention focused as much on the food offerings, material markers of the connection that persisted between them.

CHAPTER 5

Put a Little Salt

In November 2007, having already eaten many dozens of meals cooked by others in Juubche', my husband and I decided that we would prepare pizza for our hosts and their neighbors. We asked one of the itinerant bakers who sold his breads from the back of his van if he could bring us some pizza dough. We shopped in a nearby city for ingredients, and I even picked some basil, much to the dismay of those we were feeding, for whom it is only used for medicinal purposes. Although my husband and I preferred plain cheese, at the request of our friends, we also prepared what is known as Hawaiian pizza, topped with ham and pineapple. While our cheese pizza, topped with fresh basil, was met largely with ambivalence, the Hawaiian pizza was a hit. The next day doña Esmeralda told me she had mentioned our meal to her niece Elena, telling me, "I told Elena that you made us pizza last night. She asked me if it had cheese. I said yes. She asked me if it had ham. I said yes. She asked me if it had pineapple. I said yes." Elena's seeming attempt to confirm that we had made the "right" kind pizza, and doña Esmeralda's visible pleasure in confirming that indeed we had, struck me, not only for the clear attention to detail, in this case in the form of ingredients, but also because this exchange exemplified an approach to cooking and eating that I had been consistently observing in the community.

In contrast to the North American emphasis on creativity in food preparation, culinary and gastronomic culture in rural Yucatán is marked by a preference for standardization, even in the adoption of new foods. Palates appear largely in sync, reflecting and reinforcing standardized methods of preparation and reproducing, to some degree, shared bodily disposition in matters of taste. Ayora-Diaz (2012) writes of what he calls the "naturalization of taste" on the peninsula of Yucatán, in which a perception of cultural coherence contributes to a distinctive regional identity while obscuring the diverse origins of "Yucatecan" dishes. In rural communities such as Juubche', identity is often linked most tightly to the community itself, rather than to broader regional or ethnic identities (Armstrong-Fumero 2009; Castillo Cocom 2007). Additionally, access to ingredients that are not locally produced is more limited than in major urban centers, and many residents lack the cash to purchase such ingredients even if they are available. As such, the naturalization of tastes is perhaps even more intense in rural communities such as Juubche', developing in part through a narrower range of foodstuffs and a more ethnically homogeneous population. Furthermore, it is often thought to reflect not just what Ayora-Diaz (2012) calls "the spirit of the 'people'" (114) but also the bodily needs of the rural people themselves. Chapter 2 examines the attribution of bodily difference on the basis of labor activities, generation, and gender, but common residence and experience can also shape seemingly shared tastes. In Juubche' the value of standardization may endure because of the kaj-centric focus of many rural communities, related assumptions about the life and work in a particular place, and continuities in food labor. Moving from the conceptual spaces of the economic and supernatural, this chapter narrows in on those realms of life in Juubche' that are most directly related to food: preparation and consumption. The gendered division of food labor remains similar to that of decades past, and fairly predictable culinary milestones continue to punctuate the lives of girls and women. The desire for standardization persists, but cuisine, in both its preparation and consumption, is dynamic and constantly changing in Juubche'. In the early twenty-first century, access to new foods and related knowledge is challenging hierarchies of expertise, contributing to shifting identities, and gradually transforming tastes and bodies.

An examination of culinary and gastronomic fields offers a view of how diverse experiences unfold, both at the sites of individual bodies and within the larger community. This chapter analyzes the development of culinary expertise and the shaping of the tastes of Juubche' residents. Following that, an analysis of the adoption of several new foods provides a chance to identify the confluence of continuity and change within the everyday experiences of some residents of Juubche'. These new foods still reinforce gendered modes of caring, though they typically lack the cosmological significance of older foods. Other new foods, those that are sold packaged and ready-to-eat, require little to no knowledge with regard to preparation, but as the final section suggests, their potential to transform local palates may hold profound implications for food work and consumption in this community. Together, these cases reveal the inseparable but often-asynchronous transformations of bodies and the worlds they inhabit.

Learning to Cook and Eat

The acquisition of culinary and gastronomic knowledge in rural Yucatán has historically been a gradual process that accelerates with marriage and upholds established ties between knowledge and advanced age (Gaskins 2003; Greene 2002). Women accrue such knowledge over the course of their lifetimes, and those who demonstrate exceptional culinary skills may take on specialized roles in the preparation of ceremonial foods. Concurrent with the development of these skills is, not surprisingly, the development of a particularized palate. Although their participation in food preparation is usually limited to a narrow range of ceremonial dishes, men, too, refine their palates and their culinary skills over time. Older individuals and those who develop into local culinary experts acquire prestige through their displays of knowledge and aesthetic sensitivity, but these displays are also crucial in the culinary and gastronomic education of the rest of the community. In rural Yucatán assumptions about what makes food "good" reflect the value placed on consensus, tranquility, and, more generally, balance. Connoisseurship as it is performed with regard to established foodstuffs serves to preserve these values while also upholding long-standing hierarchies of knowledge.

Despite changes in the origins of many staple foods, the gendered division of food labor has not radically changed in recent decades in Juubche' and in other rural communities in the region (Heusinkveld 2008; O'Connor 2014). Although men continue to prepare certain ceremonial foods such as the breads for the ch'a-chak, women are still responsible for daily cooking. Daily cooking remains their most valued caregiving activity. The processes by which girls and young women learn to do this work are similar to the culinary initiations of earlier generations, albeit with the addition of some technologies that have reduced the physical drudgery. As school-age children, girls are often sent out to have soaked corn ground at one of the local mills. They return home with ground corn dough ready to be patted out into tortillas. All of my female informants, ranging in age from eighteen to eighty-six, learned to *pak'ach* (prepare tortillas) between the ages of eight and fourteen. Some women learned on their own out of necessity after a mother fell ill or passed way. One woman remembered: "My mother's head was hurting. . . . Who made my father's serving? Me! With a spoon! With a knife! . . . I learned on my own like that." More frequently girls learn through observation and then by joining older girls and women at the table, subjecting their tortilla-making techniques and final products to critique. This learning process is often a slow one. Not all women, especially those who are younger, are experts in tortilla making. Girls are very rarely those manning the fire; they tend to play a supporting role, patting out tortillas while an older woman judges "cooked-ness" on the griddle. In some cases girls who marry particularly young, at fifteen or sixteen, may not yet have perfected their tortilla-making skills. Still, even in those families for whom hand-patted tortillas are not the norm, tortilla making is required female knowledge, understood as crucial to the complementary gender roles that have organized household production for centuries (Landa 1941; O'Connor 2010; Redfield and Villa Rojas [1934] 1962).

Learning to prepare savory dishes, or ki' waaj, is an even lengthier process. Many girls are too busy patting tortillas, running errands, or attending to younger siblings to study the more extensive food preparation usually undertaken by their mothers. They may observe and even participate in chopping vegetables and herbs, juicing oranges and limes, and beating eggs. Those activities that require more skill and are thus more highly valued, such as cutting meat, judging cooked-ness, and seasoning dishes, are generally left to the older women in the household. Preparing more basic everyday dishes such as boiled black beans, scrambled eggs, and sautéed squash are learned through trial and error or casual observation, rather than direct instruction. One woman recounted to me how she learned to make ki' waaj by beginning its preparation and having her mother or mother-in-law taste it and make suggestions throughout the process: "Put a little salt." Many of my young female informants, those in their twenties and younger, including some who have been married for almost a decade, professed little ability to cook well. They largely rely on the culinary skills of female elders in their extended household and typically share kitchens with in-laws until they and their husbands have the funds to build a separate home. Mothers-in-law are often particularly feared culinary critics; it is perhaps for this reason, and the demands of raising small children, that many younger women tend to eat meals cooked by their mothers-in-law.[1] When it comes to meat, seasonal dishes, or special occasion foods, older women are the authority. Younger and middle-aged women take care to invite female relatives in their fifties, sixties, and older to supervise the preparation of these foods on a regular basis. These women determine when a dish is sufficiently salty, spicy, or sweet; they cut the best pieces of meat and stuff the sausage; and their criticisms, small and large, are accepted without argument.

However, the less authoritative roles many younger women hold, especially in extended family households, is not only the result of a perceived lack of expertise. The time devoted to learning how to cook and to cooking itself is not universally valued. Some younger women may use new, processed foods that free time for media consumption and personal grooming. These women are still able to perform the required duty of feeding kin, yet they are better poised to shape themselves into the feminine images they choose to project, or the images they believe their male partners want them to project. For some women the adoption of these foods reflects participation in an imagined middle-class lifestyle, one that tempers the ideals of machismo with an emphasis on the power of female consumers. While the gendered norms that largely restrict women's sexual experiences to marriage limit their participation in the new sexual possibilities available to men, as examined in chapter 3, women may seek alternate means of integrating new practices and sensory experiences into their lives, as in the case of these culinary novelties. Such practices reveal some women's inclinations to embrace some aspects of social change in ways available to them, but they also suggest the persistence of more established approaches to care and pleasure. These women accrue status through the long-standing role of women as family cooks, but they do so in a way that situates such work in Western middle-class ideologies of care through consumption (Clarke 2014; Miller 1998; Parkin 2006). Their embrace of such practices also rejects the premise that such work should be burdensome, embracing the common market message that convenience is not contrary to care. Nonetheless, women's ability to avoid more taxing forms of food labor is constrained by economic status; there are many young women in Juubche' who avidly consume bits and pieces of an imagined middle-class life through watching television cooking programs or skimming through magazines, but far fewer can afford to regularly purchase prepared foods.

These foods and even more established dishes can provoke anxieties about status and jealousy. One Christmas Eve in Juubche' I was invited to several parties. Two of those hostesses who had invited me to their parties in rapid succession were sisters. The second, knowing full well that I'd already committed to her sister's party, promised that she would serve an abundance of food, some of which, she pointed out, her sister did not know how to prepare. Indeed, at her party, the second sister unveiled a large *sandwichón*, a savory dish that resembles a frosted layer cake but is composed of white bread, mayonnaise, Cheez Whiz, and other processed foods.[2] Women might attempt to outdo each other in the quality and variety of foods they prepare. They make or interpret minor slights, late or nonexistent invitations to events, and less-prime pieces of meat, and they tempt members of their competitors' households to eat their food. In these ways established caregiving practices can manifest desires for recognition and power, challenging some of the effects, equality and balance, that reciprocity might ostensibly seek to achieve via hospitality. Wealth inequalities in extended families, while frequently sources of tension, sometimes lead female members to find culinary niches. One sister may become an expert on novel foods such as salads and sandwiches, while another hones her skills in the preparation of ceremonial foods such as relleno negro. The salad and sandwich expert remains able to enjoy handmade tortillas and more established local meals. In the meantime, her sister may gradually widen her own repertoire to include some more novel dishes. Food remains a focus of reciprocal relations in Juubche', even as it reflects the diversification of local diets.

The X-k'uus: Expertise and Ritual Life

The work of the x-k'uus, a local culinary expert, plays a critical role in ensuring the success of established rituals such as weddings and saints' day feasts. Despite the often-limited economic resources of the families who contract x-k'uuso'ob, such events figure largely into how locals envision the "good life" and are seen, by many residents, to be essential in the maintenance of social and cosmological well-being. The work of the x-k'uus, though never lucrative, provides material benefits for the expert and her family and, perhaps more importantly, reinforces the centrality of food in Yucatec Maya ritual; x-k'uuso'ob guide sensorial encounters that remind kin and neighbors of the value of established dishes and their deep ties to older practices of care.

A x-k'uus is typically a woman in her forties or older who is invited to oversee food preparation and distribution for larger events, even though she may be unrelated or only distantly related to the hosts. Most frequently the hostess of an event hires a x-k'uus to oversee the preparation of relleno negro, pork and chicken in a blackened chile sauce. The x-k'uus will provide instructions to the hostess for the purchase of ingredients, where, for example, to purchase the precooked chile mixture and how many kilos of pork. The x-k'uus will come alone or sometimes with a daughter or daughter-in-law to manage the labor of the hostess and the kin who are helping her. The x-k'uus delegates tasks, reserving the most authoritative duties, including tasting for spiciness or saltiness, for herself. She typically remains through or returns for the distribution and consumption of the meal, directing the portions to be circulated.

Like most other cooks in this community, the x-k'uus cooks from memory and embodied experience. Above all the x-k'uus must have a reputation for cooking well, producing food that tastes the way in which those who are dining expect it to taste. The x-k'uus needs to have a clear understanding of the social hierarchy, not only the more general rules linked to age and gender in this community, but also the prestige of less familiar guests: wealthier kin from urban areas or a visiting teacher or doctor. If necessary, the hosts can assist the x-k'uus in managing the distribution of food to the latter category, by pointing out who should get the most favorite cuts of meat, for example. Other traits are important too; the x-k'uus should be reliable; the events for which she is hired are often large and intended to fulfill important ritual functions. Even body size can be an indication of the x-k'uus's suitability. During one family gathering I attended, a woman named doña Susana complained that there are very few x-k'uuso'ob anymore. The slender doña Susana told her plump sister doña Anita that she ought to learn to take on this role, matter-of-factly commenting, "Why not you? You're fat."

The origins of the role of the x-k'uus are unclear. Ethnographic and historical work using the term is scant. Two Yucatec Maya language dictionaries, using distinct orthographies, gloss the term as "servant" or "maid" (Bastarracha Manzano and Canto Rosado 2003; Bricker, Po'ot Yah, and Dzul de Po'ot 1998). Bastarracha Manzano and Canto Rosado also note another curious use for the word: it can refer to chickens who are entrusted with the care of baby turkeys. This care includes teaching the baby turkeys to eat. The seeming flexibility of the term might caution us against reifying the word and the role it often, though apparently not always, signifies.

That being said, the term *x-k'uus* as it is commonly used in Juubche' is a marker of identity, but it is a fluid one. When I asked doña Elodia, a woman in her sixties, to introduce me to some x-k'uuso'ob, she could only come up with one woman, one of her sisters. Yet a few weeks later, she told me that lots of women still took on the role of x-k'uus. Such seeming inconsistencies appeared in the accounts of other local women too, eventually making it clear to me that one's status as a x-k'uus was not fixed but rather contingent on one's level of expertise and whether it was sufficient for a particular event. Generally the more important the event, the further outside of a woman's kin network she might go in order to procure a x-k'uus. In exchange for the lending of her knowledge and skills at a wedding or saint's day affair, a x-k'uus receives more food to bring home than would the average female guest who patted out some tortillas or cut onions. As wedding planning becomes increasingly complex for some young couples, their families may opt to pay multiple local women to serve as x-k'uuso'ob in the preparation of the wedding meal, freeing the couple and their kin of any food preparation responsibility. The fluid and informal placement of individual x-k'uuso'ob within a hierarchy of women who take on this role fits within a larger culinary hierarchy in Juubche'. As described earlier in this chapter, more complex and consequential culinary labor is generally left to the older women in the household. Yet even a fiercely critical mother-in-law may be silenced by the expertise of the x-k'uus procured for a particular event; when x-k'uuso'ob are in that role, they always exercise more authority than others, their culinary knowledge embodied in sharp minds, savvy hands, and refined palates.

The first chapters of this text explore how social changes of the last half century have altered food production and consumption in Juubche'. New religious diversity has weakened what were once community-wide religious and agricultural rituals, and events such as the annual fiesta in honor of the town's patron saint, once an opportunity for redistribution and commensality, are increasingly commodified, relying upon the sale of food, drink, and entertainment. The local decline in farming, a pattern seen elsewhere in Mexico especially since the early 1990s, the growing availability of Mexican-produced processed foods, and the post-NAFTA influx of imported foodstuffs have contributed to diets that include fewer local ingredients and more packaged foods (Gálvez 2018; Leatherman and Goodman 2005). In Juubche' these changes have expanded the local culinary hierarchy. Later this chapter examines how the increasing consumption of foods made mostly with nonlocal ingredients, dishes such as sandwiches and pasta salads that are often served for birthdays and other events, has elevated the status of women who demonstrate expertise and confidence in their preparation. Furthermore, at least one young man in Juubche' is perusing formal culinary training, and other men in the community perform paid food labor in tourist areas, working as cooks or waiters. The culinary hierarchy has never been entirely stable here, but the work of the x-k'uus has nonetheless been a realm in which continuity is valued and expected.

This book argues that culinary and gastronomic fields in rural Yucatán

8. *X-k'uus* at work preparing *relleno negro*. Courtesy of author.

attach value to standardization. The expectation for particular tastes and presentation appears strongest, not surprisingly, with regard to those foods that are most well established, such as those included within the category of *janal* and, even more specifically, those linked to important ceremonial events, such as the aforementioned relleno negro. Perhaps as much as food that is *ki'* (tasty), x-k'uuso'ob aim to prepare food that is *tun p'iis* or *tiibil* (as noted in chapter 1, "balanced" or "just right"). It is the x-k'uus who, throughout the preparation of a dish, renders this judgment. During spring 2017 I watched a x-k'uus I call doña Patricia strain the sakam or corn dough to make a broth of the correct thickness and crush the right quantity of tomatoes by hand. Later, when an enormous pot full of the ingredients was placed in the píib, the underground pit dug for roasting, I watched doña Patricia stir with a long thick stick until she needed a break. Before the píib was covered with banana leaves, banana stalks, a woven sack, and dirt, doña Patricia encouraged the other women to take a taste with her using a large ladle. Although each voiced her opinion about saltiness and spiciness, none deviated much from the other, and it was doña Patricia's conclusion that the taste was just right. Although some residents of Juubche' confess that they find relleno and other ceremonial foods heavy, most everyone looks forward to their starring role in what is always a hearty meal. Indeed, for several hours after consumption of the relleno doña Patricia prepared, I joined the hostess in delivering small pots and bowls full of it to kin and friends across this small town.

The importance of relleno negro and time- and resource-intensive dishes like it is, in part, linked to its place in valued rituals such as weddings and the annual fiesta in honor of the town's patron saint. Unlike other spirits who are assigned to protect particular elements, the patron saints are thought of as guardians of the entire communities who worship them; they can bestow favor on individuals and groups alike. Yet part of the value of these foods and consequently the work of the x-k'uus rests in the processes of creation itself. The preparation of relleno, for example, requires both material resources and social connections, the access to the collective labor that makes cooking and serving the dish possible. Similarly, its consumption, given that it is cooked in large quantities in a place where many lack access to refrigeration, necessitates commensality and generosity. Those who are fed include the human and nonhuman, the dogs and chickens who receive the dregs or drippings; and the living and nonliving, with bowls filled and placed on altars to provide nourishment to the spirits of the deceased. The process of preparing and consuming relleno is no mere reflection of idealized social relations but rather an important way in which doña Patricia, the hostess of this meal, and her guests work to achieve rich and reciprocal relationships, a critical part of the good life by most residents' standards in this community. However, would any of this occur if the dishes did not suit the tastes of the living humans who consume them? The crafting of tasty, "just right" food is a critical part of the continued value of these dishes and the rituals in which they are embedded. Of course, it is not the taste of relleno negro alone that leads individuals to plan weddings or host a feast for the patron saint, but the value of the food, including its taste, reaffirms the worth of the rituals. The case of the occasional bad meal only reaffirms the importance of the quality of these dishes; as in Holtzman's work on the memorability of bad food (2010), disgusting meals loom large in the collective memory of certain social affairs in Juubche', such as a relleno made with blackened chiles that tasted so strange they could have only been blackened with ink.

Avoiding such disasters is thus foremost in cooking, especially for a crowd. The talent that a few decades ago enabled a woman to master more complicated dishes and become a respected x-k'uus today facilitates the rapid absorption of culinary knowledge via sources external to Juubche'. For young women the ability to establish oneself as a culinary expert in this community often occurs through the mastering of novel foods. However, the continued affection for more established ceremonial foods is not just a function of attachment to the rituals in which these foods play a prominent role. The x-k'uus plays an essential role in employing her expertise to create food that is also valued and meaningful because of its own material qualities, not just the context in which it is consumed. The food itself lends value to the rituals, a critical function in a community in which increasing religious diversity has fractured collective ritual life.

Novel Foods: Recent Additions to the Culinary Landscape

Disconnected from popular religious practice, recent additions to the culinary repertoire in Juubche' impact social life in other ways. Most notably, they hold the potential to partially dismantle longer-standing hierarchies of expertise and enact class distinctions. They do so through the privileging of ways of preparing and tasting food that have been, and in some ways still are, materially and ideologically limited to a minority in rural communities. Although the processes of preparation and consumption that characterize these foods are no less standardized than those of established foods, the conditions under which these processes occur are often radically different. Not surprisingly, then, the introduction of these foods holds implications for individual human bodies, for the larger community, and for the practices of care by which they are constituted.

For many young women in Juubche' there is a perceived link between consuming new foods and identifying oneself as a member of larger Yucatecan and Mexican societies. Yet rather than disavowing a link to their rural community, these women are establishing themselves as versatile, respected, and middle-class members of that community. Part of this process is asserting oneself as someone who can manage new foods and successfully integrate them into the everyday rhythms of local life, including habits of care. In doing so these women render themselves local culinary experts, complicate stereotypes about indigenous Yucatecans and their food practices, and expand the possibilities of alimentary pleasure for themselves and their community. At the same time, however, these new culinary practices and the claims that come with them challenge accepted notions of care and understandings of the body.

As described earlier, the substance of what most Juubche' residents eat on a daily basis is fairly similar to that consumed several generations ago: corn tortillas, beans, eggs, chicken or, less frequently, pork or beef, and a small but satisfying array of vegetables from cornfields or home gardens. Some of these foods are not locally produced to the degree that they used to be, but the ways in which they are prepared is largely similar to earlier culinary practices described by my informants. Purchased snacks and drinks are crucial parts of the gastronomic landscape in this town—and they require unique sets of cultural knowledge to guide their purchase and consumption—but they do not demand preparation and, thus, no culinary know-how. The foods with which this section is interested are occasionally served for everyday meals, though usually for the lighter dinner than the main meal of lunch. They are most often served for secular events such as birthdays or New Year's Eve celebrations, which have been adopted from mainstream Mexican culture in recent decades. No one prepares these foods for ceremonies honoring the saints, other deities, or the souls of the deceased. These new foods are not what I term "well established"; rather, new foods have entered into the local diet only in the last generation or two. Well-established foods, on the other hand, have been consumed consistently over the lifetimes of all of my informants, the oldest of whom was born in the early 1920s.[3]

Among the most prominent of these new foods are three dishes. The first is *sándwich*, or "sandwich" in English. Yet the sándwich of Juubche' is not like the sandwiches of the United States. There is no vast array of ingredients from which to choose, nor an appreciation for creative and original combinations. The Juubche' sándwich is highly standardized: mass-produced white bread, a thin spread of mayonnaise (full fat and unflavored), shredded chicken, sliced tomato, and a few pieces of pickled jalapeño. For parties sándwiches are often wrapped in white paper napkins to keep them clean and to make for easy distribution. The second dish is *sopa fría*. Although it translates to "cold soup," in Juubche' it refers to a pasta salad with canned pineapple chunks, bits of processed ham, canned peas, and mayonnaise. In Juubche' sopa fría is always served with soda crackers for scooping. The third dish is called *ensalada*, "salad" in English, but this recipe refers to a very specific version of potato salad, with boiled carrots, canned peas, mayonnaise, and maybe a splash of the vinegar from a can of pickled jalapeños. Like sopa fría, it is always served with soda crackers for scooping. Both sopa fría and ensalada are seasoned with salt and pepper and are usually dished out onto small, disposable serving plates at various occasions.

These foods differ greatly in taste from the fare that most residents consume on a daily basis. While the inclusion of canned pickled jalapeños adds heat to a sándwich, and their juices sometimes enliven ensalada, the three dishes are bland. Well-established dishes are often simply prepared but marked by generous additions of lard, pickled or sautéed onions, spice marinades, or citrus juices. Blander foods are reserved for breakfast and light dinners, in the form of French bread and store-bought crackers or for those with illness-related food restrictions. Indeed, in the latter cases, the ill seem most bothered by this aspect of their health experience, one that restricts their food to the category of the *ma' ki'* (not tasty). Texturally as well, sándwich, sopa fría, and ensalada stray from the usual preferences.

Variations on the *torta*, a type of sandwich common through Mexico, are rarely prepared at home by Juubche' residents, though many residents purchase and consume them while attending school or working outside of town. Unlike the sándwich, the torta features a serving of meat on a large crusty roll, often with some avocado, onion, salsa, mayonnaise, or other garnish. A torta is texturally complex and less *suave* (smooth) than a sándwich, lacking the softness lent by white sandwich bread. Sopa fría and ensalada are served chilled or at room temperature and have a creamy consistency. Puréed foods, such as *tsabij bu'ul* (literally, "fried beans," but more like soupy refried beans) and *tsabij p'aak* (literally, "fried tomato," but more of a spicy tomato sauce), are commonly consumed, but they are served warm and lack the creaminess of potatoes or pasta coated in mayonnaise. In fact, creaminess is uncharacteristic of well-established foods, in which the inclusion of mayonnaise, milk, cheese, and other dairy products is rare.

In content these dishes bear little resemblance to well-established foods. The ingredients are almost all purchased and produced outside of the community. The dishes require the purchase of ingredients not used in everyday cooking. Only those few families with refrigerators can store the leftover ingredients for more than a day, with the exception of mayonnaise, which is usually left unrefrigerated anyway. And since these foods are not eaten with tortillas, women do not need to sit in front of the fire before and during a meal, nor do these dishes need to be served at a particular temperature. Practically speaking, then, these foods leave women freer to socialize or to attend to other hostess duties.

Because servings are generally contained, wrapped as individual portions or served as a scoop on a small plate, the careful judgments regarding who gets what and how much are largely unnecessary. The distribution of well-established foods at special-occasion events is important work, usually left to an older woman, the hostess in consultation with an older woman, or the x-k'uus, if one has been procured. These women carefully dole out pieces of meat and broth to men, women, and children. The equal portions in which novel foods are doled out stand in contrast to the deliberate inequities in the serving of established foods. Furthermore, these new foods do not require a table on which to consume them; guests can easily eat them in a chair with a plate or, in the case of sándwich, just in their hands. Instead of being called to eat at a limited number of tables, a hierarchy that generally prioritizes men and any esteemed guests, guests are served in a simpler and more democratic fashion: the hostess(es) and helpers distribute food by moving around the room, handing food to each and every individual in an order determined only by who is sitting or standing closest.[4]

Once distributed, these foods are also treated differently than well-established foods. A number of older people told me that they find these foods to be *ma' ki'* (not tasty), especially sopa fría. In light of the fact that these foods are often distributed at evening festivities (usually around most residents' bedtimes), some attendees choose not to eat their helpings at the event. As with established foods, however, guests must accept a first serving, so they often take the food home with them. *Ki' waaj* (meals served with tortillas) are exchanged between families on an often-daily basis in Juubche', and they are sent home with guests at many affairs (particularly when the guest helps prepare the food). It is considered poor form to throw any gifted ki' waaj away. Because most families are large, the food is consumed quickly, though smaller families may force themselves to reheat and eat it for several days. Sopa fría, ensalada, and sándwich are a different matter. According to some residents, these foods are acceptable to give to dogs, cats, or chickens as soon as guests return from an event. While it would still not be preferable for one's host to see such behavior, it is not considered poor form or even sinful as would be the tossing of ki' waaj.

The lack of reverence shown for sopa fría, ensalada, and sándwich is not merely a matter of taste, however. As noted earlier, these foods are usually served at secular affairs, such as birthday parties. These affairs are relatively new rituals, only a few decades old, and popularized over time after being encountered in larger towns and cities. Such events are unintegrated into the cosmological cycles by which food production, preparation, and commensality have long been linked. For Juubche's residents there is little sacred about the ways in which these foods' ingredients are produced. In fact, few of those who consume these foods have ever grown or prepared from scratch any of the required components, except perhaps the chicken meat and tomato that fills a sándwich. The origins of these foods are unfamiliar and abstract, mediated by cash rather than direct human labor. Their production, to the knowledge of my informants, is not dependent upon the favor of the gods of rain or the God of Christianity. Nor is their shared consumption essential to any long-standing displays of gratitude or rites of passage that reproduce established social roles. In fact, I can think of only one occasion on which I consumed one of these new foods at an event that I would categorize as religious or spiritual. *Jetsmek* ceremonies are celebrated when a young child first sits astride an adult's hip. In a symbolic act of initiation, tools are laid out to equip the child for the requirements of full membership in the community. Historically these tools have been representative of the gendered roles of household production, with machetes and other agricultural tools presented for men, and kitchen tools presented for women (Re Cruz 1996). Elena, an aspiring middle-class woman, hosted a jetsmek as the jetsmek "godmother" of her niece. Instead of kitchen tools placed in the infant's hands, a notebook and pencil represented the desired future for the infant girl. In place of the usual pork or chicken dish, Elena served sopa fría. The parallels between the choice of menu and the symbolic items given to the infant are clear, exemplifying a shifting form of gendered personhood.

Despite the differences between these foods and the foods they sometimes replace, some enduring qualities of the local culinary culture are evident. Another trait that these three new dishes have in common is the uniformity with which each it usually prepared; as with more established foods, standardization and thus predictability are more desirable than creativity or innovation. Not once have I witnessed anyone suggest an addition or variation to these foods. When older women ask whether a particular item, say, pickled onions or shredded cabbage, is included in sandwiches, younger women promptly remind them of the correct ingredients. In fact, younger women are the authorities on these foods; as one woman in her seventies announced while eating a sándwich at a birthday party, "The children really know how to make these things." In nuclear families without young women, a niece may be invited over to assist with the preparation of these foods. These women remind their older counterparts of the exact ingredients, the best places to purchase them, and the steps in which the dishes should be created. During the actual preparation, they oversee the assembly of sandwiches and the mixing of ensalada and sopa fría. They usually have the final say in how much salt and pepper must be added, and how many soda crackers should be placed with each serving. When I wondered out loud to an older woman about the safety of eating unrefrigerated mayonnaise the next day (thus revealing one of my own cultural anxieties about food), she quickly relayed the question to her much younger sister, who promptly assured her of its safety. Indeed, new foods require distinct experiential knowledge of how salty or how spicy, and older women rarely hold that knowledge in preparation or in taste.

While the preparation of sándwich, ensalada, and sopa fría reveals a certain privileging of younger women's arena of authority and expertise, the consumption of these dishes reveals the gradual development of standardized tastes. Those who eat them slowly learn, through experience, what they ought to taste like. Indeed, while new foods are being consumed, one rarely hears any commentary on the taste. The vocalized criticism, among young and old, male and female, that characterizes the consumption of more established foods is notably absent. So although these new foods are marked by the same rigidity of preparation as more established foods, the collective ability to discern their "correct" qualities is a work in progress. Food preparation has long been a realm in which some exercise more authority than others. The expertise of the younger women who prepare sándwich, ensalada, and sopa fría today now extends from the hearth to the dining table. Their ability to see, feel, and taste in ways that help them prepare these new dishes is mirrored by their expertise in assessing the finish products. Their form of connoisseurship is even more weighted than that of the older generation, for it is only their actions, instructions, and critiques that educate the rest of the community.

The Significance of New Foods

Of course, as I explore in earlier chapters, cuisine in rural Yucatán is and always has been dynamic, an amalgamation determined by multiple forces within and outside of individual communities. In the past there have been concerted efforts by the state to change food preparation and consumption in the community, as detailed in chapter 2's account of the twentieth century's cultural missions. Some women learned to prepare new dishes during time spent outside of the village. Female migration from Juubche' was not common during the twentieth century, but girls were occasionally sent to work as domestic servants in Mérida or Valladolid. Prior to the construction of a secondary school in town in the 1990s, poor families often struggled to feed older girls who remained unmarried and at home. Primary school teachers would sometimes arrange domestic work for these girls in the homes of their urban acquaintances. Employers or other household staff instructed girls from Juubche' in the preparation of new foods while doing this domestic labor; other girls simply observed and consumed the foods prepared by the household cook. Natalia, who worked as a nanny to a Valladolid family in the early 1990s, remembered, "There was a cook, too. I watched how she cooked. Because I liked cooking, I would get close and see how she made it. That's how I learned." However, she noted that she doesn't often cook these meals at home: "Foods like that require money." In other cases men acted as culinary conduits; having traveled to work in Cancún or other parts of the peninsula, they may have been party to unfamiliar culinary practices. Don Martín, a highly inquisitive man, remembered having visited an acquaintance in the Cancún home where she worked as a domestic servant. She offered him a *refresco* (soft drink). Expecting Coca-Cola, he agreed, but she handed a green drink. He found it tasty and inquired as to its contents. His friend told him that it was made from aloe vera juice. Upon his return home, he prepared it for his wife and children. Unimpressed by its taste, however, don Martín's wife was not interested in integrating the beverage into her culinary repertoire.

If residents have always been somewhat interested in trying new foods, what is new about the acquisition of culinary expertise by young women today? Despite a lack of roads and electricity until the 1980s, the residents of Juubche' had contact with their local schoolteachers, most of whom came from other parts of the peninsula; traveled to fairs and on religious pilgrimages; and migrated to work in chicle camps or on archaeological excavations. During this time women of many ages adopted new food practices, and many of these foods were easily integrated into, at the very least, dinner and could be used in secular, festive menus. Urban street foods, such as panuchos, used common ingredients found in cornfields and home gardens. Women did not need much cash, nor did they need to venture out of town to shop for ingredients. These foods carried with them a faint air of urban savvy, but they were also rooted in local farming practices and tastes. The processes by which they were produced, prepared, and consumed reproduced the cosmological vision widely embraced in the community and served to exercise care for human bodies and other entities. In other cases some novelties, such as the aloe vera soft drink mentioned earlier, became mere fodder for humorous anecdotes, perhaps due to the labor of preparation, a wife's lack of interest, or little connection to culturally significant practices or values.

Today, a much broader range of media influences the integration of new foods. Ayora-Diaz (2012) writes of the second half of the twentieth century in Yucatán more generally: "The advertisements distributed by national and international food corporations invited women and their families to change their tastes and promoted different aesthetic values to judge the beauty of a dish. . . . The transformations that took place in the Yucatecan culinary field during the 1960s and 1970s had effects that extended over the subsequent decades" (177). In rural communities like Juubche' these effects were indeed felt later, as the construction of highways, increased literacy, and access to media among younger generations opened up new possibilities for exposure to food knowledge. Rosa, a woman in her twenties, spent a few years working in a lingerie factory on the outskirts of a nearby city. Among her coworkers were some women from elsewhere in the region who knew how to prepare a version of *mole*, a dish with (oft-debated) origins in central Mexico. Eager to try the complicated dish, Rosa wrote down the recipe and was then able to prepare mole at home. Elena explained to me that she had one cookbook, and that she used it to prepare new foods such as fajitas and hot cakes for her husband and children. Importantly, her husband, Jose, a socially mobile young man, was regularly exposed to new foods at his job in Playa del Carmen. While there, he often traveled and dined with his middle-class boss, and both Jose and Elena became interested in eating such foods at home. Many women watched *Al sabor del chef*, a cooking show that aired on a national television network between 2007 and 2011; the ingredients were not always familiar, many representative of central Mexican and even international cuisines, but the recipes often piqued interests, for good or bad. One older woman told me that although she did watch the show, she thought many of the dishes appeared "not tasty," marked by unappetizing combinations of ingredients and strange presentations. The program's portrayal both of entirely unfamiliar dishes and of creative versions of Mexican staples was largely unappealing to viewers for whom predictability best ensures pleasure and satisfaction.

Television programming need not be overtly instructional, however, for its portrayals of food to be of interest (or not) to residents. My hosts and I were deeply committed to watching telenovelas together each weeknight. I would often find myself engrossed in a scene in which various characters discussed over a meal or drink some matter of supreme importance to the program's current plot. As I tried my best to understand the dialogue, frequently in the rapid Mexican Spanish of the nation's capital, my concentration would be broken by the exclamation by one of my hosts or a guest of "Well, look at that! They're eating..." Whether marveling in the familiarity or oddness of whatever was being consumed onscreen, my hosts and the many other friends in Juubche' with whom I watched television were deeply curious about the food practices onscreen. If they could not identify the foods on screen, a debate might ensue: are those foods entirely foreign, from different places for different bodies, or are they something one might have glimpsed ts'uulo'ob eating at a sidewalk café in Cancún or Valladolid, perhaps made from local ingredients but prepared in a strange manner and sold at exorbitant prices?

Indeed, one important characteristic of the young women who act as authorities on sándwich, sopa fría, and ensalada is their exposure to regional and national culinary practices. In some senses these resident experts are a diverse group: several are Catholic and several are Jehovah's Witnesses; a few are married, a few unmarried, and they participate in a range of labor activities in addition to regular housework, though one is a full-time housewife. However, all exercise control over the money they or their husbands earn. Thanks to their own work or that of their husbands, they are at least slightly wealthier than most women their age. In the cases of those who are married, all of their husbands rely primarily on wage labor, rather than subsistence farming, to support their families. All the young culinary experts have access to cars owned by their husbands or fathers, and they also own and regularly use appliances such as refrigerators and stoves. For these reasons they can easily purchase food products from outside of Juubche', as well as store and prepare those foods in ways that are not accessible to many of their fellow residents. For women with access to cars, going on day trips to nearby cities or touristic sites may also expose them to new foods. In families in which husbands have relatively well-paying jobs (for example, as taxi drivers, bartenders, waiters), the husbands themselves may have access to more than the basic fare consumed by construction workers while working on the coast. They may discover foods that they enjoy, carefully note their preparation, and suggest the dishes to their wives upon their return home. In contrast, lower-paid construction workers often rely on what they find to be less-tasty versions of the simple foods consumed at home, stocking up on cooked chicken and machine-made tortillas at Walmart or a budget eatery.

However, the differences between these women and others are not just a matter of material resources. Although they have varying levels of education, they strike both me and other residents as notably intelligent and ambitious. As an older woman remarked of one of these younger women, "She learns things quickly." Another woman in her mid-twenties, who had learned new dishes from a sister-in-law from Mérida, told me that her head was "suave" and that whatever she saw her sister-in-law make, she learned to make for herself. The talent that a few decades ago enabled a woman to master more complicated dishes and become a respected x-k'uus today facilitates the rapid absorption of culinary knowledge via sources external to Juubche' itself. Those young women who are particularly knowledgeable and skilled in the realm of new foods are also highly attentive to the culinary behaviors of others, and not only those of their relatives and neighbors but also of visiting tourists and of middle- and upper-class residents of nearby cities. Unlike other women who might upon first meeting me pepper me with a few food questions that referenced their own diets, anticipating my difference—Do I eat tortillas? Do I eat chiles?—these young culinary experts would tailor their questions to what they suspected I actually consume—Do I eat spaghetti? Do I eat quesadillas? Such young women are keenly aware of the relationship between food and class on the peninsula, but they correctly see the boundaries between consumption practices, ethnicity, and wealth as flexible. The appeal of these new foods is most certainly connected to the respect one receives as an expert in the domain of food and eating within this relatively small community. In fact, it is the ability to be flexible about food—to speak knowledgeably about new foods, to express a wide range of tastes, and to recognize the care potential of novel entities and practices—that lends these women respect and admiration. They continue to eat well-established foods and are as likely as anyone else to invite a x-k'uus to help prepare relleno negro for a special occasion. Yet these women have a unique relationship with a category of foods that comprises local culinary luxuries, and this strips their food practices of a locally perceived link to poverty. Two young women may both eat black beans and tortillas several days a week, but the ability of one to talk knowledgeably about and skillfully prepare, say, ensalada, would distinguish her from the other. They hold the knowledge of how to care for, and in doing so produce, new bodies.

New Foods, New Bodies

The categorization of these new foods as luxurious is based on certain understandings and bodily experiences of their material qualities, as well as on deep-rooted ideas of class and racial difference. These foods are, again, rarely treated as everyday foods. They are, perhaps, not entirely food to begin with, at least not the food of poor farmers. Older residents often explicitly mark simple, well-established staples such as beans and eggs as *u janalil otsil* (food of the poor). Assumptions about class and consumption may reflect the lingering effects of political and nutritional discourses in Mexico that linked corn and other rural staples to a host of moral qualities and social ills (Pilcher 1998). Those who have worked in the households of ts'uulo'ob or who have watched innumerable telenovelas (and the latter condition includes most everyone in Juubche') would, and often do, argue that beans, eggs, and tortillas make few appearances on the tables of the wealthy. What is perhaps most appealing to all about sándwich, sopa fría, and ensalada then is their utter frivolity. These foods are not, by local standards, the foods of poor people nor do they bear a direct relationship to the hard labor of local farming and the shameful class connotations farming holds for some residents. The foods are not valued for economy; few of my informants could afford to eat them on a regular basis. The consumption of them is pleasurable to most residents not only because of the foods' taste—or, in fact, as I point out earlier, in spite of—but because of the luxury of which these foods speak. These foods are often talked about as being *fino* (fine) or *suave* (smooth). Such qualities are what the bodies of ts'uulo'ob require; their food does not need to fuel the hard labor of planting and sowing crops. These news foods are not seen as either particularly nutritious or egregiously unhealthy. They are never, for example, classified as *ts'aak* (medicine), as some local foods are. However, they are thought to be easy on the stomach. For that reason, some socially mobile women, having adopted the novel idea that children have distinct food needs, believe these foods to be particularly good for children. Older people, on the other hand, often complain that these new foods do not fill them up.

The new foods are largely un-integrated into the hot-cold system. When older people express concern about eating new foods like sopa fría and sándwich when their óol is "hot," younger people assure them that these foods are not "cold." Assurances from younger women that new foods like ensalada and sopa fría do not have any disruptive qualities put older people at ease with foods that would otherwise be unfamiliar and anxiety inducing. That these foods do not threaten bodily balance in and of themselves negates the need to exercise certain modes of care while preparing and consuming them. Yet in not integrating these new foods into the hot-cold classificatory system, younger women are also dismantling, or at least reshaping, a cosmology in which all foodstuffs, like other natural resources, should be part of larger cycles of life, death, and exchange. The failure to classify these foods in established ways has several likely explanations. First, these women don't know how to classify these foods because they typically learn the qualities of foods from their elders; if their elders are unfamiliar with these foods, then women must develop their own classification. However, they are unsure of how the ingredients are produced and how they fit any of the patterns that characterize existing classifications. Additionally these women might not want to integrate these foods into the hot-cold syndrome out of shame that they might be perceived as "backward," thus threatening their chances at upward social mobility. Through their contact with biomedicine and the consumption patterns of urban folk, cooks in Juubche' realize the difference reproduced in their adherence to the hot-cold syndrome and its food classifications.

Younger women's confidence in preparing these foods and introducing them to others challenges local assumptions held by older people about racial difference. As discussed earlier, older people tend to pin dietary differences on these perceived racial distinctions, and many suggest that ts'uulo'ob are immune to the hot-cold imbalances to which they themselves are vulnerable. For older women in particular, generally the least well-traveled among residents, the categories of mayero and ts'uul tend to align with distinct culinary patterns, influenced by the contrast between local food practices and the consumption practices of ts'uulo'ob that they have observed on television. In contrast, men and younger people in general tend to have more contact with urban Mexicans and foreigners, giving them a broader spectrum of behaviors by which to understand food consumption. The greater willingness of younger women to experiment with new foods also provides a concrete means of testing accepted theories of difference; as they serve their children hot cakes and sándwich with no adverse effects, they begin to question the biological or racial links to food preferences. Just as some ostensible phenotypic shifts, such as taller heights and lighter skin, and changes in labor activities have convinced older residents that the bodies of the young are different from their own, so too does their apparently safe consumption of novel foods provoke doubt about the nature of human bodies, local and foreign. While older generations may believe that the anatomy of younger generations is, in some way, fundamentally different or that these more youthful bodies are adapting noticeably to change, the younger generation sees the growing similarities between their own lifestyles and those of urban, wealthier populations as evidence of commonality.

The adoption of foods such as sándwich, sopa fría, and ensalada by the residents of Juubche' has been made possible by a series of economic and cultural shifts during the twentieth century, including the decline of agriculture, the development of tourism, and the expansion of mass media. The rapid absorption and dissemination of food-related knowledge and skills by young women are the products of sharp observations of the ways in which food is prepared and consumed on television and in urban areas. The skill set young women demonstrate in preparing new foods embodies, for them and for their *etkajalo'ob* (fellow townspeople), both a mastery of a culinary realm and a mastery of the art of middle-class living. They seek to broaden their food practices and knowledge as a mechanism for personal and social advancement.

The ways in which young women have embraced these foods have themselves been productive of social change in Juubche'. There is not a systematic devaluation of established culinary knowledge in Juubche'; rather the culinary culture itself is expanding, largely due to these young women. They are assuming positions of authority within a culinary culture that continues to value standardization over creativity. In this way these women are re-creating cultural emphases on consensus and collectivity and maintaining some form of cohesion in the face of growing religious diversity and economic inequality in their community. At the same time, their knowledge of these new foods and their access to resources complicate local and regional ideologies of race, class, and biology. Sándwich, sopa fría, and ensalada do not require just new methods of preparation and consumption but also new understandings of bodies and health. As long as these foods remain outside of the established hot-cold syndrome and the logics of which it is a part, they will continue to invite Juubche' residents to reconceptualize the world in which they live. For residents there are few, if any, connections between these new foods and the hard labor, sometimes extreme weather, and often fickle supernatural forces that have aided or hindered in the production of food for generations. It is this radical difference that is, in fact, part of the appeal of sándwich, sopa fría, and ensalada. These young women's acquisition of new culinary skills and the dexterity and authority with which they exercise them bring a taste of, and for, culinary luxuries to Juubche', effectively broadening the realm of pleasure within the community.

Saltiness and the Case of Chips

Purchased foods requiring no preparation muddle the culinary and gastronomic culture norms even more. Like sopa fría, purchased snacks such as potato and corn chips have the potential to reshape hierarchies of expertise, with young people exercising authority. In the case of these snack foods, however, the lack of preparation offers a fundamental contrast to locally prepared foods, even those like sopa fría and sándwich. A determination of the "right" taste may now derive from the food science research and marketing strategies of industrial food producers. Shifting palates and the broadening of food-related expertise can be observed through an analysis of one quality in particular: saltiness.

Salt is one of the few commodity foods with a long presence in this region. For centuries prior to colonization, inhabitants of the peninsula participated in the trade of salt, much of which was obtained from salt pans on the northern and northwestern coasts of the peninsula (Andrews 1983; Glassman and Anaya 2011; McKillop 2004). Salt remained a staple in all households, largely due to the taste it imparts to food. One of the challenges most women in Juubche' face is making use of often limited resources to prepare foods that please all members of their households. According to these women, using quality ingredients and seasoning them properly is essential. Salt is one of the few items women buy in bulk; they buy pound or half-pound bags and dole out a pinch at a time. The right amount of salt is thought crucial to good tortillas; whether they use corn their husbands have grown or purchase dough from the local tortilla shop, women taste for saltiness before patting tortillas for a meal. Farmers' wives add salt to watered down corn dough for salty atole. Ki' waaj, the category of prepared dishes consumed with tortillas, always includes salt. Nearly all women boil black beans, most of which are now purchased dry, and then salt them. Other ki' waaj dishes that include meat, eggs, or vegetables are always salted as well. Fruits that are sour by nature or consumed before they ripen to sweetness are eaten with salt and sometimes powdered chile.

The use of salt has its limits, however. In many dishes, especially those that are sweet, the taste of salt should be imperceptible. In such dishes salt should bring out desirable qualities in the dish but not overpower them. Although few people in Juubche' have the kitchen equipment to bake, most consume breads and pastries on a regular basis, purchasing them from itinerant vendors who drive through the town each evening. Doña Cristina, a woman in her fifties, once explained to me that she did not like one baker's products because they were "k'as ch'ooch', k'as ch'ujuk" (somewhat salty, somewhat sweet). I was surprised by her assessment because these baked goods had tasted, to me, no different from the sweet breads and cookies of other local bakers. Upon comparing the baked goods again, I could taste a very subtle saltiness in the one baker's products, yet I am certain that I would have never perceived the difference had she not drawn my attention to it. A few other residents expressed similar critiques of this baker's products to me, piquing my interest in how such critiques, and the tastes upon which they depend, develop and come to be in sync with one another.

Saltiness is a familiar quality and one that demonstrates the ways in which connoisseurship has been displayed and reproduced, and the ways in which palates have been shaped over time to taste similarly in Juubche'. As a foodstuff that is widely available throughout this region and has been for centuries, salt and the flavor it imparts are logical foci for a study of collective tastes. Yet the use of salt is changing in Yucatán as already (heavily) salted industrial foods make their way into rural homes in unprecedented quantities. An analysis of these new foodstuffs and the new culinary hierarchies to which they are linked suggest shifts in connoisseurship and the palates that it presents and shapes.

For residents of Juubche' the socially knowable qualities of well-established foodstuffs embody a host of social and cosmic relations. These relations are often obscured in the case of newer mass-produced foods. The mysterious conditions behind the production of such foods and their novel tastes challenge the local culinary hierarchy and deeply rooted habits. Mass-produced foods that do not require additional culinary "tinkering," such as the addition of salt, re-educate eaters in novel ways. Among the most heartily embraced of new commodity foods in this region are mass-produced potato and corn chips. These foods are different from more established or locally produced foodstuffs, even those we might classify as snacks, for several reasons. First, unlike in the United States, where many eaters consume chips alongside a sandwich, residents of Juubche' always consume chips as snacks, usually with soft drinks. In the past, local snacking was largely confined to fruit consumption, most often fruits that one had available in a home garden and could share generously with kin and guests. Such norms for hospitality persist: when women initiate the purchase of snack foods such as chips, they almost always share them, usually with everyone present. Still, few families have the resources to purchase large quantities of such food on a regular basis. Furthermore, as described in chapter 3, adults rarely buy them just for their own consumption while in Juubche'. With the exception of pregnancy cravings, women cannot justify the expenditure of precious funds on snack foods for themselves. While some men purchase such foods during work or travel outside the village, they tend to eat home-cooked foods in Juubche'. The individual consumption of store-bought snack foods is largely limited to children, who are often indulged with regard to food, especially in their younger years.

Second, consumers of such foods in Juubche', children and adults alike, often lack knowledge about the origins and conditions of production of purchased chips. In the case of locally produced foods, their composition, place of origin, and the labor entailed by their production are embedded in local practice and knowledge. New industrial foods hold unclear qualities and emerge from unfamiliar processes of production. Unlike even sopa fría and ensalada, the ways in which one consumes them and how they "ought" to taste are entirely separate from any local culinary practice and hierarchy of knowledge. Mass-produced food commodities such as chips require unique sets of cultural knowledge to guide their purchase and consumption, but they do not demand preparation and, thus, no culinary know-how. The experts on their consumption are quite often those least skilled in any, new or old, culinary arts: children, the most avid consumers of these foods. Children are the connoisseurs and actively educate the rest of the community in the consumption of these snacks, especially about when they ought to be consumed and what health qualities they do or do not hold. Integrating nutritional information acquired in school with corporate claims, they teach their elders which chips have the highest fat content and which taste best.

Hence these snacks are different from well-established dishes not only in the conceptual and geographical distance between their production and their consumption, but also in the span within which knowledge about them circulates. Unlike with older dishes, the culinary knowledge of which moves mostly in Juubche' and similar communities, knowledge about how to consume industrial snacks comes largely from corporate advertising. There is the occasional local spin put on a food—some children in Juubche' like to eat Charritos, a mass-produced corn chip, with the juice from a can of pickled jalapeños—but, for the most part, chips are eaten as is, out of the bag and between meals. Austin and Kohn (1990) describe how Sabritas, Mexico's most popular brand of snack foods and, since 1966, a subsidiary of PepsiCo, pursued a "small bags in small stores" approach to distributing and marketing. In rural and urban communities across the nation, the company touted chips as a modern food to be consumed immediately after purchasing or "on the go" more generally. Indeed, consumption of chips in Juubche' largely mirrors this marketing message; I never saw the "party-size" bags common in the United States. Individual-sized bags were most common and were usually consumed in a single sitting.

Corporate instructions for consumption differ radically from the gradual acquisition of gastronomic skills by earlier generations: knowledge and bodily practices passed down by generations with occasional revisions inspired by biomedicine or urban lifestyles. Of course, the connoisseurs of these new snacks, children, do pass on knowledge of how one ought to consume them, but this is an inversion of the established culinary and gastronomic hierarchies. Perhaps even more importantly, learning how to consume these foods and to accept and enjoy their tastes might be reshaping palates that have been taught to taste in other ways—to be attentive to subtle over- or undersalting, for example. In previous generations and even still today, children might consume orange slices with a sprinkling of salt, remarking on and debating a preferred quantity of that salt with those in their company. As purchased snack foods replace locally grown or produced foodstuffs, industrially salted foods demand less of their consumers. The elderly sometimes lament their grandchildren's refusal eat the most healthful and well-established dishes. Like foodstuffs themselves, palates increasingly exhibit industrial origins, requiring no tinkering by local cooks. Korsmeyer (1999) writes, "The ability to educate one's palate is an almost uniquely human trait" (93). While tastes are often naturalized, they are always subject to change, and the influx of highly palatable, industrial foods in Juubche' is doing just that, perhaps more quickly than in the past.

For the time being, established foodstuffs and the gastronomic hierarchies that they support remain a central part in Juubche'. Furthermore, the reproduction of culinary standardization through connoisseurship helps to maintain local ideals of consensus and tranquility. New foodstuffs broaden the possibilities of connoisseurship and challenge older hierarchies, but for now their preparation and consumption continue to fit within this pattern of culinary standardization: there are, according to the newest gastronomic connoisseurs, proper times, places, and manners of consuming ensalada and corn chips. Novelty comes to coexist alongside the pleasures of predictability. What remains to be seen is whether the qualities of these new foodstuffs, as they are experienced in Juubche', and the education of palates that they require, will reshape tastes enough to dismantle older hierarchies.

Conclusion

The oldest residents of Juubche' occasionally remarked on the stories they had heard from their own elders about the times of *esclavitud* (slavery), when many indigenous Yucatecans labored on haciendas, producing profit for the regional and global elites. While no one, young or old, harbored any romantic illusions about milpa agriculture being easy, and indeed some young people made strong associations between poverty and the milpa, that form of labor is distinguished from esclavitud in popular discourse in the community. Even in a context of intense precarity, when one's fate as a food producer is vulnerable to forces ranging from the weather to trade policies, the work of the milpa and its attendant activities remains meaningful labor, for a multitude of reasons elaborated throughout this book. But as wage labor practices supplant milpa agriculture, this history of esclavitud looms large, with some wage labor opportunities bearing an appalling resemblance to the exploitative haciendas of the past.[1]

In February 2008 labor recruiters came to Juubche' looking for workers to harvest papayas on the property of a larger grower. Workers were promised earnings of 120 pesos each day of the six-day workweek. Two buses would bring them there, and they would be fed free of charge. They were to leave Juubche' at 5 a.m. and return at 6 p.m. About one hundred people from Juubche' boarded the bus the next day, heading to a plantation about an hour and a half away. Don Máximo, don Tino, and doña Patricia all went. They didn't return until 7:30 that evening and reported that the next morning they had to leave even earlier, 4:30 a.m. Apparently they were not fed for free either; they were charged fifteen pesos for a meal. On the second day don Máximo opted to bring his own food (tortillas and eggs with tomato, onion, and chile). At the end of the second day, they did not return until almost 9 p.m., and they were told that they would have to leave Juubche' at 3:30 a.m. on the third day, with no increase in daily wage. Don Máximo decided he would not return.

Don Tino and doña Patricia, who were in more dire financial straits than don Máximo, boarded the bus to the papaya plantation on the fourth day, along with what they estimated to be about seven hundred workers from Juubche' and other rural communities. They finished the workweek before giving up; earning roughly eleven U.S. dollars a day for over twelve hours of hard labor and three hours of travel was simply unbearable. Still in need of cash, doña Patricia sold her gold chain to another sister-in-law for some quick cash, and don Tino gathered firewood for sale.

Then in their fifties, doña Patricia and don Tino had never attended school. They lived on a rocky parcel of land with few fruit trees, and their home was relatively spare compared to those of others in the community. Don Tino began hauling water for his mother at the age of seven and begin accompanying his stepfather to his milpa a few years later. He was a skilled butcher, hired to slaughter cattle and pigs on an informal basis by relatives and neighbors. Doña Patricia, the daughter of a midwife, knew many plant-based remedies. She had a quick tongue, a gift for witty *báaxal t'aan* (play-talk), and a wonderfully deep laugh that I could recognize from a block away. The couple raised their children, now parents themselves, during the development of regional tourism, the peso devaluation of 1980s, and the implementation of NAFTA in the 1990s. For most of his adult life, don Tino has migrated temporarily to Cancún, Cozumel, and other tourist hubs, taking time away from his work in the milpa to earn much-needed cash. The couple has frequently struggled, often unable to seek medical care when they need it and often in need of loans from kin. Although not entirely devalued by their family and neighbors in Juubche', their skills—honed in the milpa, the forest, and the kitchen—bring few returns in contemporary Mexican society.

The Future

Early in the development of Cancún as a tourist destination, state planners hoped to develop relationships between local farmers and tourist hotels and restaurants. Yet, for the most part, these relationships never materialized, and small-scale food production on the peninsula has suffered.[2] Meanwhile rural farmers such as don Tino have struggled to balance milpa agriculture with temporary migration, producing yet smaller yields on increasingly degraded lands (Torres and Momsen 2005). Scholars such as Levy (2008) raise concerns about a reduction of land holdings among Mexico's rural poor due to population growth and continued depletion of the land as a result of agricultural overuse. The implementation of NAFTA in 1994 and the dismantling of price controls, among other neoliberal policies in the 1980s and 1990s, greatly reduced the profit potential of small-scale agriculture (Gálvez 2018; Vega-Leinhert 2008); if farmers are lucky enough to produce a surplus on a small and degraded plot of land, they are unlikely to make a significant profit on the sale of those surplus crops. It is not hard then to understand the necessity for wage labor, even when it pays poorly and demands hard, often dangerous work. For many families, such labor is the only way to earn enough cash to purchase food, build masonry homes, and buy children's school materials. In communities such as Juubche' and elsewhere in the eastern part of the Yucatán Peninsula, the wage labor opportunities provided by tourism have served as a release valve, mitigating the devastating effects of Mexico's neoliberal turn in the 1980s and preventing large-scale waves of transnational migration to the United States, like those from other rural regions of Mexico.

But just as a tumultuous economy and unjust detention and deportation policies in the United States have threatened transnational migrants' abilities to survive and flourish, the tourist industry and domestic policies in Mexico jeopardize the well-being of those who remain at, or close to, home. There are growing concerns about the sustainability of tourism in the Yucatán Peninsula. As Cancún has lost its allure with the wealthiest of tourists, the industry is looking to cut costs on the wages it pays workers and on the price it pays for foodstuffs, disproportionately affecting small-scale local producers (Torres 2003). While the industry continues to grow and spread south toward the border with Belize, the extension of what's referred to as the "Riviera Maya," recent increases in violence in the region have caused some concern (Glusac 2018). Tourists are attracted most of all to the region's beaches and archaeological sites, and yet these spaces are vulnerable to overuse, threatening their very appeal to visitors (Kandelaars 2000; Redclift 2005). For government officials and tourist industry executives, the potential loss of "pristine" natural spaces with which to lure tourists seems of greater concern to them than do the long-term ramifications of the industry for the region's working poor. Yet the most recent example of "mega-development" in the region appears to demonstrate concern for neither environmental or human well-being (Narcia 2019). Current president Andrés Manuel López Obrador's plan to proceed with a project known as Tren Maya (Maya Train) would bring large numbers of tourists inland, including to some parts of the peninsula and elsewhere in southern Mexico that have been relatively inaccessible due to their distance from airports and a lack of roads. Critics of the plan have pointed to the likely adverse environmental effects of the project, as well as the incursions onto the land of indigenous communities that the train network's construction would require (Lichtinger and Aridjis 2018).

Although the Tren Maya would not run through the community of Juubche', its effects would reverberate through the region. Perhaps the network would provide jobs closer to home, reducing the need for circular and transnational migration across southern Mexico. But if the development of Cancún and the Riviera Maya is any indication of what is to come, political and cultural elites, Mexican and foreign, would likely gain the most. The role of rural indigenous migrants in the development of coastal tourism on the peninsula has been crucial but constrained by structural inequalities and deeply ingrained racism: often relegated to the hard labor of construction, the majority, and the most marginalized, of these migrants rarely receive permanent jobs once construction is complete (Daltabuit and Pi-Sunyer 1990). Their labor positions are usually precarious, and their economic welfare has become dependent upon the growth of an industry that continues to expand in fits and starts but with signs of slowing down (hence tourism's move inland). The participation of rural migrants in wage labor on the Caribbean coast has brought some benefits according to those workers and their kin: more material goods above all but also some easing of the population pressure that made farmland scarce, as some of those migrants settle permanently in urban centers. However, others living and working in the region—non-indigenous Yucatecans, Mexicans from outside of the peninsula, and foreigners—have enjoyed more benefits from the development of regional tourism. For many rural indigenous people in this region, as both Castellanos (2010) and Reyes-Cortes (2011) poignantly demonstrate, the changes of recent decades present a predicament: in particular, men no longer know how to or have any desire to farm, and yet the skills they have acquired in school or on work sites rarely bring them the economic security or social status they desire. Even the potential increase in earnings the Tren Maya may bring to rural communities comes with its own risks. As Gálvez (2018) argues in her analysis of post-NAFTA Mexican diets, increased access to cash in a context of increasingly ubiquitous industrial foods (in Juubche', consumed in place of janal), together with the rapid decline of milpa agriculture, creates conditions for tremendous suffering, most visible in bodily ailments such as diabetes and kidney disease.

This book does not claim that such social and economic shifts exert transformative forces on a "traditional" or "folk" community. An essentializing argument would ignore centuries of engagement with colonial influence, the Mexican state, and foreign tourists, among others entities. Like any community, Juubche' has changed since its settlement. Many residents have left and settled in urban centers or other rural towns, while some current residents grew up in cities such as Valladolid and Tulum. At the same time, the people of Juubche', like all of us, live in bodies and within communities that are repositories of the past with residual structures and dispositions, despite constant transformations. For many rural indigenous Yucatecans, these structures and dispositions have been shaped by subsistence practices and the cosmologies that have supported them. Reflected in a myth of creation, in which human flesh was formed by ground corn, and reproduced through many forms of ritual life (Gustafson 2002; Hanks 1990; Redfield and Villa Rojas [1934] 1962), rural indigenous assumptions about the essence of human materiality and the nature of human morality have been rooted in an understanding of humanity as deeply tied to and sustained by the natural world. This relationship is one of care between humans and the other living entities, such as deities, natural forces, plants, and animals, upon which they depend for food. The reliance on food is a source of bodily vulnerability—humans must ingest foodstuffs in order to survive—and a motive for human practice in the world. In their need for food, humans must sustain the cycles of the universe and contribute to the survival and reproduction of its other inhabitants. Many people in Juubche' perform these duties with awareness of the agentive potential of these other inhabitants, and the networks of action unfolding in the universe are not always mutually beneficial. Nonhuman entities sometimes care in ways that support human interests and the larger social order, but they can also challenge and disrupt, as they are prone to many of the weaknesses with which humans too are cursed. Unlike plants and animals, however, humans and deities are capable of *tuukul* (thinking), and while they recognize the unpredictability and unruliness of the world, they hold greater responsibility for maintaining order.

Despite a move away from subsistence practices for many residents, order for the people of Juubche' is still envisioned and experienced as balance. This sense of balance applies not only to the body as an individual entity seeking to survive. The logics enacted in care practices reveal interpersonal imperatives as well. From pre-Hispanic rites of renewal to the payment of colonial tribute to the contemporary system of ejido, the insecurity of survival at the level of the household, the unit within which everyday food production and consumption usually occurred, was eased by established practices of collective labor and ritual activity. Survival was, as Farriss (1984) calls it, a "collective enterprise," a social endeavor that itself had implications for individuals and their abilities, on their own or in groups, to keep the universe in balance. Throughout this work, I stress the ways in which forms of balance—bodily, social, and cosmic—have been deeply intertwined for residents of Juubche' and how care practices, in their motives, their processes, and their implications, echo and strive to achieve this. At the same time, I have tried to make clear the incoherencies and tensions that arise when forms of balance and the care practices that work to produce them call each other into question. So many of the daily pleasures and pains of the people of Juubche' are contingent upon diverse and sometimes contradictory forms of care (and a lack thereof), upon their own successes and failures, those of people close to them, those of the state and its neoliberal economic policies, and those of supernatural entities. Widespread poverty in Juubche' reflects a long history of residents' structural vulnerability vis-à-vis the Mexican state and the economic and political interests it has historically prioritized. But I also take seriously in this work the literal agency of other forces largely beyond residents' control, such as the vipers that slither through the brush or the unexpected wind that turns the burning of a milpa into a deadly endeavor. The threat of disorder is constant and compels human action to contain it. The changes of the last few decades are significant because, for many people in Juubche', these changes do not just threaten the conditions for balance and survival; they transform them.

The first time I visited don Erasmo in his home in Juubche', I was startled by his appearance. The former farmer in his early seventies lay in his hammock, extremely thin with constantly trembling hands. He had developed *nervios*, his wife told me, after an argument with a relative four years ago, and he had been bedridden since. Don Erasmo's voice shook like his hands, and I could not always understand his words. However, he spoke more clearly when he reflected on life today compared to the past. He told me, "Today nothing is cheap. Everything is expensive. Today life is very difficult. If you don't go work, you won't earn anything. You won't survive." His survival was made possible by the care of his kin, especially through food: the broths his wife spooned into his mouth, the crackers she broke up into small pieces for him.

In her analysis of beauty ideals among Azawagh Arabs in Niger, Popenoe (2004) reminds us that some cultural forms shift more slowly than others. Bodies, for all of their concrete links to the material world around them, may still hold tight to the habits and values of the past. Bodies are always in flux, shaping and being shaped by that which is outside them. Yet the pace of change can be uneven: as limits are drawn and redrawn, the material within them transforms at varying speeds. Throughout this book, I look back to the past of my informants' ancestors not to make claims for broad cultural continuity but rather to demonstrate why certain cultural forms have persisted despite shifts in these individuals' worlds. This persistence is crucial to understanding why and how care is important to the people of Juubche' and why it is exercised largely through food, for it has worked enough, on levels that we might define as material, psychological, or social, to continually serve as an organizing logic for many valued practices.

Although care strategies are often habits, they have always been experimental, ways of tinkering and adjusting to always changing conditions. Today, established care practices are even more experimental, for residents of Juubche' are not always sure if these practices are effective in rapidly changing worlds and for rapidly changing bodies. Meanwhile, residents are also testing novel ways of caring in contexts recognizable and strange. They eat new foods, mull over the bodily sensations those foods produce, and try to make sense of the processes of production and consumption that surround them. They understand familiar and unfamiliar forms of suffering through multiple systems of knowledge and pursue well-being through diverse and sometimes conflicting healing practices. Self-interest becomes embedded in more varied notions of the self, creating doubts about what kinds of balance one ought to pursue. Again, it is not that such gaps and questions did not plague rural Yucatecans in periods past, but rather that they were then able to reconcile them within the space for disorder provided by the established cosmology, rooted in food production and preparation. That cosmology, although it was often reshaped in response to sometimes radical political and economic shifts, continued to resonate with some rural people, due to its deep connections to the material conditions of their everyday lives. Sustained during periods of tumult through continued participation in milpa agriculture and related ritual activities, these connections shaped sensory fields and bodily dispositions that, as my findings suggest, have been enduring. If care as an organizing logic developed in response to life under difficult conditions and was shaped by the possibilities for pleasure within those conditions, how will it transform under significantly altered conditions full of new possibilities (and, of course, new constraints)? As it comes to enact a multiplicity of influences and desires, will it unfold with

9. Lunch of *puchero*, rice, and tortillas. Courtesy of Justin Nevin.

intentions and implications too disparate for it to comprise an organized logic? Does this merely reflect new conditions for survival for rural Yucatecans, or will it also hinder their ability to act under such conditions? Will food remain both an object and actor in practices of care?

Don Erasmo was kept alive by the care of his family. No longer able to produce food, he relied on others for sustenance. His hammock was hung in the front room of the family's compound, a place where he could listen and sometimes join in conversations among kin and visiting guests. If the post-NAFTA economy renders those cannot work "nobodies" and "*ni-nis*" (Gálvez 2018; Green 2011),[3] then care, as it is practiced by don Erasmo's kin, resists this violence and erasure. In Juubche' practices of care were long partnered with feelings of being cared for by other actors: foodstuffs, deities, and kin especially. Established ways of caring, such as working the milpa as though one is part of a dynamic and care-dependent social order, or preparing, distributing, and consuming food as a member both of an economically interdependent household and of a greater cosmos, must now contend with new forms of practice. Of course, such adjustments are part of human experience, of the constant tinkering we all must do, but over the last four decades, the people of Juubche', like other rural poor in Mexico, have been disproportionately affected by the economic policies and political agendas of Mexico and North America more generally.

On my most recent stay in Juubche' in 2017, I visited a woman I'd known since my first visit, a quiet neighbor without children. Doña Ximena slowly pulled a sock off her foot to show me where her toes had recently been amputated. Her diabetes had worsened in the couple of years since I'd last seen her. Food remains a way in which life and that which is good is sustained in Juubche'. I ate and laughed with dozens of residents on that visit, marveling, as I always do when I am there, at the hard work and expertise that went into the creation of delicious meals, all of which were shared beyond the limits of individual households. In the heat of the late spring weather, I could even romanticize the cold Coca-Cola we shared, the generosity with which hosts topped off glasses. At that time, as I had done on other steamy days, while eating flavorful food with a cold soft drink, I thought how very good the two tasted together: complementary, balanced. But visiting doña Ximena reminded me that care through food may have its limits, especially when food carries risks that are unknowable, at least at first, or unavoidable, under a rapidly shifting and murky food system. Does care carry the same meanings, accomplish the same good, when is it detached from janal? Indeed care's power, its effectiveness in this region, has been both its attentiveness to risk and its adaptability, but as it is slowly severed of its connection to and its origins in particular ways of living—of making food and sustaining life—perhaps it risks adapting too well.

NOTES

INTRODUCTION

1. Berkley (1998) found that in a town not far from Juubche' *meyah* refers to multiple forms of work—men's and women's labor, subsistence agriculture, and wage labor—while *trabaahoh* refers only to wage labor. In Juubche' *trabaajoj* refers to situations or things that are annoying or burdensome, such as preparing separate meals for children or having to deal with a bureaucratic nuisance such as medical paperwork.

2. Disparities in economic and political power are not a product of colonization alone. Ancient Maya commoners lived under constraints imposed by elite Maya and, at times, by outside groups.

3. Of the eighty-three Juubche' residents I interviewed over the age of thirty, all reported that farming is or had been their fathers' primary labor activity. Within that same group fifty-four reported they or their husbands currently or previously farmed. Among interviewees under the age of thirty, only two out of thirty-three reported they or a spouse pursued agriculture as a primary form of labor.

4. See also Castellanos (2010); Eiss (2010); Loewe (2010).

5. See also Kray (1997); Re Cruz (1996).

6. See also Castellanos (2010); Greene (2002).

7. See also Bascope (2005); Loewe (2010).

8. See Eiss (2010, 225) for a description of the sip in one town in western Yucatán.

9. Whether a Yucatec Maya speaker uses *kalan* or *kanan* often seems to vary regionally or with context. In Juubche' residents use both, and I could not ascertain any pattern with regard to which word was used when or by whom (e.g., those native to Juubche' as opposed to those born in other parts of the region).

10. English translations of the Spanish words are from Merriam-Webster (2012).

11. Stross notes that some speakers of the Mopan Maya language refer to a certain plant as *x-kanan* (guardian [of the forest]) (2006, 583).

12. Excluding, say, personal or natural disaster.

13. See Eiss (2010) and Loewe (2010) on contemporary acts of religious devotion. See Greene (2002, 90–92) on changes in *jetsmek* ceremonies, a rite of passage for infants. See Castellanos (2010, 182) on the trend of holding more distinctly "Maya" weddings.

1. THE FORCE WITH WHICH WE LIVE

1. Distribuidora Conasupo (DICONSA) is the current incarnation of what used to be CONASUPO (Compania Nacional de Subsistencias Populares) and is intended to supply marginalized populations with low-cost food staples (Secretaría de Desarollo Social 2012). As CONASUPO, the program long provided price supports that aided local farmers, but Mexico's trend toward neoliberal economic policies led to the elimination of this part of the program in the late 1990s. Many of the products sold through DICONSA today are imports from a handful of large corporations (Vega-Leinhert 2008).

2. Ebel and Castillo Cocom (2012) find similar perceptions of farming among young men in another rural community.

3. In contrast, cattle raising is a high-status activity that has long been associated with ts'uulo'ob. Men perform nearly all related labor, and many ranchers hire workers to do this work. I knew only one young woman who performed ranch labor; she helped her brothers feed their father's cattle until she married.

4. For an exhaustive account of food consumption in several indigenous Yucatecan communities in the 1920s and 1930s see Benedict and Steggerda (1936).

5. Many of my informants recall that Juubche' was home to at least three bakers from the 1960s through the 1980s. The construction of roads linking the community to neighboring towns increased competition from itinerant bakers, and the original bakers' children opted out of their families' businesses.

6. Other dishes prepared *onsikil* (with many squash seeds) include *onsikilbil bu'ul* (beans with squash seeds), *onsikilbil kej* (venison with squash seeds), and *onsikilbil chay* (chaya with squash seeds).

7. One older, well-off couple had a *fogón* (stone stove) in their kitchen. They explained to me that they had it built out of concerns for the smoke produced from the more common three-stone hearths. Compared to others of their generation, they subscribed to many biomedical assumptions, perhaps encouraged by their daughter who worked as a nurse.

8. See, e.g., Bourdieu ([1979] 1984); Sutton (2001).

2. GIVING LIFE TO OURSELVES

1. Povinelli (2006) writes of sickness acquired in her research with Aboriginal Australians, "I, too, must decide whether I will inhabit a life-world in which sharing a sore is a necessary precondition of being together, side-by-side, one cup, food that travels from mouth to mouth" (57). As with Povinelli in her Australian field site, the decision to share in Juubche' did not preclude the privilege of particular forms of care, such as biomedical treatment, available to me, but not to my friends in the community.

2. Chile peppers are one of a number of foods that residents avoid while taking biomedical drugs. They believe that potential interactions cause one to become "intoxicated" and develop a rash.

3. By the Late Preclassic period, 400 BC to 100 AD, maize came to form much of the Yucatec Maya diet (Farriss 1984).

4. Of particular concern to the Yucatec Maya was that they were no longer permitted to use municipal funds, over the bulk of which they had long exercised control, to fund their fiestas and other practices devoted to the saints. At the same time, the bishop decided to take control of the indigenous *cofradías*, the local groups designed to ensure the good of the community, especially in religious matters. The common lands held by the cofradías were soon appropriated as well; the Yucatec Maya retained access only if the Creoles did not desire the land to expand their commercial enterprises (Farriss 1984).

5. The commonly shared story tells of Leandro Poot, the son of one Yucatec Maya rebel leader, recounting: "All at once the *sh'mataneheeles* (winged ants, harbingers of the first rain) appeared in great clouds to the north, to the south, to the east, and to the west, all over the world. When my father's people saw this they said to themselves and to their brothers, 'Ehen! The time has come for us to make our planting, for if we do not we shall have no Grace of God to fill the bellies of our children'" (quoted in Reed 1964, 99).

6. The Yucatecan army made several unsuccessful attempts to pacify them, but it did not succeed until the early twentieth century, after five decades of rebellion, much of it indirectly funded by the rebel Yucatec Maya's sale of chicle to American gum manufacturers (Redclift 2004).

7. The Mexican state had declared Quintana Roo a territory, separate from the state of Yucatán, in 1902, striking the state of Yucatán political and economic

blows (Joseph 1988). The Revolution arrived earlier in Quintana Roo, in 1912, than in Yucatán, and at first the Mexican state attempted to make alliances with the rebel Yucatec Maya there (Redclift 2004).

8. The óol can also be thought of as a type of soul, though it must be distinguished from *pixaan*, which I will address in more depth chapter 3. As mentioned earlier in this chapter, pixaan are souls that survive after physical death. Surviving kin must tend to the pixaan periodically. Kray (1997) explains, "Rather than being strictly contained by the body, the pixaan floats in and around it" (345).

9. Given the description of the *tíip'te'* as the center of the circulatory system, it is unclear whether Bourdin and his informants are using "heart" to refer to the tíip'te', the *puksi'ik'al*, a locally recognized organ, or the biomedical heart.

10. As with other Yucatec Maya nouns that begin with vowels, consonants are added to *óol* to indicate its possession: *w* for the first and second persons, and *y* for the third person.

11. I use quotation marks where "hot" and "cold" refer to classification within the hot-cold syndrome.

12. The roots of the hot-cold syndrome are highly debated. Foster (1978, 1986, 1994) argues that the humoral theories common in sixteenth-century Spain profoundly influenced health beliefs and practices in that country's Latin American colonies. López Austin (1969, 1975, 1980, 1986) and Chevalier and Sánchez Bain (2003) counter by suggesting that the pre-Conquest Mesoamerican worldview structured human relationships with the natural and supernatural worlds through the classification of hot and cold foods, plants, objects, bodily states, and bodily organs. The influence of European humoralism is evident, but as Chevalier and Sánchez Bain (2003) detail, there are numerous features of that belief system that are entirely absent in the Latin American hot-cold syndrome (12). Chevalier and Sánchez Bain's argument that the hot-cold syndrome has mostly indigenous roots suggests that similarities in the syndrome across Mexico and other parts of Central America may be the product of cultural exchange both pre- and post-Conquest. Indeed, archeological evidence points to regular trade and conflict across Mesoamerica prior to the arrival of the Spanish (Roys [1943] 1972; Smith and Berdan 2010), suggesting that indeed features of the hot-cold syndrome were likely diffused throughout the region well before the colonial period. Although many common principles can be observed, the categorization of foods, elements such as wind and rain, activities, and organs can vary greatly. McCullough (1973) posits that the hot-cold syndrome in Yucatán is adaptive in that it may prevent heatstroke. Yet

even in parts of rural Yucatán with nearly identical climates, professed beliefs and observed practices differ.

13. Older residents distinguish puksi'ik'al from the coorazon and locate it at the base of the ribcage, above the navel. Some of my younger informants classified the coorazon and the puksi'ik'al as the same organ.

14. In Juubche', in contrast to other communities, the cold to hot transition is not generally a source of anxiety, and states that may be "cold" elsewhere are considered "hot" here. While Kray (1997) finds that her informants worry about a "cold" sleeping body's adjustment to the hot beverages of the morning, my informants believe the body is "hot" while asleep and that one must be careful to avoid the shock of "cold" air or substances upon waking.

15. Water is classified as "cold" unless it has been heated. In the mornings residents are careful to rinse their mouths with water that had been heated over the fire.

16. Of course, on other occasions our illnesses worried those same hosts, who urged us to care for our bodies in the ways they cared for theirs.

17. The four types of assistance include cash transfers to the following: the elderly; pregnant or lactating women and mothers of infants, young toddlers, and malnourished children up to age four, designed to supplement nutrition; mothers of children attending school (cash transfers depend upon grade and gender of each child attending); and female heads of household.

18. Smith-Oka (2013) presents an in-depth analysis of women's interactions with the Oportunidades program in one rural Mexican community.

19. As Re Cruz (1998) and Kintz (1998) also argue, women, especially those whose husbands migrate for work, have maintained more established gender roles— caring for children, preparing food, laundering clothes—while taking on important duties outside of the home as well, such as making decisions about education and business.

3. IF IT TASTES GOOD

1. In speaking of marriage, female residents of Juubche' form the phrase for "giving themselves in marriage" from the root *sii*. Bastarracha Manzano and Canto Rosado (2003) gloss *sii* as the Spanish *regalar* (to gift) (216).

2. See Callahan (2005, 344–46) for his analysis of privacy in the town of Coba. In Juubche' talk of these intimate practices is not nearly as closely guarded as the practices themselves are.

3. Callahan (2005) argues that open doors themselves can be seen to clear inhabitants of suspicions about unseemly behavior indoors (346).

4. Elsewhere (Wynne 2015), I have written about how, in this way, male migration makes possible something comparable to what Williams-Forson (2011) calls a "culinary cooperative" (142).

5. See also Holmes (1978) and Kramer (2005) for more descriptions of everyday food exchanges.

6. Few homes in Juubche' have adequate storage space to keep larger quantities of foodstuffs fresh and safe from animals and insects. A large box of crackers would go stale in the humid climate before a family could consume it, and most families do not have refrigerators to keep larger bottles of soft drinks cold. Second, many households have sporadic and limited incomes. They might purchase a small packet of instant coffee, enough to last a few days, rather than invest in a jar that would last several weeks at five or six times the price.

7. Of course, as I explore later this chapter, the marital relationship structures the flow of most goods and services within the household, but other than clothes and other personal items, few possessions are thought of individually.

8. Holmes (1978) finds that fear of appearing stingy with one's kin leads many indigenous Yucatecan men and parents to indulge their wives and children while out in public (80–81).

9. That both *chingar* and *top* have sexual and gendered connotations is not surprising, but among many Mexicans and Mexican Americans *chingar* is also a racialized term that refers back to La Chingada, or Malinche, the indigenous woman who is thought to be the mother of the first mixed-race Mexican, hence her fucked-ness (Anzaldúa 1987; Paz [1961] 2008). As such, for some populations *chingar* harkens back to a hierarchy of power based on racial and wealth distinctions that remains highly relevant (Castellanos 2011).

10. Perhaps I was not privy to its use in reference to foreigners because I myself was a foreigner. Additionally, I certainly observed and participated in many more conversations with women than I did with men, the latter of whom usually have more contact with outsiders. Still, interactions with relatives and neighbors seem to evoke the feeling of being screwed more than relations with outsiders or structural inequities.

11. Here again, kin and community members seem most threatening. In his examination of Yucatec Maya folklore Rugeley (2001b) finds that evildoers were most often kin or other members of the community (22).

12. Such qualities are encouraged in children; Castellanos (2003) writes, "Indeed, the desire for their children to not be screwed or harmed in life constitutes one

of the main reasons why Yucatec Maya parents constantly push their children to be alert" (251).

13. Of course, food refusals are sometimes based on distrust of the giver's cooking skills or hygiene. Don Máximo once listed for me the homes from which he would not eat food. A few of the women cooking in those households simply did not make good ki' waaj, he explained. In some homes he was disturbed by other factors: one neighbor, he noted with disgust, used her floor, where dogs walked, as a workspace for filling tamales.

14. Similarly, Greene (2002) describes elderly informants' memories of sharing a sole egg with many siblings (114). At the same time I also heard stories of periods of great abundance: tall piles of corn and sweet potatoes, large populations of deer and other wildlife, and trees weighed down by fruit.

15. Her actual words were: "Xla-Coka ku otsilkintiko'on!" Andrade (1955) translates the *xla*- prefix to "old" but notes that the *x*- indicates femaleness, often in a disparaging way. For example, residents in Juubche' might prefix the name of a young woman they see as morally suspect with the *x*- or even *xla*- but would not use those prefixes if talking about a respected woman.

16. See Castellanos (2003), Greene (2002), and Juarez (1996) for comparisons between male and female migration experiences in the region. Few women from Juubche' migrate to Cancún or other coastal cities.

17. Smith-Oka (2013) argues that while the program's premise rests upon women's empowerment, it often coerces them into a project of social engineering in which their own knowledge and desires are devalued.

18. Sigal (2000) writes of ancient Yucatec Maya attitudes toward desire: "The Maya nobles claimed desire to be a problematic presence, one that could destroy society. Yet it was also a presence that could replicate society and make it grow. Those with sexual desires most often were those with power, those who could create and destroy the world. Desire was a powerful and dangerous force, a flow which, when unleashed, could either destroy society or enhance life. It had this power because desire could please or displease the gods, the nobles, and the commoners alike" (41).

19. See also Holmes (1978, 103–4). Adapon (2008) describes one woman's response— and culinary revenge—to her husband's adultery in a semi-rural community near Mexico City. Doña Marta, knowing that her husband would have eaten a full meal with his lover before returning to his marital home, prepared him a meal that she then served to him in a large portion, which according to local

norms he had to eat (81). Men too can exact food-related revenge on their wives. After a domestic dispute over his drinking, the husband of Noemi, a young woman in Juubche', refused to eat her cooking. When he returned home from the milpa, he would first head to his mother's home where he dined, fully aware that Noemi was also preparing food for him. After three days of this, Noemi left with her children for a visit to her home village a half an hour away.

20. Presumably, young men, especially those who begin working in coastal resort areas after secondary school, have ample opportunity to pursue premarital sexual relationships if they so desire. Later in life, some men take on more permanent adulterous relationships outside of the village; as I discuss later, these often present economic and emotional challenges for wives at home.

21. Woodrick (1995) notes, "Within a month after an elopement the bride's mother-in-law ought to visit the home of the girl's parents and present them with gifts of food. During her visit she assures the girl's parents that she and her husband accept their new daughter-in-law. She asks the couple to pardon their daughter's elopement" (223). Regardless of how marriage is formalized, legal divorce is very rare in Juubche', especially after church weddings, but a few cases of abandonment, by either husband or wife, seem to occur most years. The social pressure against such actions is great enough that, according to my informants, the abandoning partner never remains in the community if a formal marriage occurred or if the union has born children. Occasionally an "escaped" girl chooses to return to her natal home, but this almost always occurs only if she has not yet become pregnant.

22. This is the case for second marriages as well, and these marriages almost always occur after the death of a current spouse. In those occasional cases in which an adulterous relationship becomes long-term, the newly formed couple usually leaves the village.

23. Such exchanges were common for earlier generations as well. Older informants recalled gifts of drinking chocolates, sugar, liquor, and pastries. In *Chan Kom* Redfield and Villa Rojas ([1934] 1962) describe a more prolonged series of gift giving, detailing multiple visits by the groom's family to the bride's home to give such items. The process culminates with the offering of the *muhul* (marriage gift), as requested by the bride's family. The muhul includes a gold necklace, cloth, personal items for the bride, and yet more foodstuffs. After accepting the muhul, the bride's family agrees to the marriage (192–94).

24. Of course, as Castellanos (2007) notes, the reputations of migrant women from rural communities are often closely guarded. The presence of others from their

home communities in their temporary homes or neighborhoods may further limit their testing of established gender norms.

25. Holmes's (1978) earlier research notes the growing influence of *fotonovelas* (romance-oriented magazines) and *radionovelas* (radio soap operas) (227–28).

26. Of course, congregations such as those of the Jehovah's Witnesses more strongly condemn adultery and other acts of sex outside of marriage. While this is significant, I argue that more than official doctrine and regular rhetoric, the continued abstinence from gender-specific consumption of romantic and sexual media shapes bodily desires and moral values that make hermanas and hermanos more compatible in marriage. In interviews in Juubche', women in evangelical and Pentecostal homes report less domestic strife than women in Catholic homes in Juubche'; the alcohol consumption of many Catholic men appears to be a factor in most instances.

27. Castellanos (2010) and Greene (2002) both find that although young, single cash earners usually give a portion of their wages to their families, they do keep some for their own purchases, including clothing, makeup, and other goods.

28. There is an expansive literature on the many ways in which machismo emerges as an ideology, is embodied, and is challenged. For more in-depth and nuanced analyzes on machismo see Gutmann (1996) and Lancaster (1992).

29. While women may do all or most of the work in caring for larger domestic animals such as pigs, it is men who carry out the slaughter, the act that immediately precedes the sale of meat for cash. Similarly, it is almost always men who raise the crops that can be sold on a large scale.

30. Kray (1997) attributes this double standard to the emphasis in rural communities on women's sexual purity, arguing that those girls who have been "taken care of" by their families make more desirable candidates for marriage (100).

31. Callahan (2005) captures the dilemma that arises through the realization of such a task: "One can never really trust in one's spouse's fidelity because one can never really trust in one's own fidelity" (236).

4. SO THAT WE WON'T DIE

1. As in other communities in the region (Kray 2007), ritual activity begins on October 31, in commemoration of deceased children, rather than the Catholic calendar's November 1, followed by commemoration of deceased adults on November 1 (what is All Souls' Day, November 2, in the Catholic calendar). Events continue throughout the full month, though only the first eight days feature daily prayer sessions.

2. Watanabe (1990) uses the descriptions of Nash (1970, 207) and Reina (1966, 163) to describe the relationship between Maya individuals and the patron saints of their communities as, respectively, "standardized" and "utterly impersonal." He argues that the impetus to honor the saint is more the consequence of one's residence in a place rather than any personal appeal the saint might hold (138).

3. Numerous scholars of Maya groups have explored the potential causal relationship between the abandonment of agriculture and conversation to non-Catholic Christian denominations (see Annis 1987; Green 1993; O'Connor 2012).

4. In a small community in Quintana Roo, O'Connor (2012) finds that evangelical converts come to see farming as a "pagan" activity and often farm just enough to receive federal assistance for farmers.

5. See Anderson et al. 2005; Castañeda 2003.

6. Based on research conducted in a highland Chiapan community, Eber ([1995] 2000) writes that "Traditionalist" Catholics see ritual drinking as an integral part of relationships between humans and deities.

7. Moral critiques are applied to clear religious displays as well. During the annual fiesta, doña Patricia and don Eliecer, Catholics but not terribly active in the church, complained about how the *sacristanes* (lay leaders) had been parading the Holy Cross around the bullfight ring to collect coins almost every day rather than just on the Day of the Holy Cross. Don Eliecer called the sacristanes *loco* (crazy) and said that they just wanted to make money (for the church).

8. The fiesta is such an anticipated event that many individuals, Catholics and non-Catholics, asked me within minutes of meeting whether I would be attending the event, even when it was months away. Further evidence of its significance can be seen in the business flow of those women who sew clothing; beginning about three months before the fiesta, clients flood these women with custom orders for new dresses to wear to the event.

9. Such ritual activities were the only regular occasions during which men prepared food.

10. See Eiss (2010, 224–27) for a description of the precaution hunters take and the punishments they sometimes receive in one town in western Yucatán.

11. Norget (2006) notes that food offerings are not a part of the official Catholic form of All Souls' Day but are a central part of its celebration throughout Mexico.

12. In fact, the prohibition of alcohol consumption among Jehovah's Witnesses is a particularly attractive feature to many potential converts in Juubche'. Among other Maya groups as well, women sometimes encourage their families'

conversions to Protestant faiths so that their husbands will stop drinking (Eber [1995] 2000; Green 1993; Stoll 1993).

5. PUT A LITTLE SALT

1. Several generations ago women often had no choice but to learn to cook as well as they possibly could; prior to the local construction of roads and the labor opportunities presented by tourism, many young nuclear families moved deep into the forest where more land was available for farming. Without automobiles or even bicycles, they had to walk for hours to reach kin and larger settlements.

2. Sandwichón is a popular dish in Spain and Latin America, though it strongly resembles the "sandwich loaf" popular in mid-twentieth century American cookbooks.

3. Gálvez (2018) uses "traditional" to describe those foods representative of what she calls "milpa-based cuisine" (2). Despite the many critiques of "tradition" in anthropology, Gálvez notes that it is the way that many of the people with whom she spoke in Mexico described milpa-based foodstuffs and meals (209n8). In Juubche' people used a range of terms to distinguish well-established foods from newer foods, such as discussing them as "new" versus "old", but, as explained in chapter 1, the distinction between *janal* and other foods, which were talked about using their specific names (e.g., *sandwich*, *pizza*), was most common. These foods were not explicitly referred to categorically, but I categorize them as comprising a distinct group because of their very exclusion from the category as *janal*. For this reason I rely on the descriptor "newer" here to distinguish them.

4. Another example of a subversion of the typical guest hierarchy can be witnessed during the serving of cake at children's birthday parties. The hostesses always serve children their slices first.

CONCLUSION

1. The very title of M. Bianet Castellanos's 2010 book, *A Return to Servitude: Maya Migration and the Tourist Trade in Cancún*, suggests a similar parallel between the history of haciendas and the contemporary tourist industry.

2. Of the local food suppliers to the region's tourist establishments, many are agribusinesses that have benefited from the neoliberal economic reforms of the last few decades (Torres 2003).

3. Gálvez (2018) defines *ni-nis* as "short for *ni estudiando, ni trabajando*, people who are neither working nor studying" (xvi).

REFERENCES

Abarca, Meredith E. 2006. *Voices in the Kitchen: Views of Food and the World from Working-Class Mexican and Mexican American Women*. College Station: Texas A&M University Press.

Abel, Emily K. 1990. "Family Care of the Frail Elderly." In Abel and Nelson, *Circles of Care*, 65–91.

Abel, Emily K., and Margaret K. Nelson, eds. *Circles of Care: Work and Identity in Women's Lives*. Albany: State University of New York Press.

Abu-Lughod, Lila. 1991. "Writing against Culture." In *Recapturing Anthropology: Working in the Present*, edited by Richard G. Fox, 137–62. Santa Fe NM: School of American Research Press.

Adapon, Joy. 2008. *Culinary Art and Anthropology*. London: Berg.

Anderson, E. N. 2009. "Managing Maya Landscapes: Quintana Roo, Mexico." In *Landscape Ethnoecology: Concepts of Biotic and Physical Space*, edited by Leslie Main Johnson and Eugene S. Hunn, 255–78. Oxford: Berghahn Books.

Anderson, E. N., Aurora Dzib Zihum de Cen, Felix Medina Tzuc, and Pastor Valdez Chale. 2005. *Political Ecology in a Yucatec Maya Community*. Tucson: University of Arizona Press.

Andrade, Manuel J. 1955. *A Grammar of Modern Yucatec*. Microfilm Collection of Manuscripts on Middle American Cultural Anthropology, series 7, no. 4. Regenstein Library, University of Chicago.

Andrews, Anthony P. 1983. *Maya Salt Production and Trade*. Tucson: University of Arizona Press.

———. 1993. "Late Postclassic Lowland Maya Archaeology." *Journal of World Prehistory* 7 (1): 35–69.

Annis, Sheldon. 1987. *God and Production in a Guatemalan Town*. Austin: University of Texas Press.

Anzaldúa, Gloria. 1987. *Bordrlands/La Frontera: The New Mestiza*. San Francisco: Aunt Lute Books.

Armstrong-Fumero, Fernando. 2009. "A Heritage of Ambiguity: The Historical Substrate of Vernacular Multiculturalism in Yucatán, Mexico." *American Ethnologist* 36 (2): 300–316.

———. 2011. "Words and Things in Yucatán: Poststructuralism and the Everyday Life of Mayan Multiculturalism." *Journal of the Royal Anthropological Institute* 17 (1): 63–81.

———. 2013. *Elusive Unity: Factionalism and the Limits of Identity Politics in Yucatán, Mexico*. Boulder: University Press of Colorado.

Arroyo, L., and K. Amador. 2015. "Tourism and Male Sex Work in the Cancun Riviera, Mexico." *Estudios y Perspectivas en Turismo* 24 (4): 982–92.

Atran, Scott. 1993. "Itza Maya Tropical Agro-Forestry." *Current Anthropology* 34 (5): 633–89.

Austin, James E., and Tomas Otto Kohn. 1990. "Sabritas (Abridged)." Harvard Business School Teaching Note 390-202, HBS Case Collection, June.

Ayora-Díaz, Steffan Igor. 2012. *Foodscapes, Foodfields, and Identities in Yucatán*. Oxford: Berghahn Books.

Ball, Joseph. 1977. "The Rise of Northern Maya Chiefdoms: A Socioprocessual Analysis." In *The Origins of Maya Civilization*, edited by Richard E. W. Adams, 101–32. Santa Fe NM: School of American Research.

Barrera-Bassols, Narciso, and Victor M. Toledo. 2005. "Ethnoecology of the Yucatec Maya: Symbolism, Knowledge and Management of Natural Resources." *Journal of Latin American Geography* 4 (1): 9–41.

Bascope, Grace L. 2005. "The Household Ecology of Disease Transmission: Childhood Illness in a Yucatán Maya Community." PhD diss., Southern Methodist University.

Bastarracha Manzano, J. R., and J. M. Canto Rosado. 2003. *Diccionario Maya Popular: Maya–Español, Español–Maya*. Mérida, Mexico: Academia de la lengua maya de Yucatán, A.C.

Benedict, Francis G., and Morris Steggerda. 1936. *The Food of the Present-Day Maya Indians of Yucatan*. Contributions to American Archaeology, no. 18. Washington DC: Carnegie Institution.

Berkley, Anthony R. 1998. "Remembrance and Revitalization: The Archive of Pure Maya." PhD diss., University of Chicago.

Besky, Sarah. 2013. *The Darjeeling Distinction: Labor and Justice on Fair-Trade Tea Plantations in India*. Berkeley: University of California Press.

Bey, George J., III, Craig A. Hanson, and William M. Ringle. 1997. "Classic to Post-classic at Ek Balam, Yucatan: Architectural and Ceramic Evidence for Defining the Transition." *Latin American Antiquity* 8 (3): 237–54.

Bocci, Paolo. 2017. "Tangles of Care: Killing Goats to Save Tortoises on the Galápagos Islands." *Cultural Anthropology* 32 (3): 424–49.

Boehm, Deborah A. 2012. *Intimate Migrations: Gender, Family, and Illegality among Transnational Mexicans.* New York: New York University Press.

Bonfil-Batalla, Guillermo. 1987. *México profundo: Una civilización negada.* Mexico: Grijalbo.

Bourdieu, Pierre. 1977. *Outline of a Theory of Practice.* Cambridge: Cambridge University Press.

———. (1979) 1984. *Distinction: A Social Critique of the Judgement of Taste.* Translated by Richard Nice. Cambridge MA: Harvard University Press.

Bourdin, Gabriel L. 2007/2008. "La noción de persona en entre los mayas: Una visión semántica." *Revista Pueblos y fronteras digital* 4 (December–May).

Braha-Pfeiler, Barbara, and Anne Franks. 1992. "Preserving the Mayan Language." *Proceedings of the xvth Congress of Linguists* 4 (1): 185–89.

Brandes, B. 2006. *Skulls to the Living, Bread to the Dead: The Day of the Dead in Mexico and Beyond.* Hoboken NJ: Wiley-Blackwell.

Braziel, Jana Evans, and Kathleen LeBesco, eds. 2001. *Bodies out of Bounds: Fatness and Transgression.* Berkeley: University of California Press.

Bricker, Victoria, Eleuterio Po'ot Yah, and Ofelia Dzul de Po'ot. 1998. *A Dictionary of the Maya Language: As Spoken in Hocabá, Yucatán.* Salt Lake City: University of Utah Press.

Bullough, Vern L. 1976. *Sexual Variance in Society and History.* Oxford: John Wiley & Sons.

Burns, Allan. 1998. "Pan-Maya Ideology and Bilingual Education in Yucatán." In *Anatomia de una civilización: Aproximaciones interdisciplinarias a la cultura maya,* edited by Andrés Ciudad Ruiz, 377–89. Madrid: Sociedad Española de Estudios Mayas.

Callahan, Robey K. 2005. "Doubt, Shame, and the Maya Self." PhD diss., University of Pennsylvania.

———. 2017. "Fatalism, the Self, Intentionality, and Signs of Ill Portent in Quintana Roo, Mexico." *Anthropology of Consciousness* 28 (1): 69–95.

Caplan, Pat, ed. 1997. *Food, Health, and Identity.* London: Routledge.

Carte, Lindsey, Mason McWatters, Erin Daly, and Rebecca Torres. 2010. "Experiencing Agricultural Failure: Internal Migration, Tourism and Local Perceptions of Regional Change in the Yucatan." *Geoforum* 41, no. 5 (September): 700–710.

Castañeda, Quetzil E. 1996. *In the Museum of Maya Culture: Touring Chichén Itzá*. Minneapolis: University of Minnesota Press.

———. 2003. "New and Old Social Movements: Measuring Pisté, from the 'Mouth of the Well' to the 107th Municipio of Yucatán." *Ethnohistory* 50 (4): 611–42.

———. 2004. "'We Are *Not* Indigenous!' An Introduction to the Maya Identity of Yucatán." *Journal of Latin American Anthropology* 9 (1): 36–63.

Castellanos, M. Bianet. 2003. "Gustos and Genders: Yucatec Maya Migration to the Mexican Riviera." PhD diss., University of Michigan.

———. 2007. "Adolescent Migration to Cancún: Reconfiguring Maya Households and Gender Relations in Mexico's Yucatán Peninsula." *Frontiers: A Journal of Women's Studies* 28 (3):1–27.

———. 2010. *A Return to Servitude: Maya Migration and the Tourist Trade in Cancún*. Minneapolis: University of Minnesota Press.

———. 2011. "Becoming Chingón." In *Strange Affinities: The Gender and Sexual Politics of Comparative Racialization*, edited by Grace Kyungwon Hong and Roderick Ferguson, 270–92. Durham NC: Duke University Press.

Castillo Cocom, Juan. 2004. "Lost in Mayaland." *Journal of Latin American Anthropology* 9 (1): 179–87.

———. 2007. "Maya Scenarios: Indian Stories in and out of Contexts." *Kroeber Anthropological Society Papers* 96: 13–35.

———. 2012. "Hot and Cold Politics of Indigenous Identity: Legal Indians, Cannibals, Words, More Words, More Food." *Anthropological Quarterly* 85 (1): 229–56.

Castillo Cocom, Juan, Timoteo Rodriguez, and McCale Ashenbrener. 2017. "Ethnoexodus: Escaping Mayaland." In *The Only True People*, edited by Bethany J. bin Beyyette, 47–72. Boulder: University of Colorado Press.

Chevalier, Jacques M., and Andrés Sánchez Bain. 2003. *The Hot and the Cold: Ills of Humans and Maize in Native Mexico*. Toronto: University of Toronto Press.

Chojnacki, Ruth J. 2010. *Indigenous Apostles: Maya Catholic Catechists Working the Word in Highland Chiapas*. Amsterdam: Rodopi.

Christie, Maria Elisa. 2008. *Kitchenspace: Women, Fiestas, and Everyday Life in Central Mexico*. Austin: University of Texas Press.

Clarke, Allison J. 2014. "Designing Mothers and the Market: Social Class and Material Culture." In *Motherhoods, Markets, and Consumption: The Making of Mothers in Contemporary Western Cultures*, edited by S. O'Donohoe, M. Hogg, P. Maclaran, L. Martens, and L. Stevens, 43–55. New York: Routledge.

Clendinnen, Inga. 1987. *Ambivalent Conquests: Maya and Spaniard in Yucatan, 1517–1570*. Cambridge: Cambridge University Press.

Coe, Michael D. 2005. *The Maya*. 7th ed. New York: Thames & Hudson.

Colunga-García Marín, Patricia, and Daniel Zizumbo-Villarreal. 2004. "Domestication of Plants in Maya Lowlands." *Economic Botany* 58, Supplement: S101–S110.

Counihan, Carole M. 1999. *The Anthropology of Food and Body: Gender, Meaning, and Power*. New York: Routledge.

Culhane-Pera, Kathleen A., Cheng Her, and Bee Her. 2007. "'We Are out of Balance Here': A Hmong Cultural Model of Diabetes." *Journal of Immigrant and Minority Health* 9 (3): 179–90.

Currier, Richard L. 1966. "The Hot-Cold Syndrome and Symbolic Balance in Mexican and Spanish-American Folk Medicine." *Ethnology* 5 (3): 251–63.

Cussins, Charis. 1998. "Ontological Choreography: Agency for Women Patients in an Infertility Clinic." In *Differences in Medicine: Unraveling Practices, Techniques, and Bodies*, edited by Marc Berg and Annemarie Mol, 166–201. Durham NC: Duke University Press.

Daltabuit, Magalí Godás, and Thomas Leatherman. 1998. "The Biocultural Impact of Tourism on Mayan Communities." In *Building a New Biocultural Synthesis: Political-Economic Perspectives on Human Biology*, edited by Alan Goodman and Thomas Leatherman, 317–38. Ann Arbor: University of Michigan Press.

Daltabuit, Magalí Godás, and Oriol Pi-Sunyer. 1990. "Tourism Development in Quintana Roo, Mexico." *Cultural Survival Quarterly* 14, no. 1 (March): 9–13.

Daniel, E. Valentine. 1984. *Fluid Signs: Being a Person the Tamil Way*. Berkeley: University of California Press.

DeVault, Marjorie L. (1991) 1994. *Feeding the Family: The Social Organization of Caring as Gendered Work*. Chicago: University of Chicago Press.

Duden, Barbara. 1991. *The Woman beneath the Skin: A Doctor's Patients in Eighteenth-Century Germany*. Cambridge: Harvard University Press.

Early, John D. 2006. *The Maya and Catholicism: An Encounter of Worldviews*. Gainesville: University Press of Florida.

Ebel, R., and J. Castillo Cocom. 2012. "X-Pichil: From Traditional to "Modern" Farming in a Maya Community." Presented at VIII International Conference on Sustainable Agriculture, Environment and Forestry. Rome, Italy.

Eber, Christine. (1995) 2000. *Women & Alcohol in a Highland Maya Town: Water of Hope, Water of Sorrow*. Austin: University of Texas Press.

Eisner, Elliot. 1985. *The Art of Educational Evaluation: A Personal View*. London: Falmer Press.

Eiss, Paul K. 2010. *In the Name of El Pueblo: Place, Community, and the Politics of History in Yucatán*. Durham NC: Duke University Press.

Elmendorf, Mary. (1976) 1978. *Nine Mayan Women: A Village Faces Changes*. New York: Schenkman.

Emery, Kitty. 2003. "The Noble Beast: Status and Differential Access to Animals in the Maya World." *World Archaeology* 34, no. 3 (February): 498–515.

Engster, Daniel. 2005. "Rethinking Care Theory: The Practice of Caring and the Obligation to Care." *Hypatia* 20, no. 3 (August): 50–74.

Fabian, Johannes. (1983) 2002. *Time and the Other: How Anthropology Makes Its Object*. New York: Columbia University Press.

Fallaw, Ben. 2004. "Rethinking Mayan Resistance: Changing Relations between Federal Teachers and Mayan Communities in Eastern Yucatan, 1929–1935." *Journal of Latin American Anthropology* 9 (1): 151–78.

Farquhar, Judith. 2002. *Appetites: Food and Sex in Post-Socialist China*. Durham NC: Duke University Press.

Farriss, Nancy. 1984. *Maya Society under Colonial Rule: The Collective Enterprise of Survival*. Princeton NJ: Princeton University Press.

———. 1987. "Remembering the Future, Anticipating the Past: History, Time, and Cosmology among the Maya of Yucatan." *Comparative Studies in Society and History* 29, no. 3 (July): 566–93.

Faust, Betty B. 1998. "Cacao Beans and Chili Peppers: Gender Socialization of a Yucatec Maya Curing Ceremony." *Sex Roles* 39, no. 7 (October): 603–42.

Fernández-Sousa, Lilia. 2015. "Grinding and Cooking: An Approach to Mayan Culinary Technology." In *Cooking Technology: Transformations in Culinary Practice in Mexico and Latin America*, edited by Steffan Igor Ayora-Díaz, 15–27. London: Bloomsbury.

Fischer, Edward F. 1999. "Cultural Logic and Maya Identity: Rethinking Constructivism and Essentialism." *Current Anthropology* 40 (4): 473–99.

Fischer, Edward F., and Peter Benson. 2006. *Broccoli and Desire: Global Connections and Maya Struggles in Postwar Guatemala*. Stanford, CA: Stanford University Press.

Fiszbein, Ariel, and Norert Schady. 2009. *Conditional Cash Transfers: Reducing Present and Future Poverty*. Washington DC: World Bank.

Fitting, Elizabeth. 2011. *The Struggle for Maize: Campesinos, Workers, and Transgenic Corn in the Mexican Countryside*. Durham NC: Duke University Press.

Ford, Anabel. 2006. "Adaptive Management and the Community at El Pilar: A Philosophy of Resilience for the Maya Forest." In *Of the Past, For the Future: Integrating Archaeology and Conservation*, 105–11. Los Angeles: Getty Conservation Institute.

Foster, George M. 1978. "Hippocrates' Latin American Legacy: 'Hot' and 'Cold.'" In *Contemporary Folk Medicine, Colloquia in Anthropology*, vol. 2, edited by R. K. Wetherington, 3–19. Dallas: Fort Burgwin Research Center.

———. 1986. "La salud y el equilibrio." In *La medicina invisible: Introducción al estudio de la medicina tradicional de México*, edited by Xavier Lozoya and Carlos Zolla, 62–72. Mexico City: Folios Ediciones S.A.

———. 1994. *Hippocrates' Latin American Legacy: Humoral Medicine in the New World*. Langhorne PA: Gordon and Breach.

Gálvez, Alyshia. 2018. *Eating NAFTA: Trade, Food Policies, and the Destruction of Mexico*. Oakland: University of California Press.

Gaskins, Suzanne. 1999. "Children's Daily Lives in a Mayan Village: A Case Study of Culturally Constructed Roles and Activities." In *Children's Engagement in the World: Sociocultural Perspectives*, edited by Artin Göncü, 25–61. Cambridge: Cambridge University Press.

———. 2003. "From Corn to Cash: Change and Continuity within Maya Families." *Ethos* 31, no. 2 (June): 248–73.

Geurts, Kathryn Linn. 2002. *Culture and the Senses: Bodily Ways of Knowing in an African Community*. Berkeley: University of California Press.

Gilligan, Carol. 1982. *In a Different Voice: Psychological Theory and Women's Development*. Cambridge MA: Harvard University Press.

Glassman, Steve, and Armando Anaya. 2011. *Cities of the Maya in Seven Epochs, 1250 B.C. to A.D. 1903*. Jefferson NC: McFarland.

Glusac, Elaine. 2018. "Tourism in Yucatán Peninsula Withstands Wave of Violence." *New York Times*, April 28, 2018.

Goldkind, Victor. 1965. "Social Stratification in the Peasant Community: Robert Redfield's Chan Kom Reinterpreted." *American Anthropologist* 67, no. 4 (August): 863–84.

González, Roberto J. 2001. *Zapotec Science: Farming and Food in the Northern Sierra of Oaxaca*. Austin: University of Texas Press.

Goodner, Kenneth. 1930. "Incidence of Blood Groups among the Maya Indians of Yucatan." *Journal of Immunology* 18 (6): 433–35.

Green, Linda. 1993. "Shifting Affiliations: Mayan Widows and *Evangélicos* in Guatemala." In *Rethinking Protestantism in Latin America*, edited by Virginia Garrard-Burnett and David Stoll, 159–79. Philadelphia: Temple University Press.

———. 2011. "The Nobodies: Neoliberalism, Violence, and Migration." *Medical Anthropology* 30, no. 4 (July): 366–85.

Greenberg, Laurie S. Z. 1996. "You Are What You Eat: Ethnicity and Change in Yucatec Immigrant House Lots, Quintana Roo, Mexico." PhD diss., University of Wisconsin.

Greene, Allison C. 2002. "Huipiles to Spandex: Styling Modernity and Refashioning Gender in the Global Economy of Yucatán." PhD diss., University of North Carolina–Chapel Hill.

Guest, Gregory S. 1995. "A Tree for All Reasons: The Maya and the 'Sacred' Ceiba." MA thesis, University of Calgary.

Gupta, Akhil, and James Ferguson. 1992. "Beyond "Culture": Space, Identity, and the Politics of Difference." *Cultural Anthropology* 7 (1): 6–23.

Gustafson, Lowell S. 2002. "Mother/Father Kings." In Gustafson and Trevelyan, *Ancient Maya Gender Identity and Relations*, 141–68.

Gustafson, Lowell S., and Amelia M. Trevelyan, eds. 2002. *Ancient Maya Gender Identity and Relations*. Westport CT: Bergin & Garvey.

Gutmann, Matthew C. 1996. *The Meaning of Macho: Being a Man in Mexico City*. Berkeley: University of California Press.

Guzmán Medina, Violeta. 2010. "Youth, Poverty and Exclusion: Health Problems of Young Mayans in Yucatan." *Social Medicine* 5 (2): 100–105.

Haidt, Jonathan, Paul Rozin, Clark McCauley, and Sumio Imada. 1997. "Body, Psyche, and Culture: The Relationship between Disgust and Morality." *Psychology and Developing Societies* 9 (1): 107–31.

Han, Clara. 2012. *Life in Debt: Times of Care and Violence in Neoliberal Chile*. Berkeley: University of California Press.

Hanks, William F. 1990. *Referential Practice: Language and Lived Space among the Maya*. Chicago: University of Chicago Press.

Harbers, Hans. 2010. "Animal Farm Love Stories: About Care and Economy." In Mol, Moser, and Pols, *Care in Practice*, 141–70.

Hardin, Jessica. 2013. "Fasting for Health, Fasting for God: Samoan Evangelical Christian Responses to Obesity and Chronic Disease." In *Reconstructing Obesity: The Meaning of Measures and the Measure of Meanings*, edited by Megan B. McCullough and Jessica A. Hardin, 107–28. New York: Berghahn Books.

———. 2017. "Embedded Narratives: Metabolic Disorders and Pentecostal Conversion in Samoa." *Medical Anthropology Quarterly* 32 (1): 22–41.

Held, Virginia. 2005. *The Ethics of Care: Personal, Political, and Global*. New York: Oxford University Press.

Hendon, Julia A. 1997. "Women's Work, Women's Space, and Women's Status among the Classic-Period Maya Elite of the Copan Valley, Honduras." In

Women in Prehistory: North American and Mesoamerica, edited by Cheryl Claassen and Rosemary A. Joyce, 33–46. Philadelphia: University of Pennsylvania Press.

———. 1999. "The Pre-Classic Maya Compound as the Focus of Social Identity." In *Social Patterns in Pre-Classic Mesoamerica: A Symposium at Dumbarton Oaks, 9 and 10 October 1993*, edited by David C. Grove and Rosemary A. Joyce, 97–126. Washington DC: Dumbarton Oaks.

———. 2002. "Household and State in Pre-Hispanic Maya Society: Gender, Identity, and Practice." In Gustafson and Trevelyan, *Ancient Maya Gender Identity and Relations*, 75–92.

Herdt, Gilbert H. 1981. *Guardians of the Flutes: Idioms of Masculinity*. New York: McGraw-Hill.

Hervik, Peter. 1999. "The Mysterious Maya of National Geographic." *Journal of Latin American Anthropology* 4 (1): 166–97.

———. 2003. *Mayan People beyond and within Boundaries: Social Categories and Lived Identity in Yucatán*. New York: Routledge.

Hervik, Peter, and Hilary E. Kahn. 2006. "Scholarly Surrealism: The Persistence of Mayanness." *Critique of Anthropology* 26 (2): 209–32.

Heusinkveld, Paula R. 2008. "Tinum, Yucatán: A Maya Village and the Lights of Cancún." In *Yucatán in an Era of Globalization*, edited by Eric N. Baklanoff and Edward H. Moseley, 112–33. Tuscaloosa: University of Alabama Press.

Highmore, Ben. 2008. "Alimentary Agents: Food, Cultural Theory and Multiculturalism." *Journal of Intercultural Studies* 29 (4): 381–98.

Hirsch, Jennifer S. 2010. "The Social Production of Men's Extramarital Sexual Practices." In *Routledge Handbook of Sexuality, Health and Rights*, edited by Peter Aggleton and Richard Parker, 291–300. New York: Routledge.

Hirsch, Jennifer S., Sergio Meneses, Brenda Thompson, Mirka Negroni, Blanca Pelcastre, and Carlos de Rio. 2007. "The Inevitability of Infidelity: Sexual Reputation, Social Geographies, and Marital HIV Risk in Rural Mexico." *American Journal of Public Health* 97 (6): 986–96.

Holmes, Barbara E. 1978. "Women and Yucatec Kinship." PhD diss., Tulane University.

Holtzman, Jon. 2010. "Remembering Bad Cooks: Sensuality, Memory, Personhood." *Senses and Society* 5 (2): 235–43.

Hostettler, Ueli. 2004. "Rethinking Maya Identity in Yucatan, 1500–1940." *Journal of Latin American Anthropology* 9 (1): 187–98.

Hugh-Jones, Christine. 1979. *From the Milk River: Spatial and Temporal Processes in Northwest Amazonia*. Cambridge: Cambridge University Press.

Instituto Mexicano del Seguro Social (IMSS). 2018. "Conoce el IMSS." http://www.imss.gob.mx/conoce-al-imss.

Instituto Nacional de Estadística y Geografía. 2010. "Yucatán." http://www.beta.inegi.org.mx/app/areasgeograficas/?ag=31.

Jansen, Stef. 2008. "Misplaced Masculinities: Status Loss and the Location of Gendered Subjectivities amongst 'Non-transnational' Bosnian Refugees." *Anthropological Theory* 8 (2): 181–200.

Jordan, Brigitte. 1993. *Birth in Four Cultures: A Crosscultural Investigation of Childbirth in Yucatan, Holland, Sweden, and the United States.* 4th ed. Prospect Heights IL: Waveland Press.

Joseph, Gilbert M. 1986. *Rediscovering the Past at Mexico's Periphery: Essays on the History of Modern Yucatán.* Tuscaloosa: University of Alabama Press.

———. 1988. *Revolution from Without: Yucatán, Mexico, and the United States, 1880–1924.* Durham NC: Duke University Press.

Juarez, Ana Maria. 1996. "Epochs of Colonialism: Race, Class, and Gender among Caste War Mayas in Quintana Roo, Mexico." PhD diss., Stanford University.

———. 2001. "Four Generations of Maya Marriages: What's Love Got to Do with It?" *Frontiers: A Journal of Women Studies* 22 (2): 131–53.

Kandelaars, Patricia. 2000. "A Dynamic Simulation Study of Tourism and Environment in the Yucatán Peninsula." In *Tourism and the Environment: Regional, Economic, Cultural and Policy Issues*, 2nd ed., edited by Helen Briassoulis and Jan van der Straaten, 59–90. Dordrecht: Kluwer Academic.

Kapusta, Jan. 2016. "Maya Intimacy with the Mountains: Pilgrimage, Sacrifice and Existential Economy." *Journal of Ethnology and Folkloristics* 10 (1): 25–41.

Kintz, Ellen R. 1998. "The Yucatec Maya Frontier and Maya Women: Tenacity of Tradition and Tragedy of Transformation." *Sex Roles* 39 (7/8): 589–601.

Knight, Alan. (1990) 2004. "Racism, Revolution, and *Indigenismo*: Mexico, 1910–1940." In *The Idea of Race in Latin America, 1870–1940*, edited by Richard Graham, Thomas E. Skidmore, Aline Heig, and Alan Knight, 71–114. Austin: University of Texas Press.

Korsmeyer, Carolyn. 1999. *Making Sense of Taste.* Ithaca NY: Cornell University Press.

Kramer, Karen L. 2005. *Maya Children: Helpers at the Farm.* Cambridge MA: Harvard University Press.

Kray, Christine Anne. 1997. "Worship in Body and Spirit: Practice, Self, and Religious Sensibility in Yucatán." PhD diss., University of Pennsylvania.

———. 2002. "The Pentecostal Re-formation of Self: Opting for Orthodoxy in Yucatán." *Ethos* 29, no. 4 (December): 395–429.

———. 2005. "The Sense of Tranquility: Bodily Practice and Ethnic Classes in Yucatán." *Ethnology* 44, no. 4 (Spring): 337–55.

———. 2007. "Women as Border in the Shadow of Cancún." *Anthropology Today* 23 (4): 17–21.

Lakoff, George, and Mark Johnson. 1999. *Philosophy in the Flesh: The Embodied Mind and Its Challenge to Western Thought*. New York: Basic Books.

Lancaster, Roger N. 1992. *Life Is Hard: Machismo, Danger, and the Intimacy of Power in Nicaragua*. Berkeley: University of California Press.

Landa, Diego de. 1941. *Relación de las cosas de Yucatán*. Translated and edited by Alfred M. Tozzer. Cambridge MA: Peabody Museum of American Archeology and Ethnology, Harvard University.

Laudan, R. 2001. "A Plea for Culinary Modernism: Why We Should Love New, Fast, Processed Food." *Gastronomica: The Journal of Food and Culture* 1, no. 1 (Winter): 36–44.

Lavis, Anna. 2015. "Careful Starving: Reflections on (Not) Eating, Caring and Anorexia." In *Careful Eating: Bodies, Food and Care*, edited by Emma-Jayne Abbots, Anna Lavis, and Luci Attala, 91–108. London: Routledge.

Law, John. 2010. "Care and Killing: Tensions in Veterinary Practice." In Mol, Moser, and Pols, *Care in Practice*, 57–71.

Leatherman, Thomas L., and Alan Goodman. 2005. "Coca-Colonization of Diets in the Yucatán." *Social Science and Medicine* 61 (4): 833–46.

LeCount, Lisa J. 2001. "Like Water for Chocolate: Feasting and Political Ritual among the Late Classic Maya at Xunantunich, Belize." *American Anthropologist* 103 (4): 935–53.

Le Guen, Olivier. 2011. "Materiality vs. Expressivity: The Use of Sensory Vocabulary in Yucatec Maya." *Senses & Society* 6 (1): 117–26.

Lentz, David L., ed. 2000. *Imperfect Balance: Landscape Transformations in the Precolumbian Americas*. New York: Columbia University Press.

Levy, Santiago. 2008. *Good Intentions, Bad Outcomes: Social Policy, Informality, and Economic Growth in Mexico*. Washington DC: Brookings Institution Press.

Lichtinger, Victor, and Homero Aridjis. 2018. "The Mayan Trainwreck." *WorldPost*, partnership of Berggruen Institute and *Washington Post*, December 4, 2018. https://www.washingtonpost.com/news/theworldpost/wp/2018/12/04/amlo/.

Liebelt, Claudia. 2011. *Caring for the 'Holy Land': Filipina Domestic Workers in Israel*. Oxford: Berghahn Books.

Lock, Margaret. 1993. *Encounters with Aging: Mythologies of Menopause in Japan and North America*. Berkeley: University of California Press.

Loewe, Ronald. 2009. "Maya Reborn." *Reviews in Anthropology* 38 (3): 237–62.

———. 2010. *Maya or Mestizo? Nationalism, Modernity, and Its Discontents.* Toronto: University of Toronto Press.

Lomnitz, Larissa Adler. 1977. *Networks and Marginality: Life in a Mexican Shantytown.* Translated by Cinna Lomnitz. New York: Academic Press.

López, Daniel, Blanca Callén, Francisco Tirado, and Miguel Domènech. 2010. "How to Become a Guardian Angel: Providing Safety in a Home Telecare Service." In Mol, Moser, and Pols, *Care in Practice*, 73–91.

López Austin, Alfredo. 1969. "De las enfermedades del cuerpo humano y de las medicinas contra ellas." *Estudios de Cultural Náhuatl* 8: 51–122.

———. 1975. *Textos de medicina Náhuatl.* Mexico City: Instituto de Investigaciones Históricas, Universidad Nacional Autónoma de México (UNAM).

———. 1980. *Cuerpo humano e ideología: Las concepciones de los antiguos Nahuas.* 2 vols. Mexico City: Instituto de Investigaciones Antropológicas, UNAM.

———. 1986. "La polémica sobre la dicotomía frío-calor." In *La medicina invisible: Introducción al estudio de la medicina tradicional de México*, edited by Xavier Lozoya and Carlos Zolla, 73–90. Mexico City: Folios Ediciones S.A.

———. 2001. "El núcleo duro, la cosmovisión y la tradición mesoamericana." In *Cosmovisión, ritual e identidad de los pueblos indígenas de México*, edited by Johanna Broda and Félix Báez-Jorge, 47–65. Mexico: Consejo Nacional para la Cultura y las Artes.

Lucero, Lisa J. 1999. "Water Control and Maya Politics in the Southern Maya Lowlands." *Archaeological Papers of the American Anthropological Association* 9 (1): 35–49.

Lucero, Lisa J., Joel D. Gunn, and Vernon L. Scarborough. 2011. "Climate Change and Classic Maya Water Management." *Water* 3 (2): 479–94.

Marcus, Joyce. 2003. "Recent Advances in Maya Archaeology." *Journal of Archaeological Research* 11 (2): 71–148.

Mauss, Marcel. (1950) 1990. *The Gift: The Form and Reason for Exchange in Archaic Societies.* Translated by W. D. Halls. London: Routledge.

McCullough, John M. 1973. "Human Ecology, Heat Adaptation, and Belief Systems: The Hot-Cold Syndrome of Yucatán." *Journal of Anthropological Research* 29 (1): 32–36.

McKillop, Heather. 2004. *The Ancient Maya: New Perspectives.* Santa Barbara CA: ABC-CLIO.

Meigs, Anna. 1984. *Food, Sex, and Pollution: A New Guinea Religion.* New Brunswick NJ: Rutgers University Press.

———. 1988. "Food as a Cultural Construction." *Food and Foodways* 2 (1): 341–57.

Messer, Ellen. 1987. "The Hot and Cold in Mesoamerican Indigenous and Hispanicized Thought." *Social Science & Medicine* 25 (4): 339–46.

Miller, Cynthia J. 1998. "The Social Impacts of Televised Media among the Yucatec Maya." *Human Organization* 57, no. 3 (Fall): 307–14.

Mol, Annemarie. 2003. *The Body Multiple: Ontology in Medical Practice*. Durham NC: Duke University Press.

Mol, Annemarie, Ingunn Moser, and Jeanette Pols, eds. 2010. *Care in Practice: On Tinkering in Clinics, Homes and Farms*. Bielefeld, Germany: Transcript-Verlag.

Mulla, Sameena. 2014. *The Violence of Care: Rape Victims, Forensic Nurses, and Sexual Assault Intervention*. New York: New York University Press.

Munn, Nancy D. 1986. *The Fame of Gawa: A Symbolic Study of Value Transformation in a Massim (Papua New Guinea) Society*. Cambridge: Cambridge University Press.

Nadasdy, Paul. 2007. "The Gift in the Animal: The Ontology of Hunting and Human-Animal Sociality." *American Ethnologist* 34 (1): 25–43.

Nading, Alex M. 2014. *Mosquito Trails: Ecology, Health, and the Politics of Entanglement*. Berkeley: University of California Press.

Narcia, Elva. 2019. "Mexico's 'Tren Maya' Railway: Fat Jaguars vs. Starving Babies?" Translated by Nick Caistor. Latin American Bureau, February 21. https://lab .org.uk/mexicos-tren-maya-railway-fat-jaguars-vs-starving-babies/.

Nash, June. 1970. *In the Eyes of the Ancestors: Belief and Behavior in a Mayan Community*. New Haven CT: Yale University Press.

———. 1995. "The Reassertion of Indigenous Identity: Mayan Responses to State Intervention in Chiapas." *Latin American Research Review* 30 (3): 7–41.

Nelson, Margaret K. 1990. "Mothering Others' Children: The Experiences of Family Day Care Providers." In Abel and Nelson, *Circles of Care*, 201–32.

Noddings, Nel. 1984. *Caring: A Feminine Approach to Ethics and Moral Education*. Berkeley: University of California Press.

Norget, Kristin. 2006. *Days of Death, Days of Life: Ritual in the Popular Culture of Oaxaca*. New York: Columbia University Press.

Nutini, Hugo G. 1976. "Syncretism and Acculturation: The Historical Development of the Cult of the Patron Saint in Tlaxcala, Mexico (1519–1670)." *Ethnology* 15, no. 3 (July): 301–21.

O'Connor, Amber. 2010. "Maya Foodways: A Reflection of Gender and Ideology." In *Pre-Columbian Foodways: Interdisciplinary Approaches to Food, Culture, and Markets in Ancient Mesoamerica*, edited by John Staller and Michael Carrasco, 487–507. New York: Springer.

———. 2012. "Conversion in Central Quintana Roo: Changes in Religion, Community, Economy and Nutrition in a Maya Village." *Food, Culture, & Society* 15 (1): 77–91.

———. 2014. "Consuming the Maya: An Ethnography of Eating and Being in the Land of the Caste Wars." PhD diss., University of Texas at Austin.

Parezo, Nancy J. 2007. "To Live within Dinétah: Navajo Sandpainters and Their Quest for Place." In *Place and Native American Indian History and Culture*, edited by Joy Porter, 155–75. Bern: Peter Lang.

Parkin, Katherine J. 2006. *Food Is Love: Advertising and Gender Roles in Modern America*. Philadelphia: University of Pennsylvania Press.

Patch, Robert W. 1985. "Agrarian Change in Eighteenth-Century Yucatán." *Hispanic American Historical Review* 65 (1): 21–49.

———. 1993. *Maya and Spaniard in Yucatan, 1648–1812*. Stanford CA: Stanford University Press.

Paz, Octavio. (1961) 2008. *The Labyrinth of Solitude*. Translated by Lysander Kemp, Yara Milos, and Rachel Phillips-Belash. New York: Grove Press.

Pilcher, Jeffrey M. 1998. *¡Que vivan los tamales! Food and the Making of Mexican Identity*. Albuquerque: University of New Mexico Press.

Pi-Sunyer, Oriol, and R. Brooke Thomas. 1997. "Tourism, Environmentalism, and Cultural Survival in Quintana Roo." In *Life and Death Matters: Human Rights and the Environment at the End of the Millennium*, edited by Barbara Rose Johnston, 187–212. Walnut Creek CA: AltaMira Press.

Popenoe, Rebecca. 2004. *Feeding Desire: Fatness, Beauty, and Sexuality among a Saharan People*. London: Routledge.

Povinelli, Elizabeth A. 2006. *The Empire of Love: Toward a Theory of Intimacy, Genealogy, and Carnality*. Durham NC: Duke University Press.

Press, Irwin. 1975. *Tradition and Adaptation: Life in a Modern Yucatán Maya Village*. Westport CT: Greenwood Press.

Probyn, Elspeth. 2000. *Carnal Appetites: FoodSexIdentities*. London: Routledge.

Quintal López, Rocío, and Ligia Vera Gamboa. 2014. "Migración, etnia y género: Tres elementos claves en la comprensión de la vulnerabilidad social ante el VIH/ SIDA en población maya de Yucatán." *Península* 9 (2): 99–130.

Re Cruz, Alicia. 1996. *The Two Milpas of Chan Kom: Scenarios of a Maya Village Life*. Albany: State University of New York Press.

———. 1998. "Maya Women, Gender Dynamics, and Modes of Production." *Sex Roles* 39 (7/8): 573–87.

Redclift, Michael. 2004. *Chewing Gum: The Fortunes of Taste*. New York: Routledge.

———. 2005. "'A Convulsed and Magic Country': Tourism and Resource Histories in the Mexican Caribbean." *Environment and History* 11, no. 1 (February): 83–97.

Redfield, Robert. 1941. *The Folk Culture of Yucatán*. Chicago: University of Chicago Press.

———. 1950. *A Village That Chose Progress: Chan Kom Revisited*. Chicago: University of Chicago Press.

Redfield, Robert, and Alfonso Villa Rojas. (1934) 1962. *Chan Kom: A Maya Village*. Chicago: University of Chicago Press.

Reed, Nelson. 1964. *The Caste War of Yucatán*. Stanford CA: Stanford University Press.

Reilly, F. Kent. 2002. "Female and Male: The Ideology of Balance and Renewal in Elite Costuming among the Classic Period Maya." In Gustafson and Trevelyan, *Ancient Maya Gender and Identity Relations*, 319–28.

Reina, Ruben E. 1966. *The Law of the Saints: A Pokomam Pueblo and Its Community Culture*. New York: Bobbs-Merrill.

Remmers, Lawrence J. 1981. "Henequén, the Caste War and Economy of Yucatan, 1846–1883: The Roots of Dependence in a Mexican Region." PhD diss., University of California, Los Angeles.

Restall, Matthew. 1997. *The Maya World: Yucatec Culture and Society, 1550–1850*. Stanford CA: Stanford University Press.

———. 2004. "Maya Ethnogenesis." *Journal of Latin American Anthropology* 9 (1): 64–89.

———. 2009. *The Black Middle: Africans, Mayas, and Spaniards in Colonial Yucatan*. Stanford CA: Stanford University Press.

Reyes-Cortes, Beatriz M. 2011. "Adoring Our Wounds: Suicide, Prevention, and the Maya in Yucatán, Mexico." PhD diss., University of California, Berkeley.

Reyes-Foster, Beatriz. 2012. "Grieving for Mestizaje: Alternative Approaches to Maya Identity in Yucatan, Mexico." *Identities: Global Studies in Culture and Power* 19 (6): 657–72.

Rice, Prudence M. 2008. "Time, Power, and the Maya." *Latin American Antiquity* 19 (3): 275–98.

Rivera, Marie-Odile. 1976. *Una comunidad Maya en Yucatán*. Mexico City: Secretaría de Educación Pública.

Rosaldo, Renato. (1989) 1993. *Culture & Truth: The Remaking of Social Analysis*. Boston: Beacon Press.

Roys, Ralph L. (1943) 1972. *The Indian Background of Colonial Yucatan*. Norman: University of Oklahoma Press.

———. 1957. *The Political Geography of the Yucatan Maya*. Washington DC: Carnegie Institution.

Rozin, Paul. 1999. "Food Is Fundamental, Fun, Frightening, and Far-Reaching." *Social Research* 66: 9–30.

Rugeley, Terry. 2001a. *Maya Wars: Ethnographic Accounts from Nineteenth-Century Yucatán*. Norman: University of Oklahoma Press.

———. 2001b. *Of Wonders and Wise Men: Religion and Popular Cultures in Southeast Mexico, 1800–1876*. Austin: University of Texas Press.

Saethre, Eirik J. 2007. "Conflicting Traditions, Concurrent Treatment: Medical Pluralism in Remote Aboriginal Australia." *Oceania* 77 (1): 95–110.

Saldaña Oropesa, Román. 1952. *Imágenes más antiguas y veneradas en Tlaxcala: De documentos desconocidos o muy poco conocidos relativos a historia de esta entidad*. Mexico City: Editorial Xicotli.

Sandoval, Erika M. 2009. "Extranjero en Mi Tierra (Stranger in My Homeland): Migrant Realities in Mexico's Riviera Maya." MA thesis, University of Kansas.

Santos-Fita, Dídac, Eduardo J. Naranjo, Erin I. J. Estrada, Ramón Mariaca, and Eduardo Bello. 2015. "Symbolism and Ritual Practices Related to Hunting in Maya Communities from Central Quintana Roo, Mexico." *Journal of Ethnobiology and Ethnomedicine* 11 (71): 1–13.

Scheper-Hughes, Nancy. 2000. "Ire in Ireland." *Ethnography* 1 (1): 117–40.

Searcy, Michael T. 2011. *The Life-Giving Stone: Ethnoarchaeology of Maya Metates*. Tucson: University of Arizona Press.

Secretaría de Desarollo Social. 2012. "DICONSA: Qué hacemos?" (DICONSA: What do we do?). https://www.gob.mx/diconsa/que-hacemos.

Shattuck, George C., and Francis G. Benedict. 1931. "Further Studies on the Basal Metabolism of Maya Indians in Yucatan." *American Journal of Physiology* 96 (3): 518–28.

Sigal, Pete. 2000. *From Moon Goddesses to Virgins: The Colonization of Yucatecan Maya Sexual Desire*. Austin: University of Texas Press.

Smith, Michael E., and Frances F. Berdan, eds. 2010. *The Postclassic Mesoamerican World*. Salt Lake City: University of Utah Press.

Smith-Morris, Carolyn. 2018. "Care as Virtue, Care as Critical Frame: A Discussion of Four Recent Ethnographies." *Medical Anthropology* 37 (5): 426–32.

Smith-Oka, Vania. 2013. *Shaping the Motherhood of Indigenous Mexico*. Nashville: Vanderbilt University Press.

Solomon, Harris. 2016. *Metabolic Living: Food, Fat, and the Absorption of Illness in India*. Durham NC: Duke University Press.

Staller, John E. 2010. "Ethnohistoric Sources on Foodways, Feasts, and Festivals." In *Pre-Columbian Foodways: Interdisciplinary Approaches to Food, Culture, and Markets in Ancient Mesoamerica*, edited by John E. Staller and Michael Carrasco, 23–70. New York: Springer.

Stebbins, Kenyon Rainier. 1993. "Constraints on Successful Public Health Programs: A View from a Mexican Community." In *Health and Healthcare in Developing Countries*, edited by Peter Conrad and Eugene B. Gallagher, 211–27. Philadelphia: Temple University Press.

Steggerda, Morris. 1943. *A Description of Thirty Towns in Yucatán, Mexico.* Anthropological Papers, no. 30, *Bureau of American Ethnology Bulletin* 136: 227–48. Washington DC: U.S. Government Printing Office.

Stevenson, Lisa. 2014. *Life beside Itself: Imagining Care in the Canadian Arctic.* Oakland: University of California Press.

Stewart, Pamela J., and Andrew Strathern, eds. 2001. *Humors and Substances: Ideas of the Body in New Guinea.* Westport CT: Bergin & Garvey.

Stewart, Susan. 1999. "Prologue: From the Museum of Touch." In *Material Memories*, edited by Marius Kwint, Christopher Breward, and Jeremy Aynsley, 17–36. Oxford: Berg.

Stoll, David. 1993. "Introduction: Rethinking Protestantism in Latin America." In *Rethinking Protestantism in Latin America*, edited by Virginia Garrard-Burnett and David Stoll, 1–20. Philadelphia: Temple University Press.

Strathern, Andrew. 1982. "Witchcraft, Greed, Cannibalism, and Death." In *Death and the Regeneration of Life*, edited by Maurice Bloch and Jonathan Parry, 111–33. Cambridge: Cambridge University Press.

Stross, Brian. 2006. "Maize in Word and Image in Southeastern Mexico." In *Histories of Maize: Multidisciplinary Approaches to the Prehistory, Linguistics, Biogeography, Domestication, and Evolution of Maize*, edited by John Staller, Robert Tykot, and Bruce Benz, 577–98. London: Elsevier.

Sullivan, Paul. 1989. *Unfinished Conversations: Mayas and Foreigners between Two Wars.* New York: Alfred A. Knopf.

Sutton, David E. 2001. *Remembrance of Repasts: An Anthropology of Food and Memory.* Oxford: Berg.

———. 2014. *Secrets from the Greek Kitchen: Cooking, Skill, and Everyday Life on an Aegean Island.* Oakland: University of California Press.

Taube, Karl A. 1988. "The Ancient Yucatec New York Festival: The Liminal Period in Maya Ritual and Cosmology." PhD diss., Yale University.

———. 1989. "The Maize Tamale in Classic Maya Diet, Epigraphy, and Art." *American Antiquity* 54 (1): 31–51.

Taussig, Michael. 1980. *The Devil and Commodity Fetishism in South America*. Chapel Hill: University of North Carolina Press.

Taylor, Sarah R. 2014. "Maya Cosmopolitans: Engaging Tactics and Strategies in the Performance of Tourism." *Identities: Global Studies in Culture and Power* 21 (2): 219–32.

Terán, Silvia, Christian H. Rasmussen, and Olivio May Cauich. 1998. *Las plantas de la milpa entre los Mayas*. Mexico City: Fundación Tun Ben Kin.

Thompson, John E. S. 1954. *The Rise and Fall of Maya Civilization*. Norman: University of Oklahoma Press.

———. 1977. "A Proposal for Constituting a Maya Subgroup, Cultural and Linguistic, in the Petén and Adjacent Regions." In *Anthropology and History in Yucatán*, edited by Grant D. Jones, 33–34. Austin: University of Texas Press.

Thompson, Richard A. 1974. *The Winds of Tomorrow: Social Change in a Maya Town*. Chicago: University of Chicago Press.

Thompson, Samantha J., and Sandra M. Gifford. 2000. "Trying to Keep a Balance: The Meaning of Health and Diabetes in an Urban Aboriginal Community." *Social Science & Medicine* 51 (10): 1457–72.

Ticktin, Miriam I. 2011. *Casualties of Care: Immigration and the Politics of Humanitarianism in France*. Berkeley: University of California Press.

Torres, Rebecca. 2003. "Linkages between Tourism and Agriculture in Mexico." *Annals of Tourism Research* 30, no. 3 (January): 546–66.

———. 2011. "Life between the Two *Milpas*: Tourism, Agriculture and Migration in the Yucatán." In *Tourism and Agriculture: New Geographies of Consumption, Production and Rural Restructuring*, edited by Rebecca Torres and Janet Henshall Momsen, 47–71. New York: Routledge.

Torres, Rebecca, and Janet H. Momsen. 2005. "Planned Tourism Development in Quintana Roo, Mexico: Engine for Regional Development or Prescription for Inequitable Growth?" *Current Issues in Tourism* 8 (4): 259–85.

Tronto, Joan. 1993. *Moral Boundaries: A Political Argument for an Ethic of Care*. London: Routledge.

Vargas, Luis Alberto, and Leticia E. Casillas. 2008. "Comer, beber, cuerpo y cosmovisión, un viaje de ida y vuelta." *Anales de Antropología* 42: 87–115.

Vaughn, Mary Kay. 1982. *The State, Education, and Social Class in Mexico, 1880–1928*. DeKalb: Northern Illinois University Press.

Vega-Leinert, Anna Cristina de la. 2008. "The Realisation of the Human Right to Food in the Context of Economic Liberalisation: A Case Study on the Access to Maize-Based Food Staples in Mexico City." MA thesis, University of Applied Sciences–Berlin.

Venuti, Lawrence. 1996. "Translation as a Social Practice: Or, the Violence of Translation." *Translation Perspectives* 9: 195–213.

Verhoeven, Elizabeth. 2007. *Experiential Constructions in Yucatec Maya: A Typologically Based Analysis of a Functional Domain in a Mayan Language.* Amsterdam: John Benjamins.

Villa Rojas, Alfonso. 1981. "Terapéutica tradicional y medicina moderna entre los mayas de Yucatán." *Anales de Antropología* 18 (2): 13–28.

———. 1983. "Enfermedad, pecado y confesión entre los grupos mayenses." *Anales de Antropología* 20 (2): 89–110.

———. 1988. "Appendix A: The Concepts of Space and Time among the Contemporary Maya." In *Time and Reality in the Thought of the Maya*, 2nd ed., by Miguel León-Portilla. Norman: University of Oklahoma Press.

Vogt, Evon Z. 1971. "The Genetic Model and Maya Cultural Development." In *Desarrollo Cultural de los Mayas.* México: Universidad Nacional Autónoma de México.

Walker, Cameron Jean. 2009. *Heritage or Heresy: Archaeology and Culture on the Maya Riviera.* Tuscaloosa: University of Alabama Press.

Watanabe, John M. 1990. "From Saints to Shibboleths: Image, Structure, and Identity in Maya Religious Syncretism." *American Ethnologist* 17 (1): 131–50.

Weiss, Brad. 1996. *The Making and Unmaking of the Haya Lived World.* Durham NC: Duke University Press.

Wilk, Richard R. (1991) 1997. *Household Ecology: Economic Change and Domestic Life among the Kekchi Maya in Belize.* DeKalb: Northern Illinois University Press.

Williams-Forson, P. 2011. "Other Women Cooked for My Husband: Negotiating Food, Gender, and Identities in an African American/Ghanian Household." In *Taking Food Public: Redefining Foodways in a Changing World*, edited by Psyche Williams-Forson and Carole Counihan, 138–54. New York: Routledge.

Wilson, Kathleen. 2003. "Therapeutic Landscapes and First Nations Peoples: An Exploration of Culture, Health and Place." *Health & Place* 9 (2): 83–93.

Wolf, Eric R. (1982) 2010. *Europe and the People without History.* Berkeley: University of California Press.

———. 1986. "The Vicissitudes of the Closed Corporate Peasant Community." *American Ethnologist* 13 (2): 325–29.

Woodrick, A. C. 1995. "Mother-Daughter Conflict and the Selection of Ritual Kin in a Peasant Community." *Anthropological Quarterly* 68, no. 4 (Fall): 219–33.

Wrigley, Julia. 1995. *Other People's Children: An Intimate Account of the Dilemmas Facing Middle-Class Parents and the Women They Hire to Raise Their Children.* New York: Basic Books.

Wynne, Lauren A. 2013. "Transformations in Body and Cuisine in Rural Yucatán, Mexico." In *Food and Identity in the Caribbean*, edited by Hanna Garth, 31–44. London: Bloomsbury.

———. 2015. "'I Hate It': Tortilla-Making, Class and Women's Tastes in Rural Yucatán, Mexico." *Food, Culture & Society* 18 (3): 379–97.

Yates-Doerr, Emily. 2015. *The Weight of Obesity; Hunger and Global Health in Postwar Guatemala.* Oakland: University of California Press.

Zivkovic, Tanya, Megan Warin, Vivienne Moore, Paul Ward, and Michelle Jones. 2015. "The Sweetness of Care," in *Careful Eating: Bodies, Food and Care*, edited by Emma-Jayne Abbots, Anna Lavis, and Luci Attala, 109–26. London: Routledge.

INDEX

Page numbers in italics indicate illustrations.

migration, 204; negative influence of, 70, 97, 207; from private sales, 204; reliance on, 8, 20, 41–42, 70, 105–6; from surplus food, 43; from tourism, 41; uses for, 51, 128, 221n27; from wage labor, 47, 72, 102–3, 117, 204, 205

Castellanos, M. Bianet, 7, 40, 77, 109, 110, 130, 150, 207, 218n12, 220n24, 221n27, 223n1

Caste War, 26, 69–70

Castillo Cocom, Juan, 7, 26, 214n2

Catholicism: alcohol consumption and, 221n26; conversions from, 96, 141–42, 222n3; criticism of, 222n7; fiestas of, 151–52, 153–54; food and, 32, 146–47, 159–60, 222n11; girls and, 221n26; importance of, 96; indigenous rituals and, 142, 144, 146–47; influences on, 148; natural and supernatural worlds and, 142; non-Catholicism and, 127–28, 145–46, 149–51, 157, 159–60, 163, 164–67, 221n26; patron saints and, 151; popular, 144–45, 148; practices and beliefs of, 144–45, 146–47, 156–58, 160–61; threats to, 95; traditional, 142, 222n6; women and, 128, 140, 221n26

cattle production, 71, 214n3

CCT (conditional cash transfer) programs, 74, 88–92, 167, 217n17, 219n17

cenotes (sinkholes), 38, 48

census (2010), 149

centers of consciousness (óolo'ob), 21, 80–81, 83, 87, 194, 216n8

Central America, 7, 216n12

Central American–Dominican Republic Free Trade Agreement (CAFTA), 7

ceremonies: agricultural, 19, 76, 113, 144, 147, 148, 156–57, 222n9; food for, 173, 176, 180–81, 183; indigenous, 144; jetsmek, 29, 187; marriage, 124–25; religious, 153–54, 160–64; secular, 167–68

Chan Kom (Redfield and Villa Rojas), 3, 220n23

Chan Kom, Yucatán, 75–76

Chevalier, Jacques M., 82–83, 216n12

Chiapas, Mexico, 25, 222n6

chicken (meat), 44

chickens, 44, 49, 139, 178

chicle industry, 70–71, 72, 122, 125, 215n6

childless people, 77, 94, 113–14

children: adult, 41, 94, 132; assistance programs for, 217n17; birthday parties of, 223n4; contributions by, 76; eating by, 46–47, 52, 77; education of, 40, 72–73; as food authority, 58–59, 199–201; free time of, 37; qualities hoped for in, 218–19n12; sitting astride a hip, 187; work role of, 40, 72, 116

chingar (to bother), 109, 110, 218n9

chingón (fucker), 110, 218–19n12

chips, 46–47, 133–35, 197, 199–200

Christ, 164

clinics. See health clinics

Coca-Cola, 26–27, 44, 115, 121, 125, 134, 145, 168, 212. See also soft drinks

"cold" in hot-cold syndrome. See hot-cold syndrome

collectivity, 10, 24, 37–38, 66, 77–78, 98, 109, 156, 196, 208

colonialism: economy of, 9; influence of, 5–6, 19–20, 48, 68, 76; Mayan identity and, 26; race theories in, 24; religion and, 142, 146, 148

commensality, 19, 54, 58, 76, 160, 181

commodification: in exchanges, 31–32; gender differences and, 97, 129; increase in, 3, 103; religion and, 154, 168, 179; results of, 49, 99, 103, 115, 117, 131, 137

commodities: care and, 15; in exchanges, 95, 109, 111, 132–33, 134; increase in, 102–4; local, 197; as necessity, 115–16; nonlocal, 51, 119–20, 199; production of, 21; qualities of, 50, 98–99

communities, Yucatec Mayan, 26, 68, 144, 172

community, sense of, 10, 26, 35, 74, 77, 95, 151, 154, 163, 164
conditional cash transfer (CCT) programs, 74, 88–92, 167, 217n17, 219n17
confraternities, 215n4
congregación practice, 20, 68
connoisseurship, 22, 59–60, 173, 188, 198, 200
Conquest, Spanish, 5
consensus: development of, 60, 196; power and, 61; on qualities of food, 54, 58; on standardization of food, 22, 201; threats to, 75, 98; as tradition, 16, 148; value of, 32–33, 57, 173
Constitution (1917), 73–74
continuity, 2, 47, 173, 179
conversions, religious: care and, 140, 167; from Catholicism, 141–42, 145–46, 155, 222n3; effects of, 96, 147, 149–51; to Jehovah's Witnesses, 73, 141–42; women encouraging, 165–66, 222–23n12
cooking. *See* men: domestic work of; women, food work of
cooperation: background of, 148; food and, 16, 22, 218n4; importance of, 68; threats to, 20–21, 24, 75, 76, 77, 98, 133
coorazon (heart, biomedical), 83, 217n13
corn, 42–43, 44, 49, 52, 68, 193–94, 207–8. *See also* maize
corn drink (*atole*), 48, 61, 94, 157–58
crear (to create), 3, 16
creation myth, 16, 67, 207
creation process, 3, 5, 10–11, 79, 81
Creoles, 68, 69–70, 215n4
crosses, 95, 151–52, 154, 222n7
Cruzob (people of the Speaking Cross), 70, 215n6

dancing, 145, 149, 153, 155
debt peonage, 5, 70
the deceased, 12, 85, 139, 140, 144, 149–50, 161–65, 169, 181, 221n1

defecation, 84
deities, 16, 159, 208
Department of Cultural Missions, 73
Department of Indigenous Cultures, 72
desire: for balance, 10, 98; for goods, 115–16; new, 133; for recognition, 114, 176; sexual, 127, 135; for sharing, 113; as threat, 23, 219n18; for tranquility, 77
Devil, 146, 165
diabetes, 50, 51, 212
Día de los Muertos (All Souls' Day), 140, 168, 221n1, 222n11
DICONSA (Distribuidora Conasupo), 37, 214n1
diputados (male sponsors), 151–52, 152–53, 154, 155
disease. *See* sickness
Distribuidora Conasupo (DICONSA), 37, 214n1
distrust, 75–76, 97–98, 116, 120, 132, 221n31
doors, open, 99–100, 217n3
dresses, regional (*iipiles*), 40, 133, 155, 168
Dzul de Po'ot, Ofelia, 16–17, 80

Ebel, R., 6, 214n2
economic crisis (2008), 102
economy, global, 20, 23–24, 89, 102, 117–18
economy, local: balance in, 14; changes in, 5, 6–10, 15, 68, 94, 96–97, 196, 207; in exchanges, 103–4; influences on, 209, 223n2; status in, 176; variations in, 38, 108
education, 7, 23, 40, 53, 72–73
eggs, 44, 45, 49
ejido (collective land ownership), 20, 95, 156, 208
elderly people, 9, 75, 86, 112, 217n17, 219n14
Elmendorf, Mary, 3
elopements, 124, 128, 220n21
encomienda system, 67–68. *See also* tribute
engagements, marriage, 124–25, 220n23
Engster, Daniel, 12, 13, 15

global marketplace, 15, 65

God, 16, 89, 145, 146, 147, 157–58, 159, 164–67, 215n5

González, Roberto J., 18

gossip, 9, 32, 77, 119, 132–33, 136, 137

government programs, 37, 73, 88–92, 217n17, 219n17

Greenberg, Laurie S. Z., 118

Greene, Allison C., 14, 214n13, 219n14, 219n16, 221n27

gringas and *gringos* (tourists), 26–27, 114

Guatemala, 8, 19, 25, 146, 162

gum industry, 70–71, 72, 122, 125, 215n6

Gupta, Akhil, 6

gustos (tastes), 54, 77

Hanks, William F., 55, 80, 81

health: centeredness and, 81; food and, 49, 50, 184, 194, 196, 200; hot-cold syndrome and, 86, 91–92, 216n12; labor and, 94

health clinics, 30, 37, 73–74, 88–89, *90*, 92

heart, 80, 216n9, 217n13

hearths, 51–52, 214n7

hermanas and *hermanos*, 127–28, 140, 141, 145, 154–55, 157, 221n26

hexis, 75, 96

Holmes, Barbara E., 114, 121, 218n5, 218n8, 219n9, 221n25

Holy Cross (*Santa Cruz*), 95, 151, 154, 222n7

hot-cold syndrome, 51, 65, 81–84, 85–86, 88, 90, 92, 194–95, 216n12, 217nn14–15

humans. *See* bodies, human

humoralism, 216n12

hunting, 14, 44, 59, 71, 158, 159

hypersexuality, male, 117, 123, 129

identity, 24–26, 35, 168, 172, 183

idolatry, 145–46, 163

iipiles (regional dresses), 40, 133, 155, 168

illness. *See* gastritis; sickness

imbalance, 11–12, 74–78, 79, 81, 82, 85–86

IMSS (Mexican Institute of Social Security), 74

indigenismo policies, 5

indigenous peoples. *See* Yucatecans, indigenous

inequalities: Cancún representing, 75; commodities and, 98; cooking expertise causing, 114; economic, 176, 196; in gender issues, 9, 72, 117–18, 196; migration and, 39, 117–18, 129–30, 206

infidelity. *See* adultery; sex: extramarital

informants: attitudes of, 14; background of, 29; on care, 17, 107, 164; on ceremonies, 157–58, 161–62; on cooking, 52, 174–75, 178; on economic situation, 6–7, 96, 98, 108; on food, 1, 48–50, 60–61, 112–13, 139, 156, 169, 171, 187, 189, 190–91, 214n5, 219n14; on human body, 86, 217nn13–14; on marriage, 220n21, 220n23; on *pláticas*, 89; on religion, 107–8, 145, 156–57, 159, 164–65, 166, 222n7; on sex, 12, 132, 135–36; on sickness, 17, 51, 83–84, 87, 209, 211, 212; on work, 47–48, 55, 110, 203–4, 205. *See also* informants, by name

informants, by name: doña Cristina, 41, 48, 83–84, 110, 161–62, 198; doña Esmeralda, 1, 5, 26, 49, 55, 63, 65, 91–92, 99, 106–7, 113–15, 139–40, 168–69, 171; doña Fernanda, 146, 155, 159–60, 165–66; doña Katy, 63, 89–90, 93, 107, 136, 151, 152; doña Patricia (spouse of don Elicier), 49–50, 169, 222n7; doña Patricia (spouse of don Tino), 203–4; doña Patricia (*x-k'uu*), 180–81; doña Susana, 88, 93–94, 152, 154, 178; doña Tina, 73, 112, 146, 165; don Máximo, 5, 26, 49, 63, 65, 139, 163, 203–4, 219n13; don Teodoro (shaman), 16. *See also* informants

jalapeños, 184

janal (food), 45, 180, 212, 223n3

Yucatecans, indigenous: background of, 24–25; balance and, 2, 12, 23, 78–79; care and, 10, 14–15; change and, 7–9, 22, 75–76, 103–4, 118, 203, 206–7; character of, 15–16; desire and, 219n18; food and, 19–20, 79, 94, 111–14, 177, 207–8, 215n3; history of, 213n2, 215nn4–6; identity issues and, 71, 168, 183; influences on, 5–6; land issues and, 69–71; marriage and, 122–25; Mexican government and, 69–70, 216n7; parenting by, 218–19n12; religion and, 142, 144–46, 222nn2–3; sense of self in, 26, 79, 81, 207–8; sex and, 121–24, 219n18; Spanish Conquest and, 67–68

Yucatec Maya (language): in education, 72–73; figures of speech in, 120–21; gender in, 219n15; as informants' language, 29; possessive form in, 216n10; Spanish compared to, 3, 16–17, 109; speakers of, 27, 36, 80; words in, 2–3, 16–17, 74, 80–81, 109, 178, 213n1, 213n9

yucateco (Mayan). *See* Yucatecans, indigenous

The Food and Cooking of Eastern Europe
Lesley Chamberlain
With a new introduction by the author

The Food and Cooking of Russia
Lesley Chamberlain
With a new introduction by the author

The World on a Plate: A Tour through the History of America's Ethnic Cuisine
Joel Denker

Jewish American Food Culture
Jonathan Deutsch and Rachel D. Saks

The Recipe Reader: Narratives, Contexts, Traditions
Edited by Janet Floyd
and Laurel Forster

A Chef's Tale: A Memoir of Food, France, and America
Pierre Franey
With Richard Flaste and Bryan Miller
With a new introduction
by Eugenia Bone

Masters of American Cookery: M. F. K. Fisher, James Beard, Craig Claiborne, Julia Child
Betty Fussell
With a preface by the author

My Kitchen Wars: A Memoir
Betty Fussell
With a new introduction
by Laura Shapiro

Good Things
Jane Grigson

Jane Grigson's Fruit Book
Jane Grigson
With a new introduction
by Sara Dickerman

Jane Grigson's Vegetable Book
Jane Grigson
With a new introduction
by Amy Sherman

Dining with Marcel Proust: A Practical Guide to French Cuisine of the Belle Epoque
Shirley King
Foreword by James Beard

Pampille's Table: Recipes and Writings from the French Countryside from Marthe Daudet's
Les Bons Plats de France
Translated and adapted by Shirley King

Moveable Feasts: The History, Science, and Lore of Food
Gregory McNamee

To order or obtain more information on these or other University of Nebraska Press titles, visit nebraskapress.unl.edu.

www.ingramcontent.com/pod-product-compliance
Lightning Source LLC
Chambersburg PA
CBHW051728260326
41914CB00040B/2021/J